Deleuze and Space

Deleuze Connections

'It is not the elements or the sets which define the multiplicity. What defines it is the AND, as something which has its place between the elements or between the sets. AND, AND, AND – stammering.'

Gilles Deleuze and Claire Parnet, *Dialogues*

General Editor
Ian Buchanan

Editorial Advisory Board
Keith Ansell-Pearson
Rosi Braidotti
Claire Colebrook
Tom Conley
Gregg Lambert
Paul Patton
Adrian Parr
Patricia Pisters

Titles in the Series
Ian Buchanan and Claire Colebrook (eds), *Deleuze and Feminist Theory*
Ian Buchanan and John Marks (eds), *Deleuze and Literature*
Mark Bonta and John Protevi (eds), *Deleuze and Geophilosophy*
Ian Buchanan and Marcel Swiboda (eds), *Deleuze and Music*

Forthcoming
Martin Fuglsang and Bent Meier Sørensen (eds), *Deleuze and the Social*

Of Related Interest
Adrian Parr (ed.), *The Deleuze Dictionary*

Deleuze and Space

Edited by Ian Buchanan
and Gregg Lambert

Edinburgh University Press

© in this edition, Edinburgh University Press, 2005
© in the individual contributions is retained by the authors

Edinburgh University Press Ltd
22 George Square, Edinburgh

Typeset in 10.5/13 Sabon
by Servis Filmsetting Ltd, Manchester, and
printed and bound in Great Britain by
CPI Antony Rowe, Eastbourne

Transferred to Digital Print 2008

A CIP record for this book is available from the British Library

ISBN 0 7486 1892 9 (hardback)
ISBN 0 7486 1874 0 (paperback)

The right of the contributors
to be identified as authors of this work
has been asserted in accordance with
the Copyright, Designs and Patents Act 1988.

Contents

For our parents

With thanks to Jackie Jones, Nicola Wood, Tanya Buchanan and Wendy Watterson for their help and support; Professor Gerald Greenburg, Associate Dean, College of Arts and Sciences, Syracuse University; and Neal Magee.

Permission to reproduce images in Hélène Frichot, *Stealing into Gilles Deleuze's Baroque House* are gratefully acknowledged from:

"*La maison baroque*" (Baroque house) from Les Éditions de minuit ©

and

Möbius house image from UN Studios ©

Deleuze and Space

Ian Buchanan and Gregg Lambert

In the opening pages of *Getting Back into Place*, Edward Casey defies us to imagine a world without place. It is impossible to do, he says, citing as proof the very terror such a thought evokes. We can scarcely think of anything more terrible, he argues, than the absence of place. 'Our lives are so place-oriented and place-saturated that we cannot begin to comprehend, much less face up to, what sheer placelessness would be like' (Casey 1993: ix). Doubtless this is because we intuit that *we* could not be, indeed would not be, if *we* did not have a place to be. The extreme of this position is Heidegger's concept of *Dasein*, there-being, which is effectively an attempt to think through this problem by dissolving the underpinning separation – or what Deleuze and Guattari term 'disjunctive synthesis' – of ourselves and place. The early mistranslation of *Dasein* as simply 'man' is instructive in this respect: it acknowledges and erases the fact that Heidegger was arguing that man is a place-being, not a being in a place. However, as Heidegger well knew, internalising place in this way does not eradicate the problem of what place is and his later work which turned more explicitly to the theme of 'dwelling' would try to find ways of articulating it as an effect and precondition of existence. In this respect, his thinking was influenced – though to how great an extent is difficult to assess – by the transformations war had wreaked on Europe.[1]

As Deleuze's account of post-war cinema argues, thinking about place in this period was (understandably) dominated by rubble-strewn vistas and notwithstanding Casey's assertions to the contrary, a number of philosophers, but also artists and film-makers as well, began to imagine a world without place, a world of 'any-spaces-whatever'.

Why is the Second World War taken as a break? The fact is that, in Europe, the post-war period has greatly increased the situations which we no longer know how to react to, in spaces which we no longer know how to describe.

These were 'any spaces whatever', deserted but uninhabited, disused ware-houses, waste ground, cities in the course of demolition or reconstruction. And in these any-spaces-whatever a new race of characters was stirring, a kind of mutant: they saw rather than acted, they were seers. (Deleuze 1989: xi)

In the US, the equivalent of bombed-out vistas, the allegedly disinte-grating inner cities, feature as the backdrop to crime films, but their metaphysical message is entirely different. The deserted streets and shabby buildings signify not that 'a people' (as Deleuze and Guattari put it) is missing, but that it has been targeted for termination. Hitchcock is treated by Deleuze as the limit point of pre-war, modernist cinema, pre-cisely because his post-war films resist this movement toward a cinema of the any-space-whatever. Although his work spans the period of both neo-realism and new wave, there are no any-spaces-whatever of the type found in Rossellini or Godard in Hitchcock; on the contrary, his films operate within highly contrived and closely observed buildings: the apartment block, the motel, the mansion, the terraced house at the end of the street (the ensuing claustrophobic atmosphere of constant surveil-lance is doubtless the element of his work that retains its most potent res-onance in contemporary society). We should not assume from this, however, that 'place' persisted in Hitchcock and vanished in Rossellini and Godard and that Hitchcock's work was somehow out of step with history. Hitchcock's famous preference for the soundstage over location resulted in an aesthetic which by using back-projections and mattes instead of the 'real' thing created a cinema of what (after Eco), and in contrast to Rossellini's neo-realism, might be termed hyperrealism.[2] It is perhaps only today when spaces are being built consciously to replicate film sets that we can appreciate the dialogue on space that Hitchcock's films were trying to broach.[3]

That dialogue has to do with habitability. This question, above, dom-inates the second half of the twentieth century as the key analytic issue concerning space. At stake is the practical problem of what it takes to make space habitable, to make places from sites where the active place-making infrastructure (tradition, memory, habit, and so forth) had been either destroyed or displaced. As Anthony Vidler shows, spatial thinking before the Second World War was concerned with the seemingly damag-ing effect space was having on the modern individual. 'Metropolis rapidly became the privileged territory of a host of diseases attributed directly to spatial conditions, diseases that took their place within the general epistemology of Beard's neurasthenia and Charcot's hysteria, but with a special relationship to their supposed physical causes' (Vidler

2000: 25–6). Agoraphobia and claustrophobia, terms that first appeared some three decades before the start of the twentieth century, became the ying and yang of spatial thinking in the modernist period. Whether it was the busy thoroughfares, the phantasmagoria of the arcades or the wide open space of the boulevards, there was an associated malady diagnosed for each new type of spatial experience. More importantly, each malady was said to hold the key to understanding contemporary life, first as a kind of indexical symptom, and then as the baseline, the unexceptional standard by which society understood itself. The social space of the city became mappable, in Deleuze's terms, by tracing points of intensity of these new maladies. Thus Benjamin focussed on arcades, but more crucially on 'passing through' (*Passagen-Werk*) as the typical activity of the late nineteenth century; Kracauer zeroed in on the hotel lobby (*Hotelhalle*) as the emblem of the new rationalism; while for Simmel it was the stranger – at once fear-inducing and seducing – that embodied the ambivalence of the new era.[4]

After the Second World War, however, thinking changed: space came to be regarded as uninhabitable by definition. Whereas before the concern had been how space affected individuals, now the emphasis shifted to the other side of the equation: could individuals affect space? In different ways, Lefebvre and Heidegger stand on the cusp of this seismic shift of sensibility in that they both argue that the individual is essential to the constitution of place, that is to say, what we now call 'lived space'. Both were able to conceive of spaces that had been emptied or otherwise rendered uninhabited, but neither was yet prepared to consider the possibility of spaces that were constitutively uninhabitable. The generation of thinkers that followed – Augé, Debord, de Certeau, Deleuze, Foucault, and many others – had no such hesitation. Doubtless it was Foucault's book on the prison that set the tone, creating a dour atmosphere of institutional triumphalism that his own later work would try to ameliorate by outlining a *modus vivendi* for life in the glare of surveillance. Taking discipline as his stipulated point of departure, de Certeau reversed the accepted polarity of thinking up to that point, using 'place' to denote the restrictive and unhomely and 'space' (hitherto the designation for the uninhabited and uninhabitable) to theorise a tenuous new form of freedom – in space one has the liberty to experiment, to try new things, but the price is one cannot keep what one gains. Emblematic of this new 'space' was the sidewalk, a space which brought together the passionate intensity of Benjamin's arcades and the chancy promiscuity of Simmel's strangers, and possessed in de Certeau's eyes, a poetry all of its own. Focussing on the proliferation of spaces whose function seems only to be

4 Deleuze and Space

to facilitate our 'passing through', airports, train stations, tram stops, and so forth, Augé takes this a step further and develops an idea of the non-place, that is, a place which no longer confers the affect of place, and in the process crushes the creative and indeed anarchic spirit of de Certeau's notion of space.[5] Debord's direction was both more anarchic and in a sense more forlorn because for him it was really only in the virtual space of art that one can find any relief from the overbearing pressures of the rationalism of the age. This position is close to Deleuze's, of course, inasmuch as he too invests great faith in art, but he doesn't confine the anarchic potential of art to the virtual; he sees its explosive potential extending to the actual, if the artist has the strength to carry it through.

In its fundamental ambivalence towards the new space, Europe was well ahead of America, in fact it is not until Fredric Jameson's essay on postmodernism of 1984 that we encounter a comparable analysis; at least part of the shock of Jameson's essay came from his willingness to pronounce the new space uninhabitable, and thus bring a continental ennui stateside.[6] In complete contrast to Europe, post-war USA literally boomed; more particularly, in the decade or so following the cessation of hostilities in Europe the basic shape of contemporary USA was put in place: the inter-state freeways, sprawling suburbs, and shopping malls, that define the landscape of middle America today all came into being at this time. It is this that Hitchcock's cinema captures – his is a cinema of the 'affect' of shopping mall, the inter-state and the suburb, or what Koolhaas calls 'junk space'. 'The modern fact,' as Deleuze put it, 'is that we no longer believe in this world. We do not even believe in the events which happen to us, love, death, as if they only half concerned us. It is not we who make cinema; it is the world which looks to us like a bad film' (Deleuze 1989: 171).[7] This describes Hitchcock's cinema precisely – his worlds do look like bad films and they have been eviscerated of belief. It is a cinema of non-places, of a 'global style' that could be anywhere and, as Koolhaas puts it, has spread everywhere like a virus.[8] If one must speak of a break between Hitchcock and Rossellini it is because Hitchcock could not reconnect the severed link between man and the world, his characters persist 'in the world as if in a pure optical and sound situation' (Deleuze 1989: 172). His worlds, like shopping malls, are interiors whose aim is to eliminate the desire for the outside by reproducing it in facsimile. Hitchcock created a radical immanence whose terrifying dimensions were perhaps only properly understood by directors like David Lynch who found a way of imbuing even location shoots with this same affect.[9] Hitchcock renders palpable the space of 'universal schizophrenia' (Deleuze 1989: 172).[10]

Given our tour through space and place in post-war European and American wastelands, somewhat like the schizoid stroll of Harry Dean Stanton's character in Wender's *Paris, Texas* (1984) (who walks a bastard line straight across the Mojave desert), it is important to notice the proliferation of new concepts of space in Deleuze and Guattari's collaborative works, and to see this attention to the problem of space as something distinctive that belongs to their philosophy. In *A Thousand Plateaus* (1987), new configurations of the spatial field abound and even the work's title and composition signals a spatial assemblage of planes, lines, and between these, points of variation (or 'becoming'). This replaces the tripartite division of the spatial field normally associated with 'mental representation': the field of reality (the world), the field of representation (the book), the field of subjectivity (the author) (Deleuze and Guattari 1987: 23).[11] Thus, the work has a 'middle' (*milieu*) from which it extracts territories for analysis, but no centre; it has no end or margins, but rather 'cutting edges of de-territorialisation'. In fact, space itself is never neutral to the particular assemblage in which it appears or that produces it as its 'a priori' condition; there are always two kinds of space: 'smooth and striated space – nomad space and sedentary space – the space in which the war machine develops and the space instituted by the State apparatus – are not of the same nature' (Deleuze and Guattari 1987: 474). And yet, as they immediately go on to qualify, this does not create a rigid dualism or opposition since any composition is always 'a mixture' (*melange*) of smooth and striated space and the point is to develop a more supple system of analysis. For example, 'lines and segments' are reserved to describe molar organisations; whereas the description of molecular organisations of flows and quanta are constantly shown to pass through, or 'between,' organised segments (or the social space implied by a State Apparatus) and by processes they define as decoding and deterritorialisation.

This mapping of the different kinds of space that mix in each assemblage (social, political, but also geological, biological, economic, aesthetic or musical, and so on) becomes the major task set out by the project they define as pragmatics or micro-politics. Thus, if above we describe a fundamental reaction of ambivalence in different post-war critical evaluations of the new spaces produced by late-capitalism, such as Jameson's expression of disorientation and dizziness in the atrium of the Bonaventure Hotel, Deleuze and Guattari's response to this problem is to set out to develop a series of maps of these spaces in a pragmatic sense of finding 'a way through', or a manner of orienting themselves (as they often say in the course of their analysis: 'now we are in a better position to draw a map'), which Kant earlier defined as the fundamental task of thinking as well.[12]

In Deleuze and Guattari's last collaborative work, *What is Philosophy?*, the problem of our 'universal schizophrenia' is taken up again in terms of the modern brain in its direct confrontation with chaos. That is, the broken links of perception and sensation produce distant and flat 'any-space-whatever' accompanied by an affective sensation ('I feel') bereft of any possible subjective orientation between interior and exterior. This often produces an uncanny *Doppelgänger* effect in the space between the uninhabitable exterior spaces that seem to proliferate and surround us, without allowing us to inhabit them. 'Further away than any external world and deeper than any interiority' is a formula Deleuze derived from Foucault and Blanchot to evoke the figure of an 'Outside' that – characterised by its formlessness – has impacted and transformed, in different respects, the modern subjects of science, philosophy, and art. This confrontation recapitulates many of the descriptions offered above concerning the problem of habitation, which can also be regarded as a problem of recognition under the regime of representation – as the state in which the modern subject no longer recognises the space in which it is located. The earlier model of recognition has become derisory and clearly inadequate with regard to the 'particle signs' emitted by new spatial configurations, which are 'a bit like turning on a television screen whose intensities bring out that which escapes the power of objective definition' (Deleuze and Guattari 1994: 209).

Yet, if Deleuze and Guattari locate the juncture of this new confrontation with chaos directly in the brain, it is not in an appeal to a new science or to some 'meta-subject' (theory) to pacify this struggle. As they write: 'Philosophy, art, science are not the mental objects of an objectified brain, but the three aspects under which brain becomes subject, Thought-brain' (Deleuze and Guattari 1994: 210). Here, the broken links of perception and sensation, even memory (made up by 'chrono-signs'), have changed the situation of thought: at the exact juncture where the space of the world and the space of man unfold, between an interior and exterior fold, intersects a space 'without distance, at ground level,' from which 'no chasm, fold, or hiatus escapes' (Deleuze and Guattari 1994: 210). If, 'according to phenomenology, thought depends on man's relation with the world, in which the brain is necessarily in agreement because it draws from these relations', what happens when this relation is reversed and the relation to the world, which is fundamentally a spatial relation, now depends on thought, on thinking *this* relation anew? In their last work, therefore, the problem first enunciated by

Kant ('time off its hinges') returns again to address the problem of a sensation of space that has fallen from its rails, a problem that they early on defined as the globalising tendency expressed by increasing deterritorialisation that is approaching an almost absolute point (chaos). Where the three 'planes' composed by science, philosophy, and art meet, the brain cannot be simply reduced to the 'mental objects' that appear to be interior to these composites, or that appear on the surfaces produced by these different aspects of thought. As Deleuze has explored very early on under the mysterious theme of 'parallelism' (drawn from Spinoza) the number cannot be reduced to a pure object of mental representation since it also traces a figure of matter, which is not simply thought-matter; likewise the line traced or created by architecture cannot simply originate in the mind, but must also find its efficient cause in the resistance posed by specific materials and by the variable forms of space that are made possible by the line traced through a multiplicity (material, social, semiotic, and so on). According to the logic of the 'the fold' (*le pli*), there is no general logic of space in the same way that Deleuze has proposed a logic of sense and of sensation. *This is because the logic of space would be that of the multiplicity itself.* In keeping with the possibility of developing such a logic of multiplicity (virtual or real), this volume proposes a series of partial descriptions of the different regions and assemblages that have been touched and transformed by the concepts created by Deleuze and Guattari.

As we mentioned at the beginning, thinking about space and place has until very recently been predicated by the understanding that place is an affirmative category, the implication being that there can be no such thing as a non-place, or a non-space. This presumption has been challenged in recent years by writers trying to come to grips with a new generation of spaces that do not confer the sense or feeling of being in a place, either because they are frictionless passageways designed as conduits or simply so vast or alien they have lost contact with human proportion. Globalisation has evicted us from the world we thought we knew. Ian Buchanan takes this as his starting point, and shows how Deleuze and Guattari's concepts of deterritorialisation and reterritorialisation enable us to think through this process. In particular he focusses on the ways in which our conception of space has had to alter in the face of the hyper-mobility of the postmodern subject.

Hélène Frichot constructs the conceptual persona of 'pickpocket' to describe the architect, deliberately setting aside those personae we are more familiar with – architect as demiurge, engineer, and so on. In this guise, we see the architect as someone who in their professional practice 'borrows' creatively from other sources, which prompts the question: Have his pockets been picked? Frichot addresses directly the issue of what architects 'borrowed' from Deleuze and shows that these borrowings are anything but inconsiderable. As is well known, Deleuze's work on the baroque house, with its scheme of folds (fold, unfold, refold) extrapolated from Leibniz has been important to Greg Lynn and Peter Eisenman, but Frichot points out this doesn't tell the whole story. Rather it has been Deleuze's attempt to conceive a philosophy of the event that has had the greatest impact. As Frichot puts it, the architect, is 'interested in how the surface effects produced by the circulation of events might be created in material forms of expression'. Folding refers not so much, or rather not only, to the bending shapes of the materials (Lynn's infamous blobs), but more especially to the convergence of thought and matter, history and substance.

Paul Harris suggests Simon Rodia's Watts Towers in Los Angeles should be apprehended as a concrete example of what he describes as the bottom-up principles of folding architecture. Refracting Deleuze through the lens of Bernard Cache's work, Harris argues that Rodia's Towers exemplify folding architecture not only in terms of its structural design and materials, but more especially in terms of its building methods which literally was bottom up. Cache, who explicitly describes his work as Deleuzian ('pursued by other means'), explores through architecture and design – everything from houses to furniture – one of Deleuze's core problems, namely the problem of variation. In the virtual realm, that of the computerised design system, say, achieving a slow dance of infinite and infinitesimal variation is relatively easy – the materials themselves can morph and remould themselves according to the architect's design algorithm. But in the actual world of concrete and steel, with materials that must not be allowed to morph and remould themselves quite so readily, this is obviously a much more difficult proposition. As romantic as they sometimes seem about the virtual, it is worth recalling that Deleuze and Guattari quite pointedly say that structures built using 'nomad' principles, rather than 'royal' science, do have a tendency to fall down. The great architects, then, are those who can use immobile pieces to carry the eye off into the horizon; who can grab hold of movement using static pincers and create a structure that is not 'frozen music', but an orchestral piece unfolding in infinite time.

As Manuel DeLanda points out, there are two kinds of variation in Deleuze's work arising from the fact that there are two kinds of substances: those with intensive properties and those with extensive properties. These terms find their most concrete meaning in physics, particularly

thermodynamics. You can section a piece of wood, but not a temperature; you can slice a loaf of bread, but not a wind velocity; you can make
love, but you can't hold 'love' in your hands. That which you can grasp,
cut, twist and turn, is extensive; that which affects you, but does not yield
to your attempt to contain it, is, like wind in your face, intensive.
Intensive differences are, as Deleuze rightly points out, indivisible. As
sensible as this distinction seems, it isn't sufficient for Deleuze to ground
his ontology, DeLanda argues, because it assumes a rather too rigorous
distinction between the intensive and extensive. For Deleuze, change is
only possible if all substances are at least partly intensive, that is, capable
of that form of variation he describes as 'becoming'. What DeLanda
shows is that 'becoming' is effectively a movement between different
forms of intensity – from very low forms, such as one finds in the more
lumpish, that is, to all intents and purposes 'extensive' objects, to very
high forms of intensity, such as one finds in computer designs. This, as
DeLanda demonstrates, requires an agile form of mathematics to grasp.

The resulting space is real, but always actual, and this, as John-David
Dewsbury and Nigel Thrift argue, makes life very difficult for geographers. Yet anyone wanting to undertake an apprenticeship in a Deleuzian
form of geography must, they say, grow accustomed to a world of virtualities, singularities, and intensities, a world they are tempted to describe
as haunted. Human geographers have for many years tried to conceive
of a means of articulating both the broad structural factors geography is
supposed to encompass – the distribution of income, for instance, or the
mix of racial groups – and the singular experiences, the narratives of
daily life. Those larger categories of necessity (or so it is generally
thought) reduce to what Deleuze and Guattari call 'strata'. Life narratives are obviously more evocative than statistical tables, yet without the
data those tables contain the life narrative risks being treated as either
exceptional, a one-off with no real currency, or the standard, obliterat-
ing all other factors. In other words, it is the balance between these two
positions that geography has been striving for and like Frichot's pickpocket architects, they've lately started to rifle through Deleuze's capa-
cious pockets. There they have found a model that suits their needs.

Geographers try to articulate the space humans make for themselves
with materials that in different ways are given to them, sometimes quite
violently. In Chapter 6, Gary Genosko and Adam Bryx take up Deleuze
and Guattari's notions of smooth and striated space to provide an analytic account of the ways in which the indigenous or 'First Nations'
peoples – particularly the Inuit – of the northernmost parts of the North
American continent coped with the rigorously stratifying practices of

their colonial overlords. Coped is probably too passive a term for in fact they creatively adopted and put into variation the very devices imposed upon them as control mechanisms. In a bid to construct a stable demographic picture of the Inuit, the Canadian government took the extraordinary step of requiring them to wear numbered identity disks, or 'dog tags' as they were immediately dubbed by their hapless wearers. This step was deemed necessary because Inuit naming practices are such that a catalogue of names is not only out of date very quickly, but soon slides into meaninglessness. The Inuit do not use surnames, they do not identify with a particular family tree in their naming, nor do they gender names; by the same token, it is common for several people to have the same name in honour of a famous hunter for example. Obviously, too, as an oral culture, there was no consistency in spelling or pronunciation, so the same name might sound or look different according to the region. What Genosko and Bryx fascinatingly narrate is a twofold process whereby the government overlaid a stable identity system and the recipients of that striated system rendered it smooth all over again.

In 'Thinking Leaving', Branka Arsic discusses Deleuze's spatial thought with reference to an American author that Deleuze seldom discusses, but who seems to be implicitly located in the frequent meditations of the figure of Melville (and Emerson), namely, Henry David Thoreau. Arsic shows how Melville 'sketched out and extended the traits of a thinking already posed by Thoreau and Emerson, a thinking that conceives the world as an archipelago (as multiplicity)'. In other words, Thoreau's wandering paths through the woods of Walden of thought is 'first of all the affirmation of a world in *process*' (Deleuze 1997: 86). In this light, Arsic includes and extends Deleuze's several meditations on the new configurations of space, territory and geological memory invented by nineteenth-century American thinkers, and adds Thoreau to the list of those thinkers who saw a future that would be composed of 'uncemented stones, where every element has a value in itself but also in relation to others: isolated and floating relations, islands and straits, immobile points and sinuous lines' (Deleuze 1997: 86).

Réda Bensmaïa addresses the concept of the 'spiritual automaton' that appears late in Deleuze's work particularly around the new images of space and time in contemporary cinema. Bensmaïa underscores the particular manner in which this concept is invented in order to account for its 'object'. Thus, it belongs to the class of other 'conceptual persona', such as the infamous 'BwO' (drawn from Artaud), which are given what

Deleuze defines as a 'rigorous and inexact' usage that underlies Deleuze's theory of concept creation as the highest task of a philosophy of expression. In tracing the origins of this concept, in particular, Bensmaïa returns to the early encounter with the philosophy of Spinoza and the principle of parallelism. However, as Bensmaïa reveals, it is not a matter of applying a concept derived from the classical philosophy of Spinoza to another theoretical field (such as modern cinema), but rather one of 'using cinema to transform an 'exact concept' into 'an *operator of analysis*' that would allow it to "give rise" in us to a new way of thinking cinema'. The import of this description of the specificity of concept-creation for the analysis of the cinematic production of spaces is that in Deleuze's hands cinema itself is revealed as 'machine' that puts thought directly into contact with an Outside that subverts the nature of the relations of representation between image and reality.

In 'Ahab and Becoming-Whale: The Nomadic Subject in Smooth Space', Tamsin Lorraine explores the alternative conception of space that emerges in the concepts of heterogeneous blocks of space-time and smooth space that are outlined by Deleuze and Guattari in their *A Thousand Plateaus*. Lorraine first examines the concepts of territoriality (or milieu) and of the refrain in Deleuze and Guattari's description of the subject as actually constituted by the various rhythms of the body's components and their relations to interior and exterior blocks of space-time that become homogenised into the lived experience of an organism. According to this new conception of the conditions of stability and identity, Lorraine argues, 'the organism as a self-regulating whole with its own spatial orientation can then be opened up to forces beyond it'. Taking up the frequent references that Deleuze and Guattari employ in *A Thousand Plateaus* to Melville's *Moby Dick*, and to the character of Ahab in particular, Lorraine explicates the concept of the 'nomadic subject' which occurs when a process of subjectivity reaches a critical threshold that pushes it into another pattern of activity, 'thus actualizing singularities that were previously only implicit, and its power to affect and be affected changes as well'. In keeping with Bensmaïa's observations on the 'spiritual automaton' as a philosophical-conceptual persona, Lorraine illustrates how the persona of Ahab (or 'Becoming-Whale') engages in an active synthesis of forces that exist outside of subject-concept of Ahab, becoming rather 'a configuration of physical and symbolic forces tapped into a virtual real unfolding forces that were previously only implicit at the expense of the conventional meanings his life could be given'.

Gregory Flaxman, in 'Transcendental Aesthetics: Deleuze's Philosophy of Space', returns to take up Deleuze's central confrontation with the regime of Representation, and in particular, with the philosophy of Kant who Deleuze once described as 'the enemy'. Of course, Deleuze is known for recognising the great reversal of time in Kant's critical philosophy, in which time is liberated from the cardinal points of representation and, instead, becomes 'the form in which everything changes and moves'. At the same time, Flaxman asks, can we imagine a correlative revolution of space? In response to this question, Flaxman underlines the importance of the observation first made by Deleuze in the preface to his *Kant's Critical Philosophy* that as a result of this discovery space would have to find new determinations as well, even though this task would mostly be left to future philosophers to create. Nonetheless, the radical task underlined by Deleuze's initial declaration 'would be that any philosophy of space must begin by transforming the very presuppositions according to which space itself has been traditionally determined'. Flaxman shows that Deleuze's own response to this provocation concerns his turn to the other arts, traditionally relegated to the field of aesthetics, in order to develop an interrogation of space that would not result from a priori conditions but, instead, from an intensive '*spatium*' in which perception and thought are immanent, and in which depth is no less an intensive quantity than extensity. In this manner, Flaxman argues, Deleuze resolves to bring together the two senses of the aesthetic – the transcendental and the empirical – in order that, as Deleuze says elsewhere, 'the conditions of experience in general must become conditions of real experience' (Deleuze 1994: 68).

In 'The Space of Man: The Specificity of Affect in Deleuze and Guattari', Claire Colebrook takes up the sense of new spatial relations, clarifying both Deleuze's and Foucault's respective historical confrontations with the phenomenology of Husserl. The new spatial concepts that result from this confrontation are discussed especially in light of Deleuze's subsequent evaluation of the 'sense of space' in *Foucault* where Deleuze claims the discovery of the 'superfold' (or 'unlimited finity') whereby the thinking of space is no longer ordered by a general horizon (a world), but where 'each located observer is the opening of a fold, a world folded around its contemplations and rhythms'. Thus, if phenomenology earlier argued that all perception and communicable meaning must presuppose a horizon, a world of possibilities which would then be given repeatable form and ideality in the structures of sense, Colebrook reveals a Deleuze who takes great pains to think the way in which different expressions of life unfold different spaces, relations, fields or trajectories, according to 'the immanent power of corporeality in all matter'

(Deleuze and Guattari 1987: 411). Consequently, as Colebrook argues, alongside the critique of the normalisation of space in the figure of a unified humanity or world, the second fundamental *problem* in post-1968 philosophy is the affirmation of difference itself, that is, 'the problem or positive possibility of the whole, the power of a singular thought to imagine space in general'.

Tom Conley discusses the import of a piece of Deleuze's juvenilia, '*Causes et raisons des îles désertes*' (*Causes and Reasons of Desert Islands*), which has only recently washed ashore to become the principle title of the first volume of Deleuze's various writings assembled by David Lapoujade in *L'Île déserte et autres textes* (*The Desert Island and Other Writings*). Conley underlines the significance of this early text as offering a blueprint of the central importance of spatial thought in Deleuze's entire oeuvre, up through the projects undertaken with Guattari to the immensely important observations concerning space and the structure of prehension in *Le pli* (*The Fold*). In his review of Deleuze's earliest recorded preoccupation with spatial forms and cartographies, Conley outlines the profile of two different islands, one based on science and the other on imagination (an island that crops up later, for example, in Deleuze's mediation of 'the Other Island' appearing in Michel Tournier's palimpsest of *Robinson Crusoe*). Conley shows the importance of this dualism for understanding Deleuze's conception of the subject of 'Man' as having a doubled origin, 'one of the creation and the other of the being of the island. As Conley describes this perspective that underscores Deleuze's 'impersonal ontology', little distinction is made between the subject as supremely thinking creature (of science and imagination that can furnish an adequate ontology for itself) and the forces of the earth itself, whether organic or inorganic (that create a sense of conscience and of being apart or separate from any necessary presence of man). The island, like whoever desires it, is of a conscience unto itself, '*la pure conscience de l'île*' (the pure conscience of the island), being at the same time of the perceiver and the perceived alike.

Finally, Gregg Lambert returns to explore the question of space from the perspective of the Earth itself. Using the occasion of Hardt and Negri's recent argument concerning the creative potential of 'deterritorialisation' that they already find at the basis of what they define as 'Empire', Lambert suggests that the conceptual apparatus that Deleuze and Guattari employ in their second volume of the Capitalism and Schizophrenia project, *A Thousand Plateaus*, must be understood in a certain sense as an abandonment of an earlier problem of 'Universal History' – and of the History of Capitalism, in particular – that had preoccupied them in the first instalment, *Anti-Oedipus*. The implications of their turn to the geological metaphors of stratification and to the problems of territory and deterritorialisation, Lambert argues, can be seen to echo Marx's own shift from the language of German idealism in the earlier writings to the new conceptual apparatus of political economy in the volumes of *Das Kapital*. Following this insight, in the remaining sections of this chapter Lambert expounds on the implications of this geological shift exhibited in the latter project by asking the question: 'If the Earth has a politics, what would it be?' In responding to this question, Lambert attempts to explicate some of the more difficult concepts found to populate Deleuze and Guattari's later writings, including stratification, the primitive territorial machine, the State-Form, and finally, the processes of territorialisation and deterritorialisation.

References

Buchanan, I. (2000), *Deleuzism: A Metacommentary*, Edinburgh: Edinburgh University Press.

Casey, E. (1993), *Getting Back into Place: Toward a Renewed Understanding of the Place-World*, Bloomington and Indianapolis: Indiana University Press.

Deleuze, G. (1989), *Cinema 2: The Time-Image*, trans. H. Tomlinson and R. Galeta, London: Athlone.

Deleuze, G. (1994), *Difference and Repetition*, trans. Paul Patton, London: Athlone.

Deleuze, G. (1997), *Essays Critical and Clinical*, trans. D. W. Smith and M. A. Greco, Minneapolis: University of Minnesota Press.

Deleuze, G. (2002), *L'Île déserte et autres textes*, ed. David Lapoujade, Paris: Minuit.

Deleuze, G. and Guattari, F. (1986), *Kafka: Toward a Minor Literature*, trans. D. Polan, Minneapolis: University of Minnesota Press.

Deleuze, G. and Guattari, F. (1987), *A Thousand Plateaus: Capitalism and Schizophrenia*, trans. B. Massumi, Minneapolis: University of Minnesota Press.

Deleuze, G. and Guattari, F. (1994), *What is Philosophy?*, trans. H. Tomlinson and G. Burchell, London: Verso.

Eco, U. (1986), *Travels in Hyperreality*, trans. W. Weaver, London: Picador.

Heidegger, M. (1971), 'Building Dwelling Thinking' in *Poetry, Language, Thought*, trans. A. Hofstadter, New York: Harper and Row, pp. 143–61.

Jameson, F. (1991), *Postmodernism, or, the Cultural Logic of Late Capitalism*, London: Verso.

Jameson, F. (2003), 'Future City', *New Left Review* 2(21): 65–79.

Kant, I. (1992), *How to Orient Yourself in Thinking*, trans. H. B. Nisbet, Cambridge: Cambridge University Press.

Klein, N. (2004), *The Vatican to Vegas: A History of Special Effects*, New York: The New Press.

Lambert, G. (2002), *The Non-Philosophy of Gilles Deleuze*, London: Continuum.

Spoto, D. (1983), *The Dark Side of Genius: The Life of Alfred Hitchcock*, London: Plexus.

Vidler, A. (2000), *Warped Space: Art, Architecture, and Anxiety in Modern Culture*, Cambridge: The MIT Press.

Žižek, S. (2000), *The Art of the Ridiculous Sublime: On David Lynch's Lost*

Highway, Seattle: Walter Chapin Simpson Centre for the Humanities, University of Washington.

Notes

1. In Heidegger's essay 'Building Dwelling Thinking' (first given as a lecture in Darmstadt in 1951) this is encapsulated in the placid-sounding euphemism 'housing shortage'. But it takes no great leap of imagination to know the cause of the shortage. Having said that, the cities that were the most affected were the industrial cities in the north, not the Bavarian villages where Heidegger himself lived. Indeed, one of the key reasons the war crimes trials were held in Nuremberg was that it was one of the least destroyed major cities (its symbolic resonance with the birth of the Nazi party itself was not of course incidental).
2. See Eco 1986. That is an aesthetic of the 'realer than the real'. There are any number of examples one could point to, but one of the more ironic (because of its 'ruse of history' undertone) is the filming of (1955) *The Trouble with Harry* – according to biographer Donald Spoto (1983: 355), Hitchcock deliberately set it in Vermont to capture the striking autumn colours. However, when he got to East Craftsbury in October 1954 to photograph it, he found he had been preceded by a storm and had to film indoors in a converted school gym prepared in case of inclement weather. The finishing touches were done on a soundstage in Hollywood using East Craftsbury leaves hand-pasted onto plaster trees.
3. On the convergence of cinematic soundstages and the space of shopping malls and casinos see Norman Klein 2004: 360.
4. See Vidler 2000: 65–79.
5. See Buchanan 2000.
6. Jameson 1991. This essay was first published in *New Left Review* 146 in 1984.
7. See also Lambert 2002: 114–31.
8. 'The virus ascribed to junkspace is in fact the virus of shopping itself; which, like Disneyfication, gradually spreads like a toxic moss across the known universe' (Jameson 2003: 77).
9. His method, as Žižek (2000) has astutely shown, is to refer to other films – effectively the only outside to a David Lynch movie is another movie. He thus uses intertextuality to create a meta-level immanence that simply compounds the affect achieved by Hitchcock by multiplying it without relief.
10. Jameson (1991: 26–8) also described postmodern space as schizophrenic, but he took his cue from Lacan rather than Deleuze.
11. Of course, this method of analysis was already forecast in their analysis of the spatial coordinates of the bureaucratic assemblage in their *Kafka: Toward a Minor Literature* (1986).
12. See Kant 1992: 235–52.

Chapter 1

Space in the Age of Non-Place

Ian Buchanan

A schizophrenic out for a walk is a better model than a neurotic lying on the analyst's couch.

Deleuze and Guattari, *Anti-Oedipus*

Swimming through

In *Critique de la vie quotidienne 1: Introduction*, published in 1947 Henri Lefebvre drew together two concepts that have effectively been inseparable ever since in studies of the human environment, namely space and everyday life. He conceived this relation dialectically such that the everyday and space are never in step, but always somehow out of kilter either because the built environment has not taken account of history ('Notes on the New Town') or because as modern subjects we have forgotten how to connect to history ('Notes Written One Sunday in the French Countryside').[1] In the half-century since, a number of scholars have followed Lefebvre both in maintaining the link between these two concepts, and their essential estrangement, albeit with quite different ideological agenda in mind. Jean Baudrillard (Lefebvre's one-time research assistant), Michel de Certeau, Guy Debord and Marc Augé all owe an obvious debt to Lefebvre. Deleuze and Guattari are sometimes taken to be part of this lineage, too, but their fit is never an easy one.

Discussions of their place in this particular canon are to be found in the work of cultural geographers such as Nigel Thrift, Derek Gregory and Edward Soja, philosophers like Edward Casey and political scientists like William Connolly, but by pathologising the everyday in the way they do, Deleuze and Guattari stand apart from the majority of theorists interested in the nexus between the everyday and the built environment who are, for the most part, not even prepared to use a term like schizophrenia as a metaphor. Fredric Jameson is a notable exception to this rule, but he nonetheless very cautiously frames his deployment of schizo-phrenia as 'description rather than diagnosis' (Jameson 1991: 26). For the most part, contemporary human geography quite willingly embraces the first part of Lefebvre's critical dyad, namely that built space has eroded our connection with history (on this score Rebecca Solnit astutely argues that memorialisation is the most pernicious form of urban erasure since it pretends to preserve the formerly living-breathing thing it now symbolises); but has been much slower in grappling with the second pole, except in quite banal ways.[2] I suspect the reason for this is that while no-one is willing to make the former the cause of the latter, they cannot see how to think the connection differently and reproduce the formula regardless of best intentions. In the context of this problematic Deleuze and Guattari's claim that the schizo lives history, but has in a sense lost the luxury of the distance of historicity, can be seen as an important advance in thinking about space and everyday life in postmodernity.

The persistence of the notion of historicity as a kind of distance that enables the self to perceive itself in the third person can be seen even in those texts such as Anthony Giddens' highly influential (1990) *The Consequences of Modernity* and Fredric Jameson's equally seminal (1991) *Postmodernism, or, the Cultural Logic of Late Capitalism* which are premised on the loss of historicity. It recurs, as I will argue in what follows, in the form of a delirious 'I feel'. Giddens' narrative describes a process of 'disembedding' whereby we have been, as it were, evicted from the world, making it impossible to experience it in the same way as our more autochthonous forebears. The fresh produce with which we provi-sion ourselves is no longer grown by us, indeed even if we buy it from the local village market it is unlikely to have all been grown locally. At my own supermarket, I can buy imported Mexican mangoes, New Zealand kiwi fruit, dates from Israel and bananas from Brazil, the point being that what we take for granted as our everyday is the result of an incredible and historically recent process of globalisation. For good or ill, without it, even something as mundane as a mango salad for my evening meal would not be possible. And although most of us embrace the opportunities globalisation affords us, we nonetheless continue to sense and long for a past none of us has actually known when the con-nections were local not global, when the food on our plate was the result of our own toil in the garden. This is the world, as imaginary as it obvi-ously is, that we have been evicted from by our own success in transform-ing our habitat. The longing underpinning this feeling of exile manifests itself in the form of disorientation: we can't seem to get our bearings in this brave new world without borders. Disorientation brought on by the disembedding process requires in its turn a compensating process of re-embedding to accommodate us to the alienatingly 'faceless' world of modernity. These processes, which Giddens collectively refers to as abstract systems of trust, are effectively what holds postmodern society together in the absence of stronger, more communal bonds.

The point I am making is that for Giddens, we have scarcely changed at all in spite of the momentous shifts that have occurred in historical terms (new technology, new social structures, new modes of production, and so on); it is only our day-to-day circumstances that have changed, and although these changes have effectively redrawn the landscape of our everyday existence they do not impinge on our constitution as subjects. Of course, they affect how we relate to ourselves, to our environment, and to each other, but at some fundamentally human level, we are not so very different from our pre-Industrial Revolution forebears. At least, not in Giddens' view. The fact that we haven't changed is registered – almost imperceptibly – in the persistence of our desire for modes of social bonding that social and historical change has rendered impossible.[3] The disorientation we allegedly feel in the face of so much and such rapid change is evidence of our own stolidness, but also of the survival of historicity. We can still see ourselves in the third person, as it were. Impossibly, we've stood still as statues as the ground beneath our feet lurched into a new millennium like an out-of-control roller-coaster. Jameson captures this paradox with unusual economy in his attempt to describe the effect of the Bonaventure Hotel as an instance of a new form of hyperspace – it calls on us, he says, to grow new organs.[4] It's like climatic change, if you don't adapt you die, but just what changes are needed isn't clear. Cyberpunk writers like William Gibson conjecture we'll need more memory space to cope with the sensory overload portended by the future, while bleaker prognosticians like Philip K. Dick see adaptability itself (whether to nuclear holocaust or alien invasion) as the key trait we'll need to foster. Jameson too argues that we have not changed to keep pace with the times and that is why we find the contemporary world so dizzying. We were formed in an age whose coordinates were different, he argues, and because the changes are so rapid this continues to be true even of that marvellous generation unaware of a time before mobile phones and can't imagine life without email.

In both Jameson and Giddens, then, but in a range of other writers too, the existential quality of everyday life in postmodernity is theorised in terms of what it feels like to be trapped in a hallucinogenic space which in its newness seems literally other-worldly and for which no existing vernacular seems appropriate. As Jameson himself puts it, he is 'at a loss when it comes to conveying the thing itself' because the old language of 'volume or volumes' no longer applies. Rather the language of immersion seems better suited to this paradoxically depthless space which he goes on to proclaim 'has finally succeeded in transcending the capacities of the individual human body to locate itself' (Jameson 1991: 43–4). Elsewhere in his work (in an essay on Robert Stone, as it happens, not particularly concerned with space), he returns to the theme of immersion and shows it offers 'a new kind of opening onto the ontology of earthly space' for which the Heideggerian term *Stimmung* no longer seems either apposite or robust enough (Jameson 1993: 44–5). In its place, he offers 'sensorium', a concept which canvasses a field Deleuze articulates in terms of sensation and affect. Jameson suggests the new space, like new machines, can only be represented in motion – but the fact he focusses on a hotel and narrates that experience as a kind of swimming through (an image – borrowed from Henry Miller – that recurs in Deleuze and Guattari)[5] perhaps indicates our analyses should extend in a different direction: it is rather the postmodern subject who has to be represented in motion, not postmodern space. We are doing the lurching, not the earth. Jameson's description of his Bonaventure visit recollects those marvellous moments in science fiction (which obviously draw on travel literature of all types) when humans land on another planet and blithely describe it as strange and alien and never once think it might be they who are out of place.

Not a plane wreck, exactly, but . . .

Obviously, it would be inaccurate to say that space hasn't changed at all, but the focus on the mobility of the subject is, I want to suggest, the necessary key to understanding the ways in which it has changed. If it is finally true that space has transcended our capacity to get our bearings in it then that is because we have taken the logic of passing through to its logical extreme and created smooth, frictionless spaces that hurry the postmodern subject onward like a slippery slope.[6] It is 'geared to keep you mobile', as Michael Herr puts it in the section from his Vietnam memoir Jameson quotes to give us a sense of how postmodern space needs to be thought about (Jameson 1991: 45). The essential lesson of one of the inaugural texts on postmodern space, *Learning from Las Vegas*, is not so much architectural as existential, or rather the architectural lessons it has to offer derive from an existential standpoint which accepts the new space has its own authentic logic, albeit one not immediately apparent. Rather than bemoan the tacky, crass commercialism of the Strip, which is easy to do but scarcely instructive, Venturi et al. recommend a more autodidactic approach: 'Learning from the existing landscape is a way of being revolutionary for an architect' (Venturi et al. 1972: 3). To begin with this means setting aside preconceptions about the urban habitat. 'The Las Vegas Strip is not a chaotic sprawl but a set of activities whose pattern, as with other cities, depends on the technology of movement and communication and the economic value of the land. We term it sprawl, because it is a new pattern we have not yet understood'(Venturi et al. 1972: 76). The dominant mode of movement is obviously the car, but the question that should be asked at this point is whether or not (as is commonly assumed) the car has destroyed the city or, on the contrary, made it what it is. Speaking only of its architecture (the authors explicitly rule out making any judgements about what goes on in Las Vegas), Venturi, Scott Brown and Izenour's point is that the buildings in Vegas are designed to be perceived by an automobile culture. As such, the city's architecture is, as they carefully calculate, built to a scale suited to being seen by a subject moving at speed.

In this respect, Venturi, Scott Brown and Izenour echo and extend Reyner Banham's summation of Los Angeles as a city monumentalised in its freeways. Freeways, Banham says, not buildings, define Los Angeles' character spatially and existentially.[7] Its urban and architectural vernacular is a language of movement. The city will never be understood, he says, 'by those who cannot move fluently through its diffuse urban texture, cannot go with the flow of its unprecedented life' (Banham 1971: 5). But one might still object that the automobile has ruined the city because priority has been given to the needs, but also the capabilities, of the car, when it could quite easily have been otherwise. Where Los Angeles is concerned, such remarks are usually the occasion to lament the passing of its streetcars, which disappeared in 1961 amid a great furore, and to denounce the scandalous lack of a workable public transport system despite the billions poured into the white elephant subway project.[8] As Banham shows, it was the public transport system, the railways in particular, which in fuelling real estate speculation gave the city its shape. With the advent of the car, this design matrix did not have to be altered and indeed many of the major thoroughfares sit atop the urban palimpsest of defunct rail lines.[9] My implication is from a design point of view complaining about the car is waste of breath. Los Angeles is a city of the automobile age – I'll leave aside the question of whether or not that makes it an 'autopia' as Banham suggests, except to say I do not find much to disagree with in Rebecca Solnit's suggestion that 'what's terrifying about these new urban landscapes is that they imply the possibility of a life lived as one long outtake' (Solnit 2004: 32).

Effectively, Venturi, Scott Brown and Izenour's point is that the car made Las Vegas, so decrying its deleterious effects (as Mike Davis quite rightly does, speaking from an environmental or sustainable development rather than urban design point of view) is to forget the city's origins. Las Vegas owes its very existence to movement. Although its famous Strip and adjoining freeways are now experiencing the seemingly inexorable law of diminishing returns suffered by all freeways and know the kind of congestion that results in such frustrating ironies as it taking longer to get from McCarran airport by taxi to the Strip than it does to fly there from Los Angeles, the fact remains, at its inception, it was a parking lot, a place to stop for soldiers and truck drivers on transcontinental journeys.[10] Davis describes its urban design as having 'the apparent logic of a plane wreck' (Davis 2002: 96). Hyperbole aside this captures at least the spirit of the place. No-one would have thought of stopping in Las Vegas unless their car broke down, or they needed fuel, before the Casinos were built, when it was just heat, dust and cacti. And even then, in the beginning at least, the stops were unplanned, impromptu, if not accidental. There, where nothing was expected to be, there were gaudy neon signs and the promise of air-conditioning, cold beer and if not a good time, then at least not restless, empty time in a neither-here-nor-there roadside motel. Consequently, it has never been a walkable city. It is too hot for that in any case. Walking is done indoors in barn-sized casinos and super-sized shopping malls that replicate other places in a manner that has become synonymous with Las Vegas itself. Not a plane wreck, exactly, but still unexpected, unplanned for, built for the moment without much of a thought for the future.[11]

Like flies complaining that the fly-paper doesn't have the same hold it used to, critics seem only to be able to write about postmodern space in terms of its failure to engage them. Whether the point of reference is Los Angeles, widely championed as the city whose present most closely resembles the planet's imaginary overpopulated, hyper-consuming, car-dominated future, or Las Vegas, the Ginza or Potsdammer Platz, descriptions of postmodern spaces are invariably generated via the matrix of a confusion about what it feels like to live in them, or more often the conviction that such places are essentially unliveable. Indeed, one could go so far as to suggest the defining characteristic of a postmodern city, that is to say, precisely what sets it apart as postmodern, is not its decorated-shed architecture or plane-wreck urban design, but rather its intractability to habitation, or better yet dwelling (in Heidegger's sense). These cities are, from an existential point of view, made of Teflon: they repel old-fashioned attempts to put down roots, ways of being that sink into the earth in search of a sturdy foundation on which to erect a new life. What is postmodern about this, as opposed to modern or classical, is that these cities resist dwelling not because they are too different, but on the contrary because they are too familiar, their lack of difference disconcerting us because after having travelled so great a distance as from Sydney to Los Angeles, say, we feel we deserve an encounter with otherness of the same intensity as Flaubert's visit to the Orient. This, I gather, is what underpins Virilio's claim that such journeys are 'empty' and 'without destination' (Virilio 1983: 66). The proliferation of sameness installs a blank, standardised, one-logo-fits-all, opacity where one expected a deeply significant enigma. The Flauberts of today express their orientalism not by fervidly fantasising about what goes on behind closed curtains, but in marvelling that 'they've got McDonald's' too.

Frictionless space designed to accelerate throughput will obviously not have the same affect as a more consciously arresting space, but that doesn't warrant the conclusion that it is either affectless or ineffable. Yet this view has a wide currency as is evident in the often evoked complaint that although generally attractive to tourists, postmodern cities (as opposed to iconic postmodern buildings) are frequently characterised as leaving their visitors disappointed because they do not bestow a lasting sense of having been there. We can sense the fear of disappointment in the hyperbole of the promotional literature which invariably promises an experience that will last a lifetime. But why we should be disappointed isn't clear. Indeed, exactly what the feeling of having been there should be like is very ambiguous. Most mysterious of all is the prejudice against speed (witness the comments from Virilio cited above) which is frequently decried as ruining travel even though it is obvious that it is the speed of jet travel that makes it possible in the first place. Speed is blamed for a disappointment spawned in all likelihood from the unrealised desire to have become Parisian for having visited Paris, however briefly, or a Berliner for having spent a night or two in Berlin, or a Melbournian for having holidayed there. I will return to this theme in a moment, but suffice it to say for now that I do not think this expectation is unreasonable or implausible, except that these life changes are meant only to add a layer of cosmopolitan varnish to an already well-wrought urn of subjectivity. Yet if a label like 'Parisian' has any substance, it must mean something more diverting than simply acquiring a chic veneer expressed as a taste for croissants or baguettes; it must imply a radical transformation of subjectivity for which Deleuze and Guattari's term 'deterritorialisation' is obviously apt.

Postmodern Orientalism

Deterritorialisation names the process whereby the very basis of one's identity, the proverbial ground beneath our feet, is eroded, washed away like the bank of a river swollen by floodwater – immersion.[12] Although such transformations are often narrated as a discovery of oneself, it would be more accurate to think of them in terms of loss, or, becoming-imperceptible, as Deleuze and Guattari put it, by which they mean ceasing to stand out, ceasing to be perceived as different, looking like everybody else, merging with the landscape.[13] The conclusion one might reach from the foregoing is that postmodern cities do not deterritorialise us in the way modern or premodern cities once did; but in fact the contrary would be true – even in his most rapturous moments Flaubert wasn't deterritorialised by the Orient. It did not change him, nor open him to change. This was essentially Said's point in *Orientalism*. Flaubert took his preformed assumptions and fantasies about the Orient to Egypt and returned with them not only fully intact, but thoroughly affirmed. Said describes Flaubert's Orientalism as 'revivalist: *he* must bring the Orient to life, he must deliver it to his readers, and it is his experience of it in books and on the spot, and his language for it, that will do the trick' (Said 1978: 185). Said rightly describes Flaubert's writing as cliché ridden and filled with grotesquerie (the lingering hospital scenes Said quotes being especially overripe), but all importantly operating according to a discernible logic, or as Deleuze and Guattari would put it, code. Flaubert writes in the expectation that his account of the Orient will be understood in a very particular manner – veils, hookahs, dates, the most mundane items betoken a fantasy world Flaubert is confident his readers will recognise and want to share. Effectively Said's purpose in *Orientalism* is to explain how this coding was formulated, disseminated and ultimately naturalised.

It is instructive to compare Said's account of nineteenth-century Orientalism with Umberto Eco's *Travels in Hyperreality* written in 1975, still a couple of years before the term postmodern gained the currency and particular valency it has today.[14] Flaubert, as have many travel writers before and since, approaches the Orient as dual space, a space that has a surface which is visible without being legible, it can be seen but its significance escapes the untutored or unsympathetic eye; and it has a depth which is invisible, but legible to the cognoscenti. The surface is blank unless you know how to decipher its code.[15] The hospital scenes that so repel and fascinate Flaubert are, to him at least, signs of an inglorious, dangerous, but clearly voluptuous Oriental decadence. The clinical precision of his description, repressing as it does any expression of sympathy or sentiment which might betray his desire, deliberately condemns significance to the depths of the unseen. In this respect, one might venture the hypothesis that Orientalism is to travel what Oedipus is to psychoanalysis, it presupposes and at the same time makes legible a subterranean other world of significance. But if this is so, then as Deleuze and Guattari say of Oedipus, attacking it is pointless since it is merely a screen behind which real desiring-production goes about its business. This blank surface/legible depth dualism is reproduced in the various theories of travel and travelling that try to distinguish between travellers and tourists, the latter being portrayed by the former as the poor unenlightened souls unable to detect the deeper meaning of things.[16] But evidently it is becoming more and more difficult to sustain: postmodern space does not seem to yield the depth of meaning its classical and modern antecedents did. This is what makes Eco's book such a fantastic artefact. It is perhaps the last of its kind – a genuine, but ultimately failed attempt to read the space of postmodernity.

Eco approaches America as a country with two faces, or rather two places – one well known and public and another one hidden in plain sight. The depth is only just below the surface in Eco's appraisal of America, but it is hidden all the same. 'Cultivated Europeans and Europeanized Americans think of the United States as the home of the glass-and-steel skyscraper and of abstract expressionism. But the United States is also the home of Superman, the superhuman comic-strip hero who has been in existence since 1938' (Eco 1986: 4). Revealing his versatility, Oedipus takes on the guise of Americanism in Eco's writing, it is that which he must explain, but also presuppose, in order to enlighten his cultivated European and Europeanised readers. His writing, too, observes a kind of clinical detachment, both to ensure the accuracy of his observations, but also to secure him from the charge of having somehow crossed over and become the thing he describes: an American. Superman isn't chosen at random, however; he is not simply a ubiquitous item of Americana in Eco's hands, of a piece with apple pie and football. It is Superman's mountainous hideaway, the Fortress of Solitude where the man-of-steel goes when he needs to be alone with his memories and 'work through' his Kryptonian otherness, perhaps, that attracts Eco's keen eye. 'For Superman the fortress is a museum of memories: Everything that has happened in his adventurous life is recorded here in perfect copies or preserved in a miniaturised form of the original' (Eco 1986: 5). Resembling a baroque *Wunderkammern*, the fortress is the one place where Superman can be himself, an alien whose past has been obliterated.[17] Eco suspects the average American reader, in contrast to himself, cannot see the significance of this private museum and doubtless would have difficulty connecting it to American tastes and sensibilities.

> And yet in America there are many Fortresses of Solitude, with their wax statues, their automata, their collections of inconsequential wonders. You have only to go beyond the Museum of Modern Art and the art galleries, and you enter another universe, the preserve of the average family, the tourist, the politician. (Eco 1986: 5–6)

Outside the museums where European culture is kept in quarantine, contained as much by the label 'high art' as the walls, there are other places, ubiquitously American or rather Americanist places that Americans themselves cannot see as such. In Eco's work there is the same expectation as Flaubert's that space be coded, but in its frustrated form. There seems not to be any depth to American culture. Eco's theory of the hyperreal is an attempt to articulate the logic of the code he assumes must be there, but can't ever quite convince himself actually exists. His suspicion is that it is simply and only hollow commercialism. 'Baroque rhetoric, eclectic frenzy, and compulsive imitation prevail where wealth has no history' (Eco 1986: 25–6). Hyperreality does not finally disclose the hidden depth of the America Eco wants to convey in the same way that Orientalism functions for Flaubert. The difference is obvious. For a start, Flaubert did not have to invent Orientalism to explain himself, it was ready-to-hand and already widely accepted and understood. By contrast, Eco is trying to explain a new kind of affect generated by a new kind of space for which commercialism is perhaps an already adequate explanation, but it is one that as Deleuze and Guattari might put it cannot be avowed. Therefore Eco feels compelled to invent something that can be believed in, the original American title of his volume of essays – *Faith in Fakes* – is telling in this regard. Ultimately, the biggest piece of fakery one encounters in Eco's text is this theory, which isn't to say he wasn't sincere in elaborating it. Hyperreality, like Oedipus, is what Deleuze and Guattari call a 'dishonoured representative' – it is a construct whose sole purpose is to attract our guilt and bile, to seduce desire into throwing in its lot with interest.

The postmodern traveller, like Eco, but more especially Marc Augé as I will show in a moment, who complains that new spaces aren't as meaningful as they used to be is essentially complaining that these spaces aren't coded. That is why the schizo is a better model than the neurotic on the couch: the latter dwells in coded space (in Deleuze and Guattari's view, everything in psychoanalysis reduces to a mummy–daddy–me code, so little Richard's toy train has to be daddy, the station mummy, and so on).

Augé's work is not only emblematic of the way thinking and writing about contemporary society has (since the early 1980s) produced descriptions of space that derive from a professed inability to connect to or properly describe the experiences the space itself makes available, it also offers a glimpse of the 'abstract machine' at work in such descriptions. While the hypermobility of the postmodern subject has, as I've argued above, changed the way we experience space, our accounts of space do not yet reflect an awareness of this mobility. In Augé we perhaps see the reason behind this lag or disconnection between space and everyday life: mobility functions as an abstract machine, influencing thinking without being itself thinkable. As Deleuze and Guattari put it, the abstract machine materialises when we least expect it – its signal feeling (I use this term deliberately, for Deleuze and Guattari 'I feel' rather than 'I see' or 'I think' is the form taken by delirium) is: whatever could have happened to for things to come to this?[18]

Non-place

I like to imagine that on the fateful morning of 20 July, 1984, the day Marc Augé narrates with such passionate introspection in *La Traversée du Luxembourg*, the author experienced what his former teacher Michel de Certeau called a 'shattering' (*éclatement*), or what Deleuze and Guattari call 'cracking' (*craquement*). He rolls out of bed at 7 a.m., taking care as usual not to put the wrong foot forward, then wanders slowly, and, frankly, a little painfully, into the kitchen to make coffee. There, still a little sleepy, he muses dreamily about the day ahead, a lecture to be given in Palermo, while in the background, his bedside radio conveys in blank tones the news of the day – catastrophes in the Orient, the Tour de France leader-board, a recent Gallup poll, and so forth. At some point, maybe while he is showering, it occurs to him that contemporary life is truly marvellous in the old-fashioned sense of the term, something literally to be marvelled at. Brazilian coffee fuels a mind half-asleep in Paris but already half-way to Sicily. Although he's yet to leave the house, he is up to date with the latest goings-on in Parisian politics and the Far East. But, he thinks to himself, it is getting harder each day to decide where the near ends and the far begins; inside and outside, too, have lost most of their meaning, as have public and private, owing to the well-nigh 'divine invasion' (to use Philip K. Dick's phrase) of the mass media, which trespasses all the old boundary lines.

What he is starting to realise, perhaps only dimly at first, he has only just woken up after all, is that the everyday, even at its most banal levels, is in fact utterly remarkable. He isn't the first to have had this thought, by any means, after all it is at the centre of everything the surrealists and the situationists did. But its effect on his thinking is perhaps more shattering than it was for any of his predecessors (Lefebvre, Debord and de Certeau) because of the apparently fatal implication it betokens for his profession, anthropology, which even to the trained eye appears suited only to the analysis of carefully circumscribed villages in faraway places. Since today it no longer seems possible either to delink oneself from the network of relations we call globalisation or find a place out of the way enough not to have been penetrated by it (either in the guise of tourism or finance capitalism, or both), it is a mode of inquiry whose object has to all intents and purposes vanished. We live in a world without others, Augé suddenly thinks, and it is a world in which anthropology will find it hard to retain a place.

If the truism that one is defined by one's professional expertise holds fast, then in noting that anthropology's object has all but disappeared, Augé could scarcely have avoided wondering just where that left him. What may have begun as an idle reverie, must suddenly have taken a shattering turn. The intensity of *La Traversée du Luxembourg* we can now understand is that of a man no longer certain of his existence – it minutely records the thoughts and reflections of a man who has begun to feel he isn't quite there any more. In the manner of Joyce's *Ulysses*, then, it attempts to avert a descent into nothingness, that is, the abject meaninglessness of the everyday in its most mundane detail, even as it embraces it as its necessary condition, by elevating the notion of the day into an epic construct in its own right. The paradox here is that by focussing on this day, this day which in fact is just like any other becomes an elected day, the full implication of which is that any other day could similarly be redeemed. This, in effect, is the fantasy of diarists: the fullness of their diaries competes with the emptiness of their lives as they themselves perceive it. For that is the precise task of the diary: to imbue emptiness with meaning, to give it a body we might also say. Augé woke up an anthropologist, only to find that his anthropological way of thinking about the world has led him to the conclusion that anthropology no longer exists because the transformations of late capitalism have rendered it a discipline bereft of a proper object.

One can readily sense the prickling here of an 'I feel' of a familiarly postmodern kind – I feel that this situation in which I find myself, rather late in life, is strange. It is in this sense, too, that the schizophrenic is a better model than a neurotic on a couch, it allows us to move outside the realm of the coded to the delirious. I can't adjust to the fact that I can have Brazilian coffee in the morning and that isn't exotic or rare, but perfectly staple. I can't get used to the idea that I can take breakfast in Paris, give a lecture in Palermo at midday and still be home in time for dinner. It is almost like being in two places at once; or, nearer to the truth, perhaps, it feels like being in neither place, at once. Somehow the sheer fact of being able to be in Palermo at midday and still get home for dinner diminishes – in ways he is yet to qualify – the existential quality of his dwelling (in Heidegger's sense) in Paris and similarly makes light of his being in Sicily. Can one really say with honesty that one has been to a city if one has merely touched down there for an hour or two? Such – not entirely idle – thoughts remind me of a game my friends and I used to play as kids. It was essentially a game of braggadocio: we used to count up all the countries we'd been to and of course the most travelled won, but fights always broke out as to whether a 'stop-over' (for example, at Changi airport on the way to England) counted. We generally agreed that you had at least to leave the airport for it to count, but still we could never quite dismiss the legitimacy of the claim to having been somewhere such global pit-stops entail. I would later come to think of these stop-overs as a kind of travel that has to be written under erasure – one has gone there, without having been there.

Augé's point, I think, is that jet travel has lightened our step on earth; we no longer dwell as heavily as we once did. We swim through places more than we dwell there and consequently a new type of social space has emerged whose precise purpose is to facilitate a frictionless passage – airports, train stations, bus terminals, fast food outlets, supermarkets and hotels. Because they do not confer a sense of place, Augé calls these places non-places. The poet, if not the philosopher, of this space is Baudrillard whose later books (*America, Cool Memories, Paroxysm*) only make sense if you read them as the feverish, inspired, jottings one makes in hotel rooms in strange cities in the lonely hours between arriving and departing. He does not write about places – places write through him. He writes about where he is, right now, without looking forward or back, unless there happens to be a TV in the room in which case 'elsewhere' is beamed in live and contextless. For this reason, he stops writing when he leaves a place. The abrupt gaps in his text between each aphoristic paragraph stand in the place of a deixis deemed irrelevant – postmodern space is neither here nor there, or rather neither here nor there has meaning except, as Deleuze and Guattari put it, as opposite poles of 'an indivisible, nondecomposable distance' (Deleuze and Guattari 1983: 87).

Deterritorialisation and reterritorialisation

The new space, which Rem Koolhaas aptly terms 'junk space' (the residue of capitalism), does not confer on us any sense of 'place', as Augé, but countless others as well, have argued.[19] It is space as mass-manufactured good, as Rebecca Solnit argues. 'Starbuck's are scariest of all, because they impersonate the sensibility of the nonchains, while McDonald's is at least honest about its mass-production values' (Solnit and Schwartzenberg 2000: 141). We might ask, then, why these chain stores, like Starbuck's, but also Borders and Barnes and Noble, which combine ruthless corporate trading practices with cornerstore ambience, are so successful. Eco's answer as we've seen is that we have faith in fakes, we are in the grip of a logic of hyperreality which willingly embraces the copy as the higher form of originality. This should not be confused with Žižek's position, adapted from Mannoni, namely that we know it is fake, but treat it as real all the same. Although there is an obvious degree of sympathy between these two positions, the difference is that ultimately Eco sees no false consciousness in the logic of hyperreality. But without getting into the complex shift in the structure of the business environment in the western world that has favoured the rise of chain stores, perhaps even necessitated them, one can still see the limitation of any attempt to read these spaces as coded. The decor of a Starbuck's cannot be read, in the sense of finding layers of significance to its carefully chosen rough hewn wood panelling or its dye-free recycled cardboard cup holders.

If we have moved into a space that isn't coded and therefore cannot be read, then as Jameson narrates in his account of the Bonaventure it would indeed be impossible to navigate. He is no doubt correct in his estimate that putting up signposts is a retrograde step. Yet however much those of us who liked cities like San Francisco before gentrification set in might bemoan the effects of its postmodernisation the reality is that these cities, smooth as their space might have become, do continue to yield a place-conferring affect, albeit one that cannot completely eradicate the feeling of having lost something we never possessed.[20] It is the mode of place-conferring that has changed. In Flaubert's age, the mode was 'oedipal' (of which orientalism is but one of the better known strains), but now its mode is deterritorialisation and reterritorialisation. These two processes go hand in hand, Deleuze and Guattari always insist, but that does not mean they are of the same order or somehow reciprocal – one cannot think of it as the left hand returning what the right hand takes away. In clarifying how these terms operate I hope better to explain how chain stores function to confer upon us a sense of place (in a place-less world) and in the process answer what Jameson describes as an 'embarrassing question' raised by this process which in his view does not seem very different 'from classical existentialism – the loss of meaning everywhere in the modern world, followed by the attempt locally to re-endow it, either by regressing to religion or making an absolute out of the private and contingent' (Jameson 1998: 150).

As Jameson rightly says deterritorialisation is absolute, therefore it would be embarrassingly illogical to conceive reterritorialisation as some kind of restorative process that can, albeit on an extremely localised scale, reverse its effects and give rise to a feeling that would have to be described as along the lines of pre-territorialisation. Reterritorialisation is not a retreat into the vestigial system of 'private gardens' and 'private religions' of Jameson's reckoning, it is rather the transposition of the effect of territorialisation from a spatial arrangement that can usefully be thought of as a home onto tokens of varying kinds which henceforth can be said to have a 'home value'. There is literally no restriction on the kinds of things – tokens – that can be imbued with this value, as such it is a distortion to relegate the effects of reterritorialisation to the private. In fact, the most obvious instances of it occur in public. The homey ambience of Starbuck's decried by Solnit could well be attributed to the way in which its decor has been made to take on a 'home value'. Indeed, this is precisely what I would argue, but that still leaves unanswered the question of how this might be made to happen. This isn't to rule out private reterritorialisation effects, however, but to qualify that refracting territorialisation through the lens of a binary distinction such as public and private is to make it into something it decidedly is not, namely a binary. Deterritorialisation and reterritorialisation are separate and distinct processes that cannot be fully understood in the absence of the primary term, territory, which has a very complex history in Deleuze and Guattari's work.[21]

So what then is reterritorialisation? 'Reterritorialisation must not be confused with a return to a primitive or older territoriality: it necessarily implies a set of artifices by which one element, itself deterritorialised, serves as a new territoriality for another, which has lost its territoriality as well' (Deleuze and Guattari 1987: 174). Accordingly, anything 'can serve as a reterritorialisation, in other words, "stand for" the lost territory; one can reterritorialise on a being, an object, an apparatus or system . . .' (Deleuze and Guattari 1987: 508, ellipsis in original). This new object which has been made to 'stand for' the lost territory is said to have 'home value', that is, it is a compensation and substitute for the home that has been lost. Rebecca Solnit's comment that memorialisation is paradoxically one of the most pernicious forms of urban erasure might be rewritten in these terms. In practically every gentrified city in the world, new apartments stand in the place where old-style manufacturing, warehousing or stevedoring businesses once thrived. Often these apartments are simply warehouse conversions, but just as often they are brand new structures built from scratch on cleared land from which every surface trace of the previous usage has been removed (I specify 'surface trace' because these so-called 'brown field' sites can often contain an invisible legacy of decidedly unhealthy traces of past use). These latter types of constructions are generally regarded as 'soulless' even by the people who buy them precisely because they seem to lack a history, by which is meant a kind of organic attachment to the fabric of the city. As de Certeau argued, speaking of the destruction of Les Halles in Paris and the subsequent conversion of the site, very far from wanting to exorcise the past, we long to be haunted by it.[22] It is the city's ghosts that make it inhabitable. This is where memorialisation steps in – it positions relics of the past as tokens that 'stand for' the lost territory.

If postmodernism is defined by the preponderance of deterritorialisation and dearth of reterritorialisation (the lack of reterritorialisation would explain why Jameson found the Bonaventure so disorienting), then in view of the design for the 'Freedom Tower' to be built on the site of the World Trade Center in New York one can perhaps declare that aesthetic officially dead. The new aesthetic, whatever one wants to call it (but hopefully something more imaginative than post-postmodernism), emphasises reterritorialisation. Both a place of mourning of national significance – it is now the most visited tourist site in New York City – and one of the most valuable pieces of real estate in the world, 'Ground Zero' poses a perplexing problem to architects and developers alike. It was clear that whatever was built there would have to respect the memory of the dead by not standing on their remains, hence all the talk about the buildings' 'footprints', but also honour them with its magnificence, which is why all the early talk about not building anything so tall again – 'leaving that to the Asians' – was quickly dropped and forgotten. All the short-listed design entries treated the 'footprints' of the original towers as sacred, Libeskind took this to its logical extreme and enshrined them.[23]

His 'Freedom Tower' will (if his original design is adhered to, something that now seems increasingly unlikely) soar 541 metres (or 1,776 feet, in remembrance of the year of American independence) above the earth, dwarfing by a large margin both the original towers which stood at 411 metres and were briefly the tallest buildings in the world and

Malaysia's own twinned structure, and until very recently the record holder, the Petronas Towers which stand at 452 metres. They have since been eclipsed by a Taiwanese project known as the Taipei 101, which at 508 metres will still be beaten by the 'Freedom Tower'. With that keen sense for the memorial he has, which served him so well in designing the Holocaust museum in Berlin, Libeskind has pulled out all the stops – from the doubly symbolic height of the structure (year of independence plus tallest building in the world) to the rendering of the basement as materialisation of the American constitution (the slurry walls which were designed to hold back the Hudson and were the only part of the original building to survive were described by Libeskind as being as 'eloquent as the constitution itself'), through to the harnessing of the sun itself to cast shadowless light into its sacred core, 'the Park of Heroes', which traces the fatal footsteps of the fireman who so bravely rushed into the towers to give assistance, not to mention its nod to the Statue of Liberty, this building will never be just another skyscraper and that is surely what the American public wanted, indeed, needed.

This new type of space is very definitely coded, but in such a stifling way that it will, given time, doubtless leave us feeling nostalgic for the allegedly bad old days of postmodernity.

References

Anderson, P. (1998), *The Origins of Postmodernity*, London: Verso.

Augé, M. (1985), *La traversée du Luxembourg, Paris: 20 juillet 1984: Ethno-roman d'une journée française considérée sous l'angle des moeurs, de la théorie et du bonheur*, Paris: Hachette.

Augé, M. (1995), *Non-Places: Introduction to an Anthropology of Supermodernity*, trans. J. Howe, London: Verso.

Banham, R. (1971), *Los Angeles: The Architecture of the Four Ecologies*, Berkeley: University of California Press.

Buchanan, I. (2002), 'Deleuze and Hitchcock: Schizoanalysis and *The Birds*', *Strategies: Journal of Theory, Culture and Politics* 15 1: 105–18.

Buchanan, I. (2004), 'Inevitable Fusion? King Kong and the Libeskind Spire' *Antithesis* 14: 170–4.

De Certeau, M. (1998), 'Ghosts in the City', in M. de Certeau, P. Mayol and L. Giard Mayol, *The Practice of Everyday Life Volume Two: Living and Cooking*, trans. T. Tomasik, Minneapolis: University of Minnesota Press, pp. 133–43.

Davis, M. (2002), *Dead Cities*, New York: The New Press.

Davis, M. (2004), 'Planet of Slums: Urban Involution and the Informal Proletariat', *New Left Review* 2(26): 5–34.

Deleuze, G. and Guattari, F. (1983), *Anti-Oedipus: Capitalism and Schizophrenia*, trans. R. Hurley, M. Seem and H. R. Lane, Minneapolis: University of Minnesota Press.

Deleuze, G. and Guattari, F. (1987), *A Thousand Plateaus: Capitalism and Schizophrenia*, trans. B. Massumi, Minneapolis: University of Minnesota Press.

Eco, U. (1986), *Travels in Hyperreality*, trans. W. Weaver, London: Picador.

Giddens, A. (1990), *The Consequences of Modernity*, Cambridge: Polity.

Jameson, F. (1991), *Postmodernism, or, the Cultural Logic of Late Capitalism*, Durham: Duke University Press.

Jameson, F. (1993), 'Americans Abroad: Exogamy and Letters in Late Capitalism', in S. Bell, A. Le May and L. Orr (eds), *Critical Theory, Cultural Politics, and Latin American Narratives*, Notre Dame and London: University of Notre Dame Press, pp. 35–60.

Jameson, F. (1998), *The Cultural Turn: Selected Writings on the Postmodern, 1983–1998*, London: Verso.

Jameson, F. (2003), 'Future City', *New Left Review* 2(21): 65–79.

Klein, N. (1997), *The History of Forgetting: Los Angeles and the Erasure of Memory*, London: Verso.

Klein, N. (2004), *The Vatican to Vegas: A History of Special Effects*, New York: The New Press.

Lacan, J. 1979 *The Four Fundamental Concepts of Psychoanalysis*, trans. A Sheridan, Harmondsworth: Penguin.

Lefebvre, H. (1991), *Critique of Everyday Life: Volume One*, trans. J. Moore, London: Verso.

Lefebvre, H. (1995), *Introduction to Modernity*, trans. J. Moore, London: Verso.

Said, E. (1978), *Orientalism: Western Conceptions of the Orient*, Harmondsworth: Penguin.

Solnit, R. (2004), 'Check out the Parking Lot' (review of S. Birk and M. Sanders, *Dante's Inferno*), *London Review of Books* (July 8) 26(13): 32–3.

Venturi, R., Izenour, S. and Scott Brown, D. (1972), *Learning from Las Vegas: The Forgotten Symbolism of Architectural Form*, Cambridge: The MIT Press.

Solnit, R. and Schwartzenberg, S. (2000), *Hollow City: The Siege of San Francisco and the Crisis of American Urbanism*, London: Verso.

Virilio, P. and Lotringer, S. (1983), *Pure War*, trans. M. Polizzotti, New York: Semiotext(e).

Notes

1. See, respectively, Lefebvre 1995 and 1991.
2. Solnit and Schwartzenberg 2000: 142.
3. In sociology, this is a longstanding problematic that was given its first effective formulation by Tönnies in his distinction between *Gemeinschaft* (community) and *Gesellschaft* (society).
4. Rebecca Solnit's account of the 1990s' dot-com fuelled real estate boom in San Francisco offers a vivid picture of a city in the process of becoming a closed-in world, as Jameson describes the Bonaventure. 'Think of San Francisco as a rainforest being razed to grow a monocrop' (Solnit and Schwartzenberg 2000: 155). I will not enter into the debate that irrupted between Jameson and Davis as to whether or not Jameson paid adequate attention to the destructive effects of property development in downtown Los Angeles, except to point out that he addresses this issue in a later essay that I deal with below (see Jameson 1998).
5. Deleuze and Guattari 1987: 187.
6. There is a much darker side to this picture and that is the reality of cities too large and too poor to provide the necessary infrastructure for all their citizens. In these cities – for example, Nairobi, Lagos, Mumbai – if one does not belong to the thin, upper stratum, one is at best permanently transient. See Davis 2004.
7. Thus Banham (1971: 183–93) famously offers only a note on downtown Los

Angeles because that is all it is worth, its heart having been shrivelled by the ubiquitous freeways.

8. Mike Davis (2002: 184) reports that so far the LA subway has cost a spectacular $290 million per mile to construct.

9. See Klein 1997: 36–8.

10. See Davis 2002: 98.

11. As Davis (2002: 85–6) points out, Las Vegas doesn't care much for the past either – none of the iconic hotels of the 1950s and 1960s, the hey-day of the 'Rat Pack', is still standing. Even if the names have remained the same – MGM Grand, Mirage, Dunes, and so on – the buildings haven't.

12. Norman Klein (2004) uses the term 'immersion' to connect postmodern spaces and more especially film with the baroque. What is startling about this connection is that it was staring us in the face in Jameson's (1991: 40) description of the Bonaventure as aspiring to be 'a total space, a complete world' for which the baroque term of the Gesamtkunstwerk would not have been inappropriate. Decrying such spaces as 'junk' as Koolhaas instructs has effectively prevented us from apprehending their logic.

13. Deleuze and Guattari 1987: 198–9; 279.

14. I take this date from that given at the end of the chapter entitled 'Travels in Hyperreality' in the book of the same name which was first published in 1986 under the title Faith in Fakes. According to Perry Anderson (1998: 21–2) 'postmodern' was first used in the way we now understand it in 1974, but didn't really find much traction until 1977 with the publication of Charles Jenck's much celebrated Language of Post-modern Architecture.

15. We have to avoid using the term 'decode' in this context because in Deleuze and Guattari's text décodage doesn't mean decipher, or interpret. It is not the translation that is ambiguous, however, but Deleuze and Guattari's usage. That said, its logic is clear: the prefix 'de' has the meaning of cutting away (as in decapitate), not reading into (as in de-cipher). A decoded text is one that cannot be interpreted because it no longer operates according to the rules of codes – surface and depth – but has instead become 'axiomatic', pure surface.

16. Deleuze and Guattari (1987: 482) make a similar distinction between what they call Goethe travel and Kleist travel, but reverse the polarity. For them, the best kind of travel is precisely that which skates across the surface, or better yet doesn't move at all.

17. There is an interesting resonance here between Eco and Klein in the way each connects the postmodern to the baroque.

18. Deleuze and Guattari 1987: 169; 194. See also Buchanan 2002.

19. See Jameson 2003.

20. In my case, this is literally true: I first visited San Francisco in 1998, long after the gentrification process had begun to 'destroy' the city. My model for understanding this process though is the transformation of Fremantle in Western Australia, a city I lived in as a student, first by property developers cashing in on the America's Cup, then by the slow encroachment of Notre Dame University which is buying up all the old seafarers' hotels and turning them into classrooms and student accommodation.

21. This is not the place to investigate that history in full, but it is perhaps worth pointing out that such an investigation would have to begin with the startling sentences in the opening pages of Anti-Oedipus where Deleuze and Guattari announce that the Freudian concept of the drive must be redefined in terms of territoriality. 'There is no doubt that at this point in history the neurotic, the pervert, and the psychotic cannot be adequately defined in terms of drives [pulsions], for drives are simply desiring-machines themselves. They must be defined

in terms of modern territorialities. The neurotic is trapped within the residual or artificial territorialities of our society and reduces all of them to Oedipus as the ultimate territoriality' (Deleuze and Guattari 1983: 35).
22. See de Certeau 1998.
23. For a more developed consideration of this point see Buchanan 2004.

Chapter 2

To See with the Mind and Think through the Eye: Deleuze, Folding Architecture, and Simon Rodia's Watts Towers

Paul A. Harris

Folding Architecture

Gilles Deleuze's thinking about space is not to be found in a single text or statement. It is rather distributed throughout his writings about topics as diverse as Francis Bacon's paintings, fractal geometry, biological morphologies, and geography. Over the past decade or so, Deleuze's diffuse philosophy of space has actually been most incisively clarified not by philosophers, but architects and architectural theorists. Several influential architects have turned to Deleuze's philosophy as a means to rethink the conceptual grounds of their field. Deleuze's spatial concepts are then implemented in architectural work, and given visible form as architects utilise new design techniques made possible by different computer programs and softwares. Thus, in a somewhat circular fashion, architectural work influenced by Deleuze becomes an exemplary means by which to understand and explicate his philosophy of space.

French philosophy entered architectural discourse in the 1980s through deconstruction, as Jacques Derrida collaborated in different ways with leading postmodern architects including Frank Gehry, Bernard Tschumi, and Peter Eisenman. While the infiltration of Deleuze's thought into architecture remains less widely known in philosophical circles, it has nonetheless been pervasive. Derridean deconstructive architecture is giving way to Deleuzian folding architecture: Susannah Hagan notes that 'As Derrida dominated the 1980s, so Gilles Deleuze and Felix Guattari dominated the 1990s, drawing to themselves like strange attractors all those ideas about topology, morphology, biology, geology and complexity that are currently swarming amongst the architectural intelligentsia' (Hagan 2001: 137).[1] The shift from deconstructive to folding architecture entails more than a change in preferred metaphors and disciplines.[2] In the seminal *Folding in*

Architecture, Greg Lynn notes that deconstructive architecture operates with 'a logic of conflict and contradiction', whereas folding architecture foregrounds 'a more fluid logic of connectivity' (Lynn 2004: 8). While deconstructive architecture foregrounds formal rupture, folding architecture seeks material heterogeneity. Lynn posits that, 'If there is a single effect produced in architecture by folding, it will be the ability to integrate unrelated elements within a new continuous mixture' (Lynn 2004: 8). Significantly, this shift also reconfigures the relation between the conceptual and perceptual dimensions of architecture. The deconstructive logic uses conceptual means to disrupt perceptual habits: deconstructionists induce conflicts between structural design and a site's topography, or between a building's axes of symmetry and the space of rectilinear convention. In contrast to deconstruction, folding favours linkage over aporia. Folding architecture creates continuities between site and structure, implementing conceptual designs that entrain perception to follow patterns that connect outside and inside, both physically and psychologically. In Michael Speaks' words, folding architecture marks 'the development of more pliant, complex, and heterogeneous forms of architectural practice – with architectural practice supple enough to be formed by what is outside or external to them, yet resilient enough to retain their coherence as architecture' (Speaks 1995: xvi). In such architecture, where the outside is a fold of the inside, the conceptual and perceptual become increasingly indiscernible.

The most provocative, explicitly theoretical extrapolations of Deleuze's thought into architecture have come from Bernard Cache and Greg Lynn.[3] Cache attended Deleuze's seminars for several years and wrote a manuscript completed in 1983; Deleuze approvingly cites Cache's then-unpublished work in *The Fold* (1992). Cache's text first reached print in 1995 in English as *Earth Moves* and finally appeared in French in 1997 under its original title *Terre Meuble*. Lynn has been a central figure in articulating the conceptual underpinnings of folding architecture, dating from the seminal *Folding in Architecture*. In subsequent essays collected in the volumes *Folds, Bodies and Blobs* (1998a) and *Animate Form* (1998b), Lynn elaborates a theory and practice assembled around a Deleuzian vocabulary of the fold, multiplicity, machinics, bodies, and the virtual. Both Cache and Lynn reformulate architecture in terms of virtual concepts and abstract diagrams, and then actualise these conceptual tools through different computerised design processes. The Deleuzian concept of space made visible in folding architecture then yields a different notion of the body, and entails thinking through a new adaptation between the body and space.

Cache and Lynn, while conceptually very similar, use different sets of terms to integrate Deleuzian thought into architecture. Cache's work is seminal in forging the link between Deleuze and architecture because it is grounded in Bergson's ontology of images. Cache utilises Deleuze–Guattari's discussion of consolidation in *A Thousand Plateaus* as a framework within which to rethink the essential elements of architecture. Cache's analysis yields a treatment of space that Deleuze drew on in *The Fold*, particularly Cache's notion of inflection. Reconceiving architecture this way leads Cache to an image of the human body losing its erect solidity and stretching out as a skin folded in space. For Lynn, the relation between the body and geometry must be the starting point for redrawing architecture along Deleuzian lines. His early work takes up 'the present static alliance between rigid geometry and whole organisms' in architecture and seeks to render it 'more flexible and fluid through the use of suppler, deformable geometries' (Lynn 1998a: 42). Lynn's essays of the early to mid-90s adduce a critique of space, geometry and the body that works through Deleuze–Guattari's discussion of a 'protogeometry' of 'anexact, yet rigorous forms' in *A Thousand Plateaus* and the ontology of curvilinear matter in *The Fold*. This work culminates in a theory and practice of 'animate form' (presented in the 1998 book of that title), where a computer-generated design process unfolds in a space shaped by the integration of topology, time, and parameters into architecture (Lynn 1998b: 20).

Deleuze's philosophy of space is thus both clarified and extended in the work of Cache and Lynn. This application of philosophical concepts in architecture raises interesting methodological issues. Inflected by philosophy, folding architecture's techniques operate top-down, in that they move from philosophical spatial concept to designing abstract diagrams to implementing them in plans and projects. There is a certain irony in this, given that the central concepts of folding architecture are all founded on bottom-up principles. In other words, folding architecture has discovered how to design bottom-up concepts, but not how to practise bottom-up building procedures. In order to reflect on how bottom-up material methods could be conjoined to the spatial concepts of folding architecture, one must venture outside the parameters of folding architecture. In light of these issues, Simon Rodia's Watts Towers of Los Angeles prove to be very productive. The site realises the bottom-up principles of folding architecture in terms of structural design, materials deployed, and building methods. From a philosophical standpoint, thinking about the Watts Towers through the lenses of Deleuze's work yields a pedagogical experience, where one learns to *see with the mind, and think through the eye*.[4]

Bernard Cache: Consolidation and Inflection

The conceptual foundation in Bernard Cache's *Earth Moves* is Bergson's ontology of images, itself a critical element of Deleuze's thinking about space. From the outset, Cache defines his book as 'a classifier of images', and his introduction moves from the specific sense in which images function as 'visual documents' in architecture (sketches and plans) to a general, critical analysis of architectural images (Cache 1995: 2). The Bergsonian trajectory of Cache's analysis is evident in his attempt 'to show or create the kind of movement that is prior to the representation of stable objects, and so to introduce a new dynamic conception of both image and architecture' (Boyman 1995: viii). Cache's theoretical classification of spatial images ranges from geography to buildings to furniture. Abstractly, Cache defines the image to include 'anything that presents itself to the mind' – a significant shift to the philosophical because with it 'we pass from visible objects to visibility itself' (Cache 1995: 3). This passage is the space where we find the play between percept and concept, where they cross into each other, and where architecture implements philosophy. As for Deleuze's influence on his work, Cache acknowledges that his book amounts to 'a pursuit of [Deleuze's] philosophy by other means' (Cache 1995: 7). Like Deleuze, Cache defines his domain in terms of operative function rather than an essence or property: architecture is the 'art of the frame' (Cache 1995: 2), just as for Deleuze philosophy is the invention of concepts. The central problem probed by Cache is how to construct frames that function as folds rather than rigid boundaries between outside and inside, so that the movement of images pervades the built structure. Thus Cache operates with:

> a logic where the whole is not given but [is] always open to variation, as new things are added or new relations made, creating new continuities out of such intervals or disparities. In the unstable dynamic world in which they figure, images are therefore no longer defined by fixed divisions between inside and outside. Rather this division itself comes to shift or move as outside forces cause internal variations or as internal variations create new connections with the outside. (Boyman 1995: ix)

The foundation for Cache's theory of architecture as the art of the frame comes directly from Deleuze–Guattari's analysis of space and milieus in section 11 of *Thousand Plateaus*, '1837: Of the Refrain'.[5] Explaining his theoretical premises, Cache posits that 'The frame reduces architecture to its most basic expression and allows us to formulate a concept that derives directly from Eugene Dupréel, whose philosophy was centred entirely on the notion of frame and probability' (Cache

1995: 22–33). Within this view, 'Architecture would be the art of introducing intervals in a territory in order to construct frames of probability' (Cache 1995: 23). When consolidation enters into the framing process itself, the interval induces 'movement on a rarefied ground that turns into an aberration' and from it 'a whole range of dynamic states are thus produced' (Cache 1995: 25). Cache's formulations here directly echo the behavioural-biological 'machinics' Deleuze–Guattari elaborate throughout *A Thousand Plateaus*, especially the distinction they make between the 'rhizomatic' and the 'arborified' and their discussion of Dupréel's notion of consolidation. The arborified imposes form or a correct structure from without or above, whereas the rhizomatic depends upon articulation from within – packets of relations evolve without a blueprint; coordination and interaction are never direct or linear, but work, like neural networks, according to release or inhibition. To account for how milieus and territories fold inwards, as it were, and take on a consistency, Deleuze–Guattari invoke Dupréel's theory of consolidation, alluded to by Cache.

Dupréel's model of consolidation is critical for a concept of the frame that functions as a fold, because it models processes whereby new parts are not integrated into a pre-existing whole, but where the process of consolidation continually modifies the milieu. Rather than working from the inside (the centre of a pre-existing whole) to the outside (the boundary), here the whole is like a membrane, and consolidation proceeds from exterior to interior. Most importantly, the exterior boundary never simply dictates interiority as a cause that produces effects. Deleuze–Guattari sum up Dupréel's model as follows: 'Consistency is the same as consolidation, it is the act that produces consolidated aggregates, of succession as well as of coexistence, by means of . . . three facts . . . intercalated elements, intervals, and articulations of superposition' (Deleuze and Guattari 1987: 329). Consolidation thus never unfolds in a linear chain of events in consolidation: intercalated elements imply that there is no beginning from which linear sequence would derive; intervals dictate that consolidation occurs through arrangement and distribution; and articulations of superposition entail that consolidation entails disparate, overlapping rhythms. Because it proceeds bottom-up, consolidation is always creative, always beginning over again at each operation; but because it is an emergent process, it also always creates consistency. The reason Cache would turn to this particular moment in Deleuze's thought becomes clear when Deleuze–Guattari pose architecture as the material realisation of consolidation. They propose a spectrum between architectural forms where consolidation is subordinated to static structure and ones where consolidation is embedded in the building process. 'Architecture, as the art of abode and territory, attests to this: there are consolidations that are made afterward, and there are consolidations of the keystone type that are constituent parts of the ensemble' (Deleuze and Guttari 1987: 329).

But Cache does more than simply cut and paste the tripartite Deleuze–Guattari concept of consolidation into his theory of architecture. It would be more fitting to say that as Cache grafts this work onto his own, the abstract machine evolves in significant ways. The three elements of the Dupréel consolidation model (intercalated elements, intervals, and superposition of disparate rhythms) are transposed by Cache into three aspects of architecture: inflection, vector and frame. In turn, the three 'abstract functions' of architectural frames are, respectively, separation, selection and arrangement. Essentially, Cache seeks to incorporate the 'outside' forces of matter into the framing of architecture – or again, to induce the frame to function as a fold between outside and inside. Any architectural frame starts from an unoriented space, that of inflection. A frame's appearance marks a separation of it from its environment, but a properly permeable frame will not demarcate a rigid boundary but open an interval. If the frame does not serve as a cause of subsequent effects, it is freed from defining the form or function of an edifice. If it is conceived of instead as a vector, a tendency, then the architectural instantiates a 'frame of probability'. The probabilistic does not enclose a prefabricated space but opens an interval: 'the notion of a frame of probability presupposes that a distance or dehiscence be maintained between a frame and its content: one never knows how the interval that is marked off by the frame will be filled' (Cache 1995: 28). Thus the frame marks a space of arrangement rather than enclosure. In the context of Deleuze's work on space, it is fascinating to mark how Cache's adaptation of the Deleuze–Guattari notion of consolidation as the conceptual foundation for architecture induces him to posit a spatial ontology that anticipates the one articulated by Deleuze in *The Fold*.[6]

Earth Moves may thus be read as a kind of fold between *A Thousand Plateaus* and *The Fold*. Cache gives a physical grounding to the images ontology in terms Deleuze repeated in the study of the baroque. Images comprise 'substance', which, like Bergson's images, are between a representation and a thing: 'For body and mind are made of the same thing, of the only thing that is, which is neither spiritual nor corporeal, and which, like others, we will call substance. This substance is a priori nothing other than a fact of curvature' (Cache 1995: 120). Once the world is seen in terms of curvature rather than empty space and linear forms, 'the texture of substance is the inclusion of envelopes that fold into one another, small circles into larger ones' (Cache 1995: 124). Within such an ontology, the Dupréel model of consolidation implies that, '[e]xperimental imprecision, the occurrence of unexpected events, are the signs that reality is a hollow image and that its structure is alveolar. Intervals always remain and intercalated phenomena always slip into them, even if they finally break the frames of probability apart' (Cache 1995: 23). In the evolution of Deleuze's thinking about space, the notion that reality is 'alveolar', a 'hollow image', subtends some discussions of space in A Thousand Plateaus, taking its most explicit form in a brief discussion of 'holey space' (Deleuze and Guttari: 1987: 413–15). However, this notion of space comes to fruition at the outset of The Fold in conjunction with Leibniz's physics:

> Matter thus offers an infinitely porous, spongy, or cavernous texture without emptiness, caverns endlessly contained in other caverns: no matter how small, each body contains a world pierced with irregular passages, surrounded and penetrated by an increasingly vaporous fluid, the totality of the universe resembling a 'pond of matter in which there exist different flows and waves'. (Deleuze 1992: 5)

For Cache, this ontology of space initiates a Bergsonian image of thought. Restated in the terms of Leibniz, this ontology implies that, '[w]e will then certainly not acquire the soul or the body that we are at such pains to secure by better enclosing our subject zones; we must rather delve down into texture or go back up into envelopes by grafting ourselves onto the world that surrounds us and by opening this world within us' (Cache 1995: 124). In his investigation of time, Bergson sought to reach back to the 'critical turn' where duration surges forth as a continuous multiplicity. The corresponding spatial substrate in Cache, taken up by Deleuze in The Fold, is inflection. Just as for Bergson duration may be apprehended only through a mental effort of intuition, for Cache a dynamic conception entails a reaching back behind the fixity of rigid bodies in three-dimensional space: 'Take any surface. Generally, we describe its relief in terms of summits and crests, basins and valleys. But if we can manage to erase our coordinate axes, then we will only see inflections, or other intrinsic singularities that describe the surface precisely' (Cache 1995: 36). Once we sense images in terms of their qualitative uniqueness, rather than according to an external metric, Cache posits that 'we accede to another regime of images that we will call primary ones' (Cache 1995: 36). For Cache, the primary image is not an ur-image or the first stage in a series; it is rather space in its sheer virtuality, what Deleuze, citing Cache, called 'not yet in the world: it is the World itself . . .' (Deleuze 1992: 15). Just as for Bergson duration would constitute the surging forth of time as a continuous multiplicity, primary images trace the welling up of space. They precede distinctions between inside and outside, before and after. Cache takes the Möbius strip as an example of how a primary image 'allows us to see, if only for an instant, a universe with no top or bottom, right or left, inside or outside' (Cache 1995: 37).[7]

Inflection and the primary image are critical to Cache's concept of space (and Deleuze's in *The Fold*) because in their virtuality they mark the 'point' where space becomes indiscernible from time. Primary images 'allow us to glimpse a pure temporality to which we can't accede as subjects' (Cache 1995: 39). This time lies beyond – or rather, prior to – subjectivity because it is not yet a flow or rhythm. Cache characterises the temporality of the primary image as 'hysteresis', 'a gap in the time of the world through which we perceive pure instantaneity. It is the time of a universal lapping of waves that cannot be represented by a straight line or even a swirl, but only by a surface of variable curvature that is perpetually out of phase' (Cache 1995: 39). 'Thus we will not say that time flows but that time varies' (Cache 1995: 41). The 'alveolar' or 'spongy, cavernous' texture of space must be understood dynamically: space as 'variable curvature' unfolds or is folded according to a multi-temporality of different co-existing rhythms rather than in a linear series of events. Thus in *The Fold*, 'inflection' as the fundamental texture of space must be understood in both graphic, mathematical terms (curvilinearity, tangents) and in a language borrowed from fluid dynamics: 'Inflection itself becomes vortical, and at the same time its variation opens onto fluctuation, it becomes fluctuation' (Deleuze 1992: 17). In Deleuze's chaos-theory inflected account of space, the vortical nature of the 'pleats of matter' is mathematically speaking a fractal and dynamically speaking turbulence: 'Dividing endlessly, the parts of matter form little vortices in a maelstrom, and in these are found even more vortices, even smaller, and even more are spinning in the concave intervals of the whirls that touch one another' (Deleuze 1992: 5).

The question Cache ultimately confronts is how to incorporate or enfold inflection into the architectural frame. Or conversely, how to transform the rigid function of the frame as a 'separation' from the outside into a permeable membrane where inside and outside become sides of a surface. Cache first produces a schematic resolution to the problem: he 'simply transfer[s] the forms of the geographical outside onto furniture to get the outside inside' (Cache 1995: 73). Geography, defined as 'the shape of the outside', is recast in terms of what Benoit Mandelbrot called 'the fractal geometry of nature'. The topographical contours of the outside become folds in a topological texture, where intervals and zones of indeterminacy can open between any points (Cache 1995: 71). This texture then passes through the architectural frame and is iterated in surfaces within the built structure. Thus Cache designs furniture with curvilinear surfaces that emerge out of the materials he uses. For instance, a figure in *Earth Moves* shows a bookcase that looks like a rectilinear set of shelves that has been stretched and had waves sent through it. This shape is 'constituted by the rise of the formal powers of its materials. As it is being sanded down, the different strata of wood dilate and appear as so many instances of fold and detour' (Cache 1995: 71). The curvilinear texture of the outside passes inside, and is reconstituted as/on the outer surfaces of the interior Cache describes throughout the book – bookcases, chairs, tables, lamps. Thus: 'It is as if architecture functioned as a topological operator: a frame crossed through by a Moebius strip. Passing over to the inside of the frame only sends us back to the outside of the strip' (Cache 1995: 72).[8]

If we pursue the idea that architecture is a 'topological operator', this folding of the formal contours of outside into the inside would only be the first iteration of a recursive function. Cache returns to his favoured spatial image to express this iterative process: 'the description of a Moebius strip presupposes that one go around it twice: once from the outside toward the inside, then a second time from the inside toward the outside' (Cache 1995: 72). In essence, the 'other side' of the question becomes: once geography enters into and transforms the abode, how does the abode transform the human animal and return it to the outside? Architecture as 'covering' also entails a 'baring': walls allow humans to peel off clothes. How, then, as the next iteration, does the inside of the body become part of its outer surface? Cache recounts Michel Serres' observation that animal forms evolved from having hard outer shells to forms where what is hard gets interiorised. He then posits, in Deleuzian terms, the next iteration: 'we might drop the bones altogether, then the flesh, then the epidermis . . . Dermic power rises: the becoming of man-as-skin' (Cache 1995: 73). The evolution to 'modern man' was marked by an orthogonal shift from horizontal movement to *homo erectus* who 'proudly raise their spine against the gravitational vector' (Cache 1995: 74). Cache imagines 'the abandonment of a vectorial status in favour of a spreading out on the surface'. Cache then evokes one of Deleuze's favourite examples, Bacon's paintings of the Crucifixion. These works stretch the human animal onto a frontal plane where 'the projected flesh spreads out, slips and bends like a surface of variable curvature on an abstract plane: the fluctuations of the flesh become the play of dermic forces' (Cache 1995: 75). Here, then, emerges a vision where body and space inhere along abstract planes of inflection and evolve in the variations allowed for by consolidation.

Greg Lynn: Multiplicitious Bodies and Animate Forms

When it comes to pushing architecture to become an implementation of the virtual, Greg Lynn's work stretches the envelope. Adopting Deleuze's philosophy of the virtual, Lynn seeks to reconfigure relations between the body and geometry in architecture. For Lynn, folding architecture must 'deterritorialise' the architecture of fixed spatial types, itself founded on a 'pact between organic bodies and exact geometric language' (Lynn 1998a: 41). Essentially, Lynn's work envisions nothing less than a new *adaptation* between the body and geometry, as each undergoes a transformation conceived along Deleuzian lines. The body becomes a multiplicity, and geometry becomes what Deleuze–Guattari call (after Husserl) a 'proto-geometry' of 'anexact yet rigorous' forms (Deleuze and Guttari 1987: 329). Lynn's work thus theorises and produces alliances between 'anexact, multiplicitious, temporal . . . bodies' and 'more supple, deformable geometries' (Lynn 1998a: 42). Like Cache, Lynn seeks to replace the fixity of the architectural frame with a notion of the frame as a probabilistic envelope within which bodies or forms may develop into different configurations.

Lynn finds tools with which to understand morphological variation in the field of biometrics (the measurement of biological objects), because such measurement and modelling techniques must be supple enough to accommodate unpredictable changes in morphology over time. Biometrics depends on 'probable geometries', because they 'occupy a provisional relationship to the matter they describe' (Lynn 1998a: 86). Bio-medical image-processing functions by integrating into a probable geometry a series of 'random sections' or transectional views of the object over time. Deploying biometric techniques in architectural design is critical because, while architecture traditionally starts from the ideal form, probable geometries can begin with the 'amorphous' and yet still yield the 'anexact yet rigorous' geometry called for by Deleuze–Guattari (Lynn 1998a: 86). Probable geometries generated by random section models 'will provide architecture with the possibility of writing volumetric indeterminacy within a precise and rigorous system of measurement: a series of serial transections along with related coefficients of size, shape, and orientation' (Lynn 1998a: 85–6). The broad terms in which Lynn conceptualises architectural design thus ultimately shares with Cache the emphasis on treating architectural frames as intervals opening probabilities, where intercalated events intervene as internal differentiation occurs in relation to external influences.

Lynn's reconceptualisation of the body in architecture essentially replaces the human form as the basis for spatial types with biological models of morphological change. Splicing together the terminology and conceptual apparatuses of *A Thousand Plateaus* and *The Fold*, Lynn defines the body as a folded multiplicity: 'Multiplitious bodies are always already entering into relations and alliances through multiple plications. Structures such as these are not identically repeatable outside of the particularities of their internal elements or their external environments' (Lynn 1998a: 45). Like Deleuze, Lynn excels in cataloguing specific, vivid examples. Instances of multiplitious bodies include a singularity capable of becoming a multiplicity: the flatworm, which can be cut and grows heads in different ways, thus holding within its body 'a very specific constellation of possibilities for the proliferation of a multiplicity of bodies' (Lynn 1998a: 45). Or, conversely, multiple bodies that fold into a singularity through parasitism: the 'pseudocopulation' between an orchid and a digger wasp where the orchid serves as a 'false female' that sexually attracts the wasp, which absorbs pollinia on its head as it rubs its genitals on the flower. 'By becoming a surrogate sexual partner to the wasp the orchid gains mobile genitalia in the wasp. The multiple orchids and wasps unify to form a singular body. This propagating unity is not an enclosed whole but a multiplicity: the wasps and orchids are simultaneously one and many bodies' (Lynn 1998a: 139).

Lynn theorises folding architecture in terms of processes that, in a sense, represent the integration of probable geometries and multiplitious bodies. Here, Deleuzian spatial concepts become dynamic techniques. Thus Deleuze's smooth space is transformed by Lynn into a functional operation, 'smoothing', which 'incorporates free intensities through fluid tactics of mixing and blending' disparate elements (Lynn 1998a: 110–11). Similarly, when Deleuze's notion of the fold (*pli*) is mobilised as folding in architecture, *le pli* becomes 'pliancy', which 'implies first an internal flexibility and second a dependence on external forces for self-definition' (Lynn 1998a: 111). The folding process itself has a certain smoothing or pliant quality: 'Folding employs neither agitation nor evisceration but a supple layering' of heterogeneous elements (Lynn 1998a: 112). As disparate components are folded into a smooth mixture, a distinctly intricate texture emerges: 'Intrications are intricate connections that affiliate local surfaces of elements with one another by negotiating interstitial rather than internal connections' (Lynn 1998a: 112–13). Ultimately, folding

architecture would seek to build structures that incorporate these processes and properties. The result, in conceptual form, would be a 'plexus',
'a multi-linear network of interweavings, intertwinings, and intrications;
for instance, of nerves or blood vessels' (Lynn 1998a: 121).

Distinctive in Lynn's writings is his ability to demonstrate incisively the
ways in which architectural design techniques are able to implement
abstract diagrams that mimic (rather than model) the characteristics and
behaviour of folding architecture. Lynn argues that architecture is now
capable of working directly with virtual concepts at the level of design,
while maintaining a careful distinction between philosophical and technological senses in which 'virtual' may be understood:

> The term virtual has recently been so debased that it often simply refers to
> the digital space of computer-aided design. It is often used interchangeably
> with the term simulation. Simulation, unlike virtuality, is not intended as a
> diagram for a future possible concrete assemblage but is instead a visual
> substitute . . . Thus, use of the term virtual here refers to an abstract scheme
> that has the possibility of becoming actualised, often in a variety of possible
> configurations. (Lynn 1998b: 10)

Lynn conceptualises the virtual, abstract diagrams he works with in
terms of 'animate form'. Animate form does not simply model or express
changes in a body's motion or behaviour over time. Thus Lynn asserts
that, 'Animation is a term that differs from, but is often confused with,
motion. While motion implies movement and action, animation implies
the evolution of a form and its shaping forces; it suggests animalism,
animism, growth, actuation, vitality and virtuality' (Lynn 1998b: 9). In
other words, animate forms are open wholes that evolve through differences that spur changes in kind rather than degree. Animate design realises or makes visible Deleuze's conceptual physics of a world where
bodies interact and undergo transformations as forces act on them. Lynn
stipulates that, 'animate form is defined by the co-presence of motion and
force at the moment of formal conception.' Animate forms are not
unified or identical forms that move around in a neutral space. Instead,
'the motion and shape of a form is defined by multiple interacting vectors
that unfold in time perpetually and openly. With these techniques, entities are given vectorial properties before they are released into a space
differentiated by gradients of force.' Thus, architectural practice implements (in the sense of a hands-on use of a tool) and explores virtual diagrams:

> Instead of a neutral abstract space for design, the context for design
> becomes an active abstract space that directs form within a current of forces

that can be stored as information in the shape of the form. Rather than as a frame through which time and space pass, architecture can be modelled as a participant immersed within dynamical flows. (Lynn 1998b: 11)

Defined in these terms, Lynn's notion of animate form perhaps sounds like a sort of opaque architectural language whose actual meaning remains elusive. But Lynn's animate form in fact represents a remarkable synthesis of Deleuzian concepts with various mathematical models and technological tools, where philosophical thinking is directly linked to and grounded in specific practices. On a theoretical level, Lynn uses Deleuzian ideas of bodies and difference as a template for how architectural design should unfold: building designs should behave like bodies which:

> emerge through processes of differentiation, yielding varying degrees of unity based on specific affiliations and mutations. By beginning with bodily matter the possibility for singularity is not precluded; but rather, bodies are sedimented, aggregated, unified and stratified through differential forces and the continual fusion of matter. An architectural model of bodily matter such as this exists as a fluid interface. (Lynn 1998a: 137)

The practical level of Lynn's work consists in seeking to find and develop models where assemblages undergo various kinds of differentiation. Thus he utilises software programs developed in the special effects and animation industries that enable him to work with blob models. A blob is a 'topological geometrical type that exhibits the qualities of multiplicity and singularity' (Lynn 1998a: 163). Similar in appearance to a puffy dough fried in hot oil, blobs are three-dimensional shapes defined by a centre and surface area. They interact through two fields of influence, called zones of fusion and inflection: respectively, an 'inner volume' within which they can merge with other blobs to form single surfaces, and an 'outer volume' within which other blobs can influence a blob's contours. Blobs are multiplicitous bodies because they are not 'parts' that link up to form different 'wholes'. A blob is rather 'simultaneously singular in its continuity and multiplicitious in its internal differentiation' (Lynn 1998a: 164). As was the case with Cache then, Lynn's Deleuzian thinking in architecture ends in a reimagining of the body and its adaptation to space.

The Plane of Folding Architecture

For both Bernard Cache and Greg Lynn, architecture unfolds as the direct investigation and implementation of virtual concepts. Deleuze's reading of Leibniz demonstrates how Leibniz's formulation of the calculus yields notions of difference and differentiation that subtend the concept of vortical space. Cache and Lynn regard contemporary architectural design as direct explorations into Leibniz/Deleuze's space. Thus Cache believes that 'numerical technologies' (computers) 'give us the tools to realize once again Leibniz's program: "Everything can be calculated"' (Cache 1995: 3). Similarly, Lynn observes that, 'The prevalence of topological surfaces in even the simplest CAD software, along with the ability to tap the time-and-force modelling attributes of animation software, presents perhaps the first opportunity for architects to draw and sketch using calculus' (Lynn 1998b: 17). Both architects draw a correlation between the curvilinear, smooth space of design and a dynamic, temporal spatial field. For Cache, computed design *'opens two great possibilities'*: First, it enables the design of new forms that, because they are composed of surfaces of variable curvatures, realise the virtual concept of space in actual built objects. Second, there ceases to be a static plan or model from which objects are made. Instead, there emerges a *'nonstandard mode of production'* where changing parameters in the computer make possible *'a different shape for each object in the series'* (Cache 1995: 88; original emphasis). Commenting on Cache's concept of the object, Deleuze marks a shift 'where the fluctuation of the norm replaces the permanence of a law', and where the object's status 'no longer refers its condition to a spatial mold – in other words, to a relation of form-matter – but to a temporal modulation that implies as much the beginnings of a continuous variation of matter as a continuous development of form' (Deleuze 1992: 19). Similarly, Lynn succinctly states that, in contrast to the 'inert medium' of paper and pencil, the computer's organising properties include 'topology, time and parameters'. Thus the computer enables new investigations of relations between time and shape to be explored because, 'Issues of force, motion and time, which have perennially eluded architectural description due to their *"vague essence"'*, can now be experimented with by supplanting the traditional tools of exactitude and stasis with tools of gradients, flexible envelopes, temporal flows and forces' (Lynn 1998b: 17). In a sense, the computer simulation as a norm whose parameters may be changed corresponds to the architectural frame as an interval, the opening of a frame of probabilities susceptible to taking on many forms.

The computer as design tool thus brings about changes in the nature of the architectural plan and hence the process by which the architectural unfolds. From this standpoint, folding architecture may be located in relation to Deleuze–Guattari's scheme (in *What Is Philosophy?*) that distinguishes between philosophy, science, and art. The work of each domain is characterised by a specific 'plane' on which it unfolds. Philosophy creates concepts on a plane of consistency, science works with functions on a plane of reference, and art works with percepts and affects on a plane of composition. In a general sense, architecture works on all three planes – it has always merged philosophy, science and art, through geometrical plans conceptualised for aesthetic reasons. Folding architecture works more closely to Deleuze–Guattari's particular scheme, though, because it seeks to translate the virtual – the fractal texture or 'consistency' of the philosophical concept and plane – into the concrete, so that the actual, material forms it produces do not resolve or untangle the consistency of the virtual. Folding architecture works with *objectiles* and *assemblages* on a plane of *technique*.[9, 10] This plane is abstract; it persists in the techniques of topology, animation, and parameter-based modelling the computer has made accessible. It allows abstract diagrams to unfold, disperse, and be actualised in objectiles and assemblages that are variations on a diagram rather than possible examples of a specific, static model.

One very crucial question remains, however: to what extent and in what ways has the project of folding architecture truly *materialised*? On the one hand, folding architecture does provide a means through which the actual may be virtualised: as we have seen, Cache and Lynn have virtualised, or articulated virtual concepts for, the realm of bodies, buildings and space. But on the other hand, the actual examples of this project remain difficult to pin down. Cache's text features discussions of his furniture as *exempla* of his theories, but the connection between them is seldom clear in more than an indicative fashion. Lynn remains more circumspect in his claims about the folding architecture project in general. Concluding his 'Animate Form' manifesto, Lynn is very clear about the status of his work:

> The effects of abstract machines trigger the formation of concrete assemblages when their virtual diagrammatic relationships are actualised as a technical possibility. Concrete assemblages are realized only when a new diagram can make them cross the technical threshold . . . It is in the spirit of the abstract technical statement yet to become concrete that topologies, animation and parameter-based modelling are being explored here. In order to bring these technologies into a discipline that is defined as the site of translation from the virtual into the concrete, it is necessary that we first interrogate their abstract structure. Without a detailed understanding of their performance as diagrams and organizational techniques it is impossible to begin a discussion of their translation into architectural form. (Lynn 1998b: 40–1)

Folding architecture, then, may be said to engage in the invention of architectural diagrams – abstract diagrams in Deleuze's sense as opposed to diagrams in the sense of architectural plans. In virtualising the actual, it remains limited in the plane on which it actualises – that of, primarily, the space of computational design.

Put differently, one could say that Cache and Lynn work on the plane of technique, directly manipulating and implementing virtual designs that present the conceptual directly to perception. But perception of the virtual remains circumscribed within what amount to symbolic representations of virtual structures: the animate forms that result from being able to 'draw and sketch using calculus' take shape as configurations of pixels. Viewed within the ontology of images, the plane of technique remains caught in the problem of representation – it represents rather than embodies the texture of the fold and smooth space. As Cache puts it, this ontology implies that, 'Our brain is not the seat of a neuronal cinema that reproduces the world; rather our perceptions are inscribed on the surfaces of things, as images amongst images' (Cache 1995: 3). In the design processes of folding architecture, the surface of things becomes the cinema of the computer screen.

A certain irony thus persists in folding architecture. In its initial formulation, it comes across as championing the local, the contingent, the material, in a bottom-up sort of way. Recall Lynn's proclamation that, 'If there is a single effect produced in architecture by folding, it will be the ability to integrate unrelated elements within a new continuous mixture' (Lynn 1998a: 101). If we accept Lynn's conclusion that folding architecture should continue its investigations of 'abstract structures' before it seeks 'their translation into architectural form', then this project remains in a rather top-down stage where virtual diagrams have yet to actualise as material structures. In essence, as Susannah Hagan points out, folding architecture has remained essentially theoretical in its project to create folds between the outside and inside of building projects. 'What it does not do,' Hagan insists, 'is produce a new material relation between architecture and site, despite the suggestiveness of the language used' (Hagan 2001: 142).

Simon Rodia's Watts Towers of Los Angeles

The Watts Towers of Los Angeles were built from 1921 to 1955 by Simon Rodia, an Italian immigrant labourer, who actually called his site 'Nuestro Pueblo', or 'our town'.[11] Rodia used skills garnered from work as a construction and steel worker, cement mixer, and tile setter to build three free-standing steel-piping towers encased in cement, and decorated with shards of glass, china, soda bottles, tiles and other debris. Although the Watts Towers have been compared to many other sites,[12] they elude or exceed attempts to classify or define them.[13] Building on our preceding discussion, the site may be seen as a work of folding architecture *avant la lettre* – the work of Deleuze, Cache and Lynn pinpoints the salient features of Rodia's methods and materials, as well as the perceptual and conceptual dimensions of the site. The Watts Towers in fact provide an almost strangely literal *exemplum* of folding architecture's definitive characteristics. At the same time, Rodia's work does more than embody the conceptual tenets of folding architecture. It accomplishes what Hagan argues folding architecture has failed to do, namely, to 'produce a new material relation between architecture and site' (Hagan 2001:137). This material relation emerges, moreover, from a bottom-up building process – rather than implementing folding concepts at the level of design on a plane of technique, Rodia realised the folding architecture project in his actual construction practices. These practices follow a logic of consolidation, moulding heterogeneous materials into a constantly changing whole.

As we have seen, folding architecture is defined by 'a fluid logic of connectivity' that 'integrate[s] unrelated elements within a continuous mixture' (Lynn 1998a: 101). There is a certain ambiguity as to what these terms mean specifically in practice – they have played out in folding architecture primarily on a formal level of design. The 'unrelated elements' may include aspects of the site environment and the inclusion of different formal types within a project. Rodia's project displays innovative forms of 'fluid logic of connectivity' on a structural level, and integrates an astonishing heterogeneity of materials. The site's skeletal structures are composed of scrap steel piping bent into curvilinear forms on nearby railroad tracks, and bound together by wrapping joints with chicken wire that were then encased in a cement mortar of his own devising. Interspersed among the three towers (that stand fifty-five, ninety-eight, and nearly 100 feet tall, the last being the tallest free-standing structure of its kind) are several other constructions, including a gazebo with a thirty-eight-foot tall spire, a ship, a cactus garden, and a fountain. The structures are interconnected by more than 150 supports to form a maze of shifting patterns, multicoloured mosaics, and a daunting amount of finely filigreed detail. The structures make an intricate meshwork that induces the eye to trace patterns that move between macro- and microscopic scales. It becomes, in Deleuze's terms, a 'labyrinth' that is 'multiple because it contains many folds', that 'not only has many parts' but is

also 'folded in many ways' (Deleuze 1992: 4). At the Watts Towers, space
and matter become 'an infinitely porous, spongy, or cavernous texture
without emptiness' (Deleuze 1992: 5).

In large part, this sense of space emerges because of the sheer range of
'unrelated elements' of debris that Rodia has arranged 'into a continuous mixture'. This debris includes 11,000 pieces of whole and broken
pottery, 15,000 glazed tiles, 6,000 pieces of coloured bottle glass, 10,000
shells, hundreds of rocks, and pieces of marble, linoleum, and telephone-
line insulators (Goldstone and Goldstone 1997: 56). Because Rodia constantly changed the materials he was using and invented new mosaic
patterns as he worked, the textures of Nuestro Pueblo continuously shift.
Along certain sightlines, both outlines and surfaces are sharply, irregu-
larly jagged. In some spots rounded cement surfaces are cluttered with
jagged hunks of harsh, heavy materials, including waste metal from the
blast furnaces of steel mills, industrial slag and telephone-line insulators
(cylindrical, grooved chunks of glass around which power lines were
wound atop telephone poles). Yet other views yield a smooth series of
concentric rings, similarly tiled surfaces, curvilinear forms hinted at
through the sheen of patchwork colours. Even a short walk through the
site leads one to a vivid experience of folding architecture's logic, 'a logic
where the whole is not given but always open to variation, as new things
are added or new relations made, creating new continuities out of such
intervals or disparities' (Boyman 1995: ix).

Rodia's construction methods and process enact the theoretical principles of folding architecture, playing out physically and materially what
Lynn and Cache formulate at the level of design concepts. For Lynn,
formal explorations of folding architecture induce a 'temporal modulation that implies as much the beginnings of a continuous variation of
matter as a continuous development of form' (Lynn 1999: 19). Rodia's
labours trace precisely such a 'temporal modulation', a bottom-up
process of local decisions made without any drawn plans. The nearly
improvisational nature of this project resonated strongly with jazz musi-
cian Charles Mingus, who recalls from his Watts childhood that Rodia
'was always changing his ideas while he worked and tearing down what
he wasn't satisfied with and starting over again, so pinnacles tall as a two-
story building would rise up and disappear and rise again. What was
there yesterday mightn't be there next time you looked, but then another
lacy-looking tower would spring up in its place' (Mingus 1991: 37). The
bottom-up notion of 'bootstrapping', where one level of a whole induces
the next to emerge, and so on, finds literal realisation in the construction
of the three towers. Working without scaffolding, Rodia built each rung

or ring of a tower, then climbed down, and toted the next load of material up to the top rung, stood on it, held onto the structure only by a window-washer's belt, and built the next ring. Rodia was always working from the middle of his project, building several sculptures at once; while waiting for the mortar to dry and harden enough to support his diminutive 4ft 10ins frame, he assembled the next piece, encasing piping with cement and setting fragments in it while wet.

For Cache, architecture is the art of making frames and folding architecture is the art of creating probabilistic frames. From the standpoint of framing, the Watts Towers present a singular case where there is no distinction between frame and interior. The outer walls delineate a boundary on the horizontal plane, but their function as frame is negated because the walls are dwarfed by the scale of the towers. The walls seem more like part of a skin that stretches invisibly across the skeletal surfaces throughout the site. The relation between external frame and internal content also breaks down when one realises that the site resembles a ship, with the three towers serving as masts, that the site's triangular shape transforms its walls into the ship's prow and hull, and that the arch motifs along the walls represent the waves of the sea. Thus Rodia constructs a frame from the inside, as it were, rather than the outside – the frame emerges from the milieu rather than enclosing it. The site as frame materialises the drive in folding architecture not only to fold the outside into the inside, but to assemble an 'unstable dynamic world' of 'images . . . no longer defined by fixed divisions between inside and outside' where 'this division itself comes to shift or move as outside forces cause internal variations or as internal variations create new connections with the outside' (Boyman 1995: ix).[14]

Cache's concept of architectural construction as 'consolidation' also finds particular means of expression at the Watts Towers. Any segment or section of Rodia's work may be seen as an 'interval', an opening or potential field within which he inserted 'intercalated elements', each one of which changed the nature of the interval. Because there is no single whole that can be taken in, each shift of the eyes essentially takes a different cross-sectional view through a whole which changes in the viewing, so that perception of the site inevitably discerns relations and patterns that emerge through 'articulations of superposition'. The density of detail invites the eye to slow down, and trace the meticulous arrangements of incidental events that fill any portion of the site one examines. Like 'nomad art' as conceived by Deleuze and Guattari, Nuestro Pueblo functions in a *close-vision haptic space* whose 'orientations, landmarks, and linkages are in continuous variation', such that there can be 'no ambient space in which the multiplicity would be immersed and which would make distances invariant' (Deleuze and Guattari 1987: 493).

Combining elements of architecture, sculpture, and art, Nuestro Pueblo is perhaps most accurately characterised as an assemblage. But it is more than an assemblage of found objects in the sense that assemblage is spoken of in the world of twentieth-century art. Like artistic assemblage (and collage as well), Rodia's work incorporates found materials that express the urban, industrial character of modern experience – but it does so on an unprecedented scale.[15] Here again, the Deleuzian spatial vocabulary proves particularly – and peculiarly – apt in characterising the Watts Towers. The abstract-seeming terminology that Deleuze–Guattari use to describe assemblages captures quite succinctly the ways in which Rodia combined heterogeneous elements into something that evolved through incremental steps and local decisions into a non-totalisable whole:

> Assemblages are defined simultaneously by matters of expression that take on consistency independently of the form-substance relation; reverse causalities or 'advanced' determinisms, decoded innate functions related to acts of discernment or election rather than to linked reactions . . . in short, a new 'pace' produced by the imbrication of the semiotic and the material. (Deleuze and Guattari 1987: 337)

To look at the Watts Towers is to be immediately engulfed in reading it – the site accrues an immanent 'pace' as each material piece fits into ever-shifting configurations, as any part becomes entangled in a whole undergoing constant variation. Rodia expresses this dynamic part-whole relation by imprinting patterns that are essentially maps of the site, such as an impression of wire basket bottoms that form three sets of concentric rings, as if to depict the towers as seen from above. The folding texture of the site, the ways in which inside and outside inhere along a surface, finds expression in the constant display of inverted motifs – an enantiomorphic mirroring ensues from imprinted twinned images of different kinds of artifacts (tools, baskets, wire chair frames). Moreover, Rodia explicitly induced the material surface of his project to take on semiotic dimensions in a number of ways. Rodia's signature is ubiquitous, and written in different signifying regimes: little tile pieces spell out his initials, name and the title and address of Nuestra Pueblo; in many panels in the outer walls, he impressed his tools into the cement, creating a distinctly hieroglyphic-feeling set of designs, a signature that is both visual and linguistic symbol.

The site's signature motif though, may be found in the rosette, a design

Rodia imprinted all over both the inside and outside of the walls, using round outdoor tap knobs. The rosette may be read as a sign expressing the specific mode of perception induced by the Watts Towers. On an atomistic scale, the rosette shows the alveolar nature of matter as 'an infinitely porous, spongy, or cavernous texture without emptiness, caverns endlessly contained in other caverns' (Deleuze 1992: 5). In the 'protogeometry' of this fractal assemblage that 'addresses vague, in other words, vagabond or nomadic, morphological essences' (Deleuze and Guattari 1987: 365), every part functions as both whole and hole. As Cache puts it, the rosette demonstrates, 'that the texture of substance is the inclusion of envelopes that fold into one another, small circles into large ones'. The rosette thus shows that, 'we will certainly not acquire the soul or the body that we are at such pains to secure by better enclosing our subject zones; we must rather delve down into texture or go back up into envelopes by grafting ourselves onto the world that surrounds us and by opening this world within us' (Cache 1995: 124). The Watts Towers both embody and induce this double dynamic, this movement of perception: a scrutiny narrowing down to elusive detail and a flight up concentric rings. It thus opens within us the world of what Deleuze calls 'perception in the folds', a swirl of 'minute perceptions lacking an object, that is, hallucinatory microperceptions' (Deleuze 1992: 86). This is a mode of perception both restless and restful:

> It is a lapping of waves, a rumour, a fog, or a mass of dancing particles of dust . . . It is as if the depths of every monad were made from an infinity of tiny folds (inflections) endlessly furling and unfurling in every direction, so that the monad's spontaneity resembles that of agitated sleepers who twist and turn on their mattresses. (Deleuze 1992: 86)

The waking dreamer walking through the Watts Towers is immersed in a world composed of constant inflection folded into an elusive consistency. Nomadic movements bring on monadic perception; one shifts *'from the cosmological to the microscopic, but also from the microscopic to the macroscopic'* (Deleuze 1992: 87). The images in this world inhere on a plane of primary images that take:

> the form of an absolute exteriority that is not even the exteriority of any given interiority, but which arises from that most interior place that can barely be perceived or even conceived, which is to say, in the paradoxical mode, that of which the perceiving itself is radically temporal or transitory: the nonsummable, the noncapitalisable. (Cache 1995: 37–8)

This 'paradoxical mode' situates nothing less than the fold between body and soul, or in Deleuze's architectural allegory, between the floors in the

Baroque house. This fold would also be the fold between folds. Rodia, through his site, becomes the '"cryptographer" [who] is needed, someone who can at once account for nature and decipher the soul' (Deleuze 1992: 3). The cryptographer must understand that in the paradoxical mode no direct communication between body and soul is possible. Thus while the astute reader of the Watts Towers assemblage sees the 'imbrication of the semiotic and the material', such an insight only presents the materials that must themselves be interpreted. As Gregg Lambert points out, when there 'can be no direct presentation, or transposition, of the perceptual', then 'perception must itself become a sign, and the sign must become a text that must be read, deciphered' (Lambert 2002: 48). The reason that Rodia's project enacts this process of perception, or that the site induces us to enact it, rests in the model of perception at play in the folds. This is a cryptic perceptual mode where 'perception takes place in the design, and must be constructed, piece by piece, apartment by apartment' (Lambert 2002: 48). The Watts Towers invites us to read its cryptic messages that are all on the surface, literally as well as figuratively. But the material itself poses a mystery, the solution to which is apparently hidden in plain sight – because the material presents itself in perception as an allegory of its own secret. On a perceptual level, the sheer profusion of detail gives the site an almost active physical presence. The structures saturate the eye with colours and textures and lines and patterns, so that the roving eye takes in more than the still mind can process. One is immersed in an aleatory, combinatoric world of elements in constant reconfiguration. This perception overload allows for a play on the conceptual level – as if, because they never crystallise as a single perceived entity, distinctly seen and captured by the eye, they continually take on different conceptual shapes and stimulate different lines of thought. Percept and concept, sight and insight, become indiscernible, to the point that the Towers entrain one to *see with the mind* and *think through the eye*.

In Deleuze's geography, his writing of space, Simon Rodia's Watts Towers of Los Angeles take shape as Leibniz's Baroque house as remodelled by Möbius, with a nod to Escher. There is no longer a vector that differentiates a lower floor with windows of perception and an upper floor with folds of soul. At the Watts Towers, one is rather going up the down staircase, caught in an escalating experience where perception and concept enter into a chase after one another; at the moment they appear as one they flip into the other. Deleuze's version of Leibniz has become entangled with his account of Kant, where faculties are left 'to evolve freely in order to form strange combinations as sources of time; 'arbitrary forms of possible intuitions' (Deleuze 1984: xii). At the fold of body and soul, when percept and concept enmesh, images form strange combinations as sources of space; aleatory forms of possible inflections. Space thus becomes saturated with and restored to its immanent connection to time. For as stable, massive, and enduring as they are, the Watts Towers are also supple, mobile, and endless. There *is* no Watts Towers; there are only Watts Towers yet to come.

References

Bergson, H. (1990), *Matter and Memory*, trans. W. S. Palmer and N. Paul, New York: Zone Books.

Boyman, A. (1995), 'Translator's Preface', in Cache, B. (1995), pp. viii–xii.

Cache, B. (1995), *Earth Moves: The Furnishing of Territories*, ed. M. Speaks, trans. A. Boyman, Cambridge: MIT Press.

Deleuze, G. (1984), *Kant's Critical Philosophy*, trans. H. Tomlinson and B. Habberjam, Minneapolis: University of Minnesota Press.

Deleuze, G. (1986), *Cinema I: The Movement-Image*, trans. H. Tomlinson and B. Habberjam, Minneapolis: University of Minnesota Press.

Deleuze, G. (1992), *The Fold*, trans. T. Conley, Minneapolis: University of Minnesota Press.

Deleuze, G. (1994), Difference and Repetition, trans. Paul Palfour, London: Athlone.

Deleuze, G. and Guattari, F. (1987), *A Thousand Plateaus: Capitalism and Schizophrenia*, trans. B. Massumi, Minneapolis: University of Minnesota Press.

Goldstone, B. and Goldstone, A. P. (1997), *The Los Angeles Watts Towers (Conservation and Cultural Heritage)*, Los Angeles: Getty Center for Education in the Arts.

Hagan, S. (2001), *Taking Shape: A New Contract between Architecture and Nature*, Boston and Oxford: Architectural Press.

Lambert, G. (2002), *The Non-Philosophy of Gilles Deleuze*, New York: Continuum Books.

Lynn, G. (1998a), *Folds, Bodies and Blobs*, La Lettre Volée.

Lynn, G. (1998b), *Animate Form*, Princeton: Princeton Architectural Press.

Lynn, G. (2004) (ed), *Folding in Architecture*, New York: John Wiley & Son.

Manley, R. and Sloan, M. (1997), *Self-Made Worlds: Visionary Folk Environments*, New York: Aperture Press.

Mingus, C. (1991), *Beneath the Underdog: His World as Composed by Mingus*, New York: Vintage Books.

Speaks, M. (1995), 'Folding toward a New Architecture', in Cache, B. (1995), pp. xiii–xx.

Ward, D. and Sheldon Posen, I. (1985), 'Watts Towers and the Giglio Tradition', *Folklife Annual*: 142–57.

Notes

1. This shift in theoretical orientation in architecture is exemplified by Peter Eisenman's turn to folding architecture around 1993. Other architects inflected by Deleuze's thought include Jeffrey Kipnis, Charles Jencks, and John Frazer.
2. For a detailed comparison of deconstructive and folding architecture, see Greg

Lynn's essay 'The Folded, the Pliant, and the Supple', in *Folds, Bodies and Blobs* (109–33).

3. Another important figure in this regard is Jacques Attali, an architect and philosopher who has collaborated with Rem Koolhaus among others. See *Le plan et le détail: Une philosophie de l'architecture et de la ville* (2001), Nimes: Editions Jacqueline Chambons.
4. This phrase is taken from Robert Hooke's writings about the microscope, quoted in a wall panel in The Museum of Jurassic Technology in Culver City, California.
5. Cache's failure to cite Deleuze's writings would appear to be almost scandalous. However, here circumstances mitigate the situation: Cache may have worked from lecture notes rather than written texts, and he apparently wrote his own work with no intent ever to publish it. This fact also sheds light on the manuscript's unconventional publication history, first in a slightly abridged form in English and subsequently in complete form in French.
6. The resemblance between Cache's work and *The Fold* is so close that one wonders whether in the seminars Cache attended Deleuze was working through the materials that would reach print in the Leibniz study. I have not ascertained which years Cache heard Deleuze, nor when or if Deleuze delivered material that would comprise *The Fold* in his lectures. Cache may also have derived his ideas from Deleuze's extensive allusions to Leibniz in *Difference and Repetition*.
7. Of course, at any specific location, a Moebius strip does have a top and bottom or inside and outside. Locally, then, there are spatial distinctions, within a global space without inside and outside.
8. In the phrase 'topological operator' one detects the influence on Cache of Michel Serres, the theorist of Leibniz and topology most similar to Deleuze in contemporary French philosophy.
9. As elaborated below, Bernard Cache redefines the architectural object as 'objectile' in *Earth Moves*, and Deleuze integrates the term in his analysis of the object in *The Fold*.
10. Throughout his work, Lynn adopts the Deleuze–Guattari notion of assemblage in *A Thousand Plateaus* as a term for architectural formations. In the later section of the present essay, we will see how the term takes on a different resonance with architecture in relation to the Watts Towers and the California Assemblage Movement.
11. Readers interested in seeing photos of the Watts Towers to put images to the following discussion of Rodia Watts Towers may view my web-based analysis of the Watts Towers at http://myweb.lmu.edu/pharris/Wattspaper.html
12. Rodia's decorative techniques are frequently compared to those used by Raymond Isodore, who in 1938 began covering his home near Chartres with broken crockery. Isodore's method was termed 'pique assiette'. Like Rodia, he became notorious with his neighbours, who mocked Isodore's fanatic devotion to his work and called him 'Picassiette', perhaps in order both to ridicule a perceived pretence to high art while also in essence calling Isodore a 'plate stealer'. Though there are definite apparent visual similarities between these sites – which, interestingly, began construction almost simultaneously – the decorative aspect of Rodia's project incorporates a greater range of materials, and of course involved much more elaborate architectural elements. In addition, Rodia's technique was less an aesthetic expertise than a locally embedded practice – he worked as a tile setter for the Malibu Tile Company, and owners of homes built in Malibu in the 1930s and 1940s wonder whether Rodia may have done the tilework in their showers or kitchens. The Towers are often compared to Gaudi's church of La Sagrada Familia in Barcelona. The sites share not only dense

decoration in mosaic styles, but a geometry of catenoidal curves. When Rodia was presented with pictures of Gaudi's work, he asked, 'Did he have helpers?' and crowed, 'Me, I did it myself!' (Goldstone and Goldstone 1997: 60)

13. The site has been called 'a collection of seventeen sculptures' (Goldstone and Goldstone 1997: 11), and is frequently cited as an example of the 'urban vernacular' style of architecture. In the more avant-garde art-critical vein, William Seitz and others have marked the Towers as the genesis of California Assemblage, a tradition that subsequently included George Herms, Betty Saar, John Outterbridge and Ed Kienholz (Bud and Goldstone 1997: 19). Roger Cardinal includes the Watts Towers in his influential 1972 study *Outsider Art*. Most generally, the Watts Towers constitute what Roger Manley and Mark Sloan call a 'self-made world', in their study of 'folk art environments' (Manley and Sloan 1997). I. Sheldon Posen and Daniel Franklin Ward, while wary of lumping the Towers into an all-encompassing 'folk art' category, have examined the specific ways that Rodia's work does in fact function in a certain tradition, while bringing innovations of his own.

14. The folding between outside and inside at Nuestro Pueblo also operates in terms of relations between local and global evoked by the site. Rodia's labours, so immersed in local materials and practices, were also functioning on an imaginative, mnemonic level, where he was working back towards his childhood and homeland. I. Sheldon Posen and Daniel Franklin Ward have shown that the Towers resemble ceremonial towers paraded annually in the Giglio festival that originated in Nola, a town near the Italian village where Rodia was born. The Giglio festival, celebrated in Brooklyn as well, commemorates the kidnapping, liberation and return of Santo Paulinus, then Bishop of Nola. The general construction and shape of the eight wood and paper towers carried in the parade are similar to Rodia's Towers. The clinching link between the Giglio festival and Rodia's work is that, in addition to the towers, a ship modelled on a medieval galleon is also carried at the festival. The first structure Rodia built closely resembles the ship in his hometown parade that commemorates Paulinus' arrival home from Africa. Rodia called his small ship the Ship of Columbo or the Ship of Marco Polo.

15. In addition to the site's industrial aspects, it also serves as something like a museum of local history, in that it records significant facets of domestic life in late nineteenth- and early twentieth-century Los Angeles. Preserved in the Towers are traces of the important porcelain manufacturing and importing companies of the time, and the site reflects trends in the decorative arts, and generally the tastes of the time: the plates people ate from and the bottles they drank from.

Chapter 3

Stealing into Gilles Deleuze's Baroque House

Hélène Frichot

In fact, the house does not shelter us from cosmic forces; at most it filters
and selects them.

Deleuze and Guattari, What is Philosophy?

Now we are at home. But home does not preexist: it was necessary to draw
a circle around that uncertain and fragile centre, to organise a limited place.

Deleuze and Guattari, A Thousand Plateaus

The great refrain arises as we distance ourselves from the house, even if this
is in order to return, since no one will recognise us any more when we come
back.

Deleuze and Guattari, What is Philosophy?

Theft is primary in thought.

Deleuze, Difference and Repetition

Stealing is the opposite of plagiarizing, copying, imitating, or doing like.

Deleuze and Parnet, Dialogues

In considering architecture as an object of investigation the house is the
most obvious starting point, perhaps too obvious. It offers us the very
first threshold beyond which we are subject to unpredictable forces.
Gaston Bachelard was well aware of this when he wrote *The Poetics of
Space*. The archetypal, immemorial spaces we visit alongside him reintro-
duce us to the erstwhile lost nooks and crannies of the house as framing
device of the blissful domestic scene, albeit a specifically European model
of said structure, with its vertical arrangement of attic, serial storeys, and
basement. We will begin here within the house, on the safe side of the
threshold. Are we surprised, what's more, to find that Marcel Proust's
lengthy search takes the country home of his childhood as its point of
departure? The house seems to be the most convincingly material of all

architectural forms, the most deceptively familiar and heart warming. The house offers us the so-called inalienable right of property ownership, of a perfect childhood, of fundamental shelter. We always begin inside the house before we are allowed to exit across its formidable threshold toward the unknown. Sense is made within the shelter it offers, the good and common sense of familial ritual frames our expectations of an orderly, successful future, and our incipient notion of self-identity. We could go so far as to suggest that the house offers us our first register of meaning, furnishing us with significations that will travel well in the outside world.

It is frequently through literature that we are invited into the affective dimension of inhabitation. Bachelard, for instance, outlines his poetics by way of a constellation of literary citations, among which we happen upon the name of Marcel Proust. Should we pause for a moment to examine closely the opening pages of Proust's search, what we find is not simply the old house in Combray, but a kaleidoscopic arrangement of all the rooms that the narrator has inhabited. The walls do not stand firm within his purview, but in his semi-aware state they writhe, seemingly suffused with breath. Expanding and contracting as though animated, one room, one temporal pocket after another envelops us, alongside the narrator, in a magic lantern display. We are now in the city, now in the country, 'the unseen walls, shifting and adapting themselves to the shape of each successive room that [the body] remembered, whirled around in the dark' (Proust 1989: 7). The body that inhabits these rooms owns now the limbs of a child, now the heavy invalid body of the adult. The restless sleeper rests fitfully. The house is not built of bricks and mortar, but straw. It does not enclose our inhabitation securely, but merely offers a provisional frame for a contingent state of affairs and a suffering body. We find that the ongoing sensations of the domestic scene cannot be tamed so easily as Bachelard suggests; one must also account for that which is unhomely, both the darkened corners of the interior and the unwelcome forces, which, like draughts, discover points of entry where the house has been ill-maintained.

With the falling into disrepair of the house and the disorganisation of its surface, stabilised ascriptions of meaning are also jeopardised. Tripping over the threshold into a new millennium, the architect discovers that the stability of meaning has been rendered untenable. Champion of architectural theory, Kate Nesbitt, suggests that in the past architecture's concern with meaning has focussed upon issues such as its origin, essence, and disciplinary limits, its requisite qualities and proper techniques of construction (Nesbitt 1996: 18–19). Such relationships between architecture and meaning have been, for the most part, severed, or at least problematised. The house is no longer a haven whose fundamental task is that of offering shelter. What does it mean to be without meaning, or to be on the outside of meaning (which is not to suggest that architecture cannot continue to produce sense)?

First, any access to a fixed and universally valid set of rules that determines the 'how' of architecture has been cast aside, or considered defunct. Key texts, from Vitruvius, through Laugier, to Le Corbusier, offer the architect an interesting genealogy, but no longer provide instructions for use. Likewise, the aspirations, both formal and socio-political of the modern project have proved unsatisfactory. The house as machine for living in has reached its expiry date. Functionalism imposed from the outside or determined in advance has been impossible to maintain, and the idea that form strictly follows function no longer holds. Postmodern architecture, in turn, and its shallow pastiche of quasi-historical motifs plastered onto mute sheds has insulted the sensibilities of its media-saturated clients.

Second, the architectural process as a teleological activity, or one that is desirous of a final and completed form can no longer find satisfaction. The 'what' of architecture can no longer be definitively located. The construction of the house is never finished, but subject to additions, renovations and, worse case scenario, demolition. What we discover instead is that the process, as distinct from the end product, of architectural design has taken on a new urgency.

Third, we can no longer ask: why? The architectural edifice has failed in its attempt to represent a beyond or some idea that is bigger than itself. Instead we must look toward the immanent conditions of architecture, the processes it employs, the serial deformations of its built forms, together with our quotidian spatio-temporal practices.

In much the same way that the architectural object, together with its affiliated discourse, has undergone certain deformations, the role of the architect has also shifted. The character of the architect has been variably conceived as demiurge, progenitor (playing the conjoint role of father and mother), engineer, for example, of the modernist house as a machine for living, ironist of postmodern pastiche ('less is a bore'), and uniting all these roles the architect still sees herself as author-creator.[1] In place of any of the above characters we will consider the role of the architect as pickpocket, in that she has become well-practised in the redistribution of concepts she has borrowed from outside her disciplinary terrain.

Despite the problematisation of architectural meaning, the discipline still expresses a strong desire to make sense of its built forms, to demarcate its territory, and to determine those activities that can be called properly architectural. Still, it is often at the threshold of its disciplinary terrain that architecture can be most productive, and across this threshold a thriving trade in ideas continues. Having given herself leave to venture backwards and forwards across a borderline she is anxious to maintain in at least working order, the architect is that agent and occasional pickpocket who searches far and wide for means of legitimising her activity. Without this traffic in ideas, the relative autonomy of architecture becomes meaningless, its containment self-consuming. Here we will consider what spoils the architect as pickpocket has gathered from the expansive *oeuvre* that is signed with the name, Gilles Deleuze.

Pursuing certain contemporary trends in architecture, this essay will argue that in pilfering some of its spoils from the body of work signed by Deleuze, architecture can be seen to participate in the circulation of nonsense and sense. In order to produce sense, architecture must admit the forces of nonsense. Ronald Bogue points out that, according to Deleuze's schema, nonsense 'is actually the full and unrestricted dimension of meaning or sense' (Bogue 1989: 74). Nonsense is the plenitude of all imagined and imaginable possibilities, corporeal and incorporeal. Assuming that architecture wants to leave the exploration of its formal permutations open-ended, we can argue that it implicitly relies on the co-presence of sense and nonsense. Through the play of sense and nonsense, we will see how the house can operate as a device of deformation, allowing, by way of our departures and returns, our sensory and conceptual becomings, a means of creating new openings and capturing the chaotic forces of the Outside. All the same, we must also remain wary. Could it be that despite their abhorrence of metaphor, Deleuze and Guattari's references to architecture remain no more than useful illustrations of the conceptual landscape they build? As for architecture, to what extent can it effectively take the conceptual spoils it has gathered and put them to theoretical, and even material use?

Deleuze and Guattari tell us that, 'architecture is the first of all the arts' and that its most crucial task requires that it 'endlessly produces and joins up planes and sections' (Deleuze and Guattari 1994: 182).[2] According to this formulation, architecture operates as a filter or sieve of chaos, that uncertain realm we discover just beyond our familiar thresholds. Deleuze and Guattari imagine their own primitive hut, which accommodates an interior space in which tasks might be carried out. 'Now we are at home,' they write, and home is where 'the forces of chaos are kept outside as much as possible, and the interior space protects the germinal forces of a task to fulfil or a deed to do' (Deleuze and Guattari 1987: 311). This modest house is the framing device of our creative activities, in fact, the house is considered the very first frame. In turn, it lends its capacity to filter, select, and extract elements from a plethora of material mixtures and immaterial forces to the arts in general, 'from painting to the cinema' (Deleuze and Guattari 1994: 186). Another rendition of Deleuze and Guattari's primitive hut is described in Deleuze's *The Fold: Leibniz and the Baroque*. This is a work that celebrity architects such as Peter Eisenman and Greg Lynn have been keen to transform into radical instructions for use for the becoming-architect. As Anthony Vidler suggests, Deleuze's Baroque house, a humble home consisting of two storeys, had secured its place in the theoretical and design culture of architecture by the 1990s (Vidler 2000: 119). Deleuze borrowed aspects of its architectonic from the seventeenth-century philosopher, Gottfried Wilhelm Leibniz, in order to develop the concept of the fold, and as Vidler argues, the material promise of this concept piqued the interest of architects, who are 'always searching for the tangible attribute of an abstract thought'. But, Vidler continues, 'it is not at all clear that folds, in the sense of folded forms, correspond in any way to Deleuze's concept, or even less to Leibniz's model' (Vidler 2000: 119).

We can observe in the upstairs apartment of Deleuze's Baroque house, the folds of the soul, and below, on the ground floor, the pleats of matter. Upstairs the voluminous space of the house is entirely dark, it has no windows to the outside, in fact, it is quite difficult to tell exactly how expansive it might be. Its exterior form gives no true indication of the cavernous space that sprawls within. Downstairs there are windows, a door, and a rather formal set of steps that allow us to enter or exit with some ceremony. This is the realm of the five senses. Here the dimensions

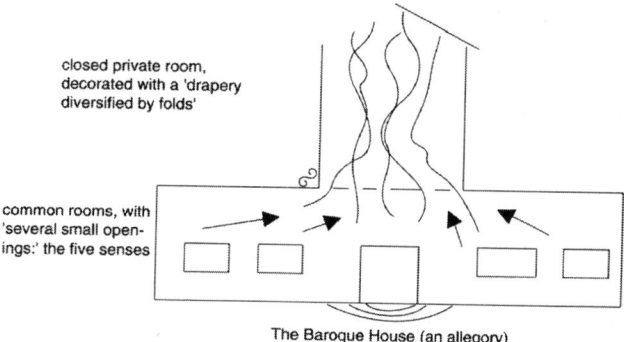

closed private room, decorated with a 'drapery diversified by folds'

common rooms, with 'several small openings:' the five senses

The Baroque House (an allegory)

Figure 3.1 Deleuze's Baroque house

might be measured, and the space quantified and assessed with more ease. The event, restless inhabitant of this house, is that which neither the material nor the immaterial, neither the ground nor upper apartment, can entirely account for. The event wanders about, ghost-like, ungraspable, in-between floors, surveying the flexible membrane that has been developed by Deleuze and Leibniz.

This threshold, or flexible membrane between material constituents and immaterial forces also recalls in its fine details the surface of sense, which Deleuze has developed from that marvellous line of separation the Stoics drew between bodies and incorporeal effects. It is upon this surface that we discover the circulation of events and the creation of innumerable surface effects. Deleuze affirms that it is this surface that renders things possible.[3] Although Deleuze cautions us that, 'the event should not be treated as something whose sense is to be sought and disentangled' (Deleuze 1990: 211), our pickpocket, the architect, remains interested in how the surface effects produced by the circulation of events might be created in material forms of expression.

In what follows, I will attempt to draw a diagram of the surface of sense, that threshold which can be located between the floors of Deleuze's Baroque house. With this diagram I will present some provisional instructions for the use of that curious collection of concepts that have been signed with the name Deleuze, and also Deleuze and Guattari. The diagram, it must be remembered, is that which initiates a work, but by no means can the diagram be presented on its own as a finished product, or a durable bloc of sensations. I will focus on those concepts that have provoked the most interest and some action among architects and architectural theorists. These will include: the event, a survey of the plane of immanence as a topological field, the complex workings of the fold, the dynamic threshold between the virtual and the actual, time conceived or rather felt as duration, and the diagram and its modes of operation. It should be noted that this list identifies only a few pilfered concepts.

A particular seduction for the becoming-architect is suggested in the way these concepts are arranged and the unexpected surface patterns that seem to emerge alongside their construction. Deleuze and Guattari describe the arrangement of concepts as the inexact fit of the rough-hewn rocks that compose a dry-stone wall, going on to suggest that concepts are linked by little bridges, and that when we consider a large number of concepts what we have is something that amounts to a plane of immanence, though the plane should not be confused with the concepts that come to inhabit or pave it. The architect, no doubt, already begins to picture a landscape of sorts, a ground that might await her activity of form making. In taking up the assemblages offered by the above philosophers, the architect must contend with the perilous threshold between sense and nonsense, or the meeting place between the framing capacity of a provisional form and the forces which both facilitate and trouble its construction.

The architectural pickpocket steals into the house of philosophy and asks: what is an event? Our first concept, the event, traverses two sides of what we have called the surface of sense; one side belonging to the material facticity, or the pleats of matter, for instance, such that might inform a provisional form or framing device, the other surface belonging to the immaterial folds or incorporeal forces without which the material could never have become actualised. It is not so much a matter of asking what is an event, as how can the surface effects marked by an event be produced in the construction of something that is minimally durable? The surface of sense, surveyed by the event, is a topological playing field, and the event is an ever-mobile force that draws places once distantly related upon the field into the proximity of one another, procuring as it does the paradox of proximal distance. Further on we will see how the concept of the fold contributes to this paradox.

The event is treated in some detail within the twenty-first series of Deleuze's *Logic of Sense* where it is described as a 'leaping in place of the whole body'. The event 'is actualised on its most contracted point, on the cutting edge of an operation' (Deleuze 1990: 149), at the threshold, so to speak. The threshold organises on either side of its fine line two different conditions, and the ever-mobile event trespasses backwards and forwards across this line or surface. That is to say, the event surveys two sides of the surface of sense and, as such, can be registered twice. On the one side it becomes actualised in a definitive present by a material state of affairs, for example, a built form that comes to be inhabited by bodies that assemble themselves in shifting arrangements. On the other, immaterial side of the surface of sense, the 'mobile instant' of the event continues to escape us by resisting the present and dividing perpetually into a past and a future. This is the slippery aspect of the event that Deleuze has borrowed from the Stoics and called a counter-actualisation. As with the dry stone wall, an inexact fit pertains between the event and its commingling with a material state of affairs, but neither can the event be accounted for solely through immaterial forces and incorporeal effects. Counter-actualisation, which doubles the work of the event, is always in excess of that which has been actualised, for instance, the built form, and effectively allows an opening for future actualisations, or future built forms.

Hence we discover such pickpockets as John Rajchman, Elizabeth Grosz, and Brian Massumi, all of whom participate in the theoretical discourse of architecture, calling for those encounters that are yet to come, and asking us to attempt to grasp the cutting edge of novel forces knocking on our door.[4] It is crucial, as Deleuze with a Stoical emphasis elaborates, that we 'not be unworthy of what happens to us' (Deleuze 1990: 148–9). With respect to the discipline of architecture this call is an attempt to arouse a groping experimentation and to dissuade the architect from simply following tried and tested methods (though established techniques should never be underestimated). The structure of the event always leaves enough in its wake for further experimentation.

Deleuze and Guattari call the topological field upon which the event roams the plane of immanence, our second concept. This plane or plan lays out only the potential logic of *topos* or place, and is, in itself, rather more complicated than the first concept. This does not mean that it cannot be successfully mapped, and here is where our diagrams are eventually going to come in handy. If there is one thing that architects love to do, it is to map, capture, frame and grasp space or, as Brian Massumi has put it, to 'flush forms' out of the chaotic state of the plane of immanence (Massumi 1998a: 18). Why is the plane of immanence chaotic? Because it gives us the plenum of everything at once, more than we could ever perceptually account for; it overwhelms our senses, and our capacity to make sense. The plan(e) is pre-philosophical in that, for the philosopher at least, it awaits the construction of concepts. The plane of immanence leaves us with bloodshot eyes, ringing ears, ground down teeth, exhausted limbs and in a thorough state of perplexity. Nevertheless, as we travel upon the plane of immanence every day, we have mostly become habituated to its continuous upsurge of novelty. As social actors, often constrained with fixed scripts, susceptible to cliché and opinion, we are happy to brush off the interfering noise of immanence, and just get down to business. Day in, day out, immanence is that which permanently pervades and sustains and yet of which we own, or have mapped, but the most rudimentary set of concepts. Whether we are philosophers, artists, scientists, or, for argument's sake, architects, we will only ever have a provisional logic by which we can negotiate our way across this topological field of endless self-variation.

With respect to the plane of immanence figured as a topological field, great interest has been aroused and has influenced the work of such architectural practitioners as Eisenman and Lynn. The topological field, they claim, offers that medium across which we can make our escape from the so-called 'Cartesian' grid, a rigid frame always fixed in advance by the x, y and z coordinates with which the computer interface has made the architectural draftsperson so familiar. The idea is that we can now take our departure from this fixed geometry of points in order to surf the indeterminate, continuously interpenetrating moments of the multitudinous number of folds that compose the elusive surface of the plane of immanence. With no small amount of perplexed fascination we have begun to register that the conceptual and material territories across which we travel, having neither beginning nor end, can only ever be approached from somewhere in the middle. This is also to say that there is no singular, omnipresent, God's eye point of view that can be claimed in order to survey the whole of the plane, or to take it all in instantaneously.

Let's slow down for a moment, and consider a shift in scale. Rather than attempt to apprehend a daunting and immeasurable field, we might consider just one fold at a time. Let us consider in more detail the concept of the fold, our third concept. The plane of immanence, our surface of sense, is complicated, and every explication complicates it further as it is composed of an indefinite number of folds, which, in turn, and in addition to the event, inform the philosophical construction of concepts. The fold (*le pli*), as Rajchman narrates, is etymologically linked to such words as complicate, explicate, implicate, replicate (Rajchman 1998: 15). The thing about a fold is that it owns, at the very least, a convex and a concave surface. The French architect and theorist, Bernard Cache, illustrates that while these curves are extrinsically informed by a maximum and a minimum point, independent of these fixed points a whole series of singular points proliferate. These singular points are what Cache calls points of inflection. Forming a serial continuum they are defined only in relation to themselves. Inflection registers the indeterminacy of the fold as a serial continuum of singular points rendered in motion (Cache 1995: 17). Very different conditions can be secreted into the pockets that a fold develops; let's say, an interior and an exterior condition. Like the event with which we began, the fold allows for diverse conditions to be brought into an erstwhile unfamiliar proximity. Not only can the fold be read across any number of heterogeneous conditions, both material and immaterial (it is an odd assortment of events and things that correspond to the fold), but we can use the fold as a device by which we can bring the work of two or more philosophers from different centuries and socio-cultural contexts into vicarious contact. Hence we discover Deleuze joining forces with Hume, Leibniz, Spinoza, Bergson, and many other personae, philosophical, literary, and so on.

The concept of the fold has as much to do with the organisation of language and sense, as it has to do with the ever-shifting material folds of our garments. Before one can fold one needs a surface, and every surface has two sides. In *The Logic of Sense*, the plane of immanence we have been speaking of above, that milieu articulated by folds, is described instead as the surface of sense and, as Deleuze writes, 'to the physics of surfaces a metaphysical surface necessarily corresponds' (Deleuze 1990: 125). On the right and reverse sides of this surface we have the immaterial and the material, the incorporeal and the corporeal, the conceptual and the practical, propositions and things, ideational flights and the murmuring depths of bodies entangled in sordid states of affair. The crucial point, or we might say, the crucial fold, is that this necessarily doubled surface of folds allows for what Massumi has described as the 'mutual envelopment of thought and sensation' (Massumi 1998b: 307). Cache, who animates the fold through his concept of inflection, suggests, 'it is in the strange nature of inflection that it changes qualities as soon as one tries to grasp it' (Cache 1995: 83). Deleuze, responding to Cache's formulation, adds that inflection configures an 'elastic point', and enthuses further that, 'inflection is the pure Event of the line or of the point, the Virtual, ideality par excellence' (Deleuze 1993: 15). The qualitative force that continues obstinately to escape us, the breeze that animates these inflected folds, as Deleuze indicates above, is the virtual.

With the dynamic threshold between the virtual and the actual we arrive at our fourth concept. Approaching this threshold, Deleuze and Guattari inform us, 'from virtuals we descend to actual states of affairs, and from states of affairs we ascend to virtuals, without being able to isolate one from the other' (Deleuze and Guattari 1994: 160).[5] Again we can observe the structure of Deleuze's Baroque house. The plane of immanence or the surface of sense operates as a threshold, or what Massumi has called a dynamic threshold, between the virtual and the actual. It is not a matter of organising a search party that can venture forth and capture virtual forces, for we are not speaking here of a computer game, the world wide web or some 'virtual' simulation. As Massumi argues, 'the virtual, as such, is inaccessible to the senses,' continuing, 'this does not, however, preclude figuring it, or constructing images of it' (Massumi 1998b: 305). The virtual always already precedes us, and proceeds in advance of us. It is the murmuring that persists just beyond the threshold of our senses, and our capacity to make sense. It is composed of all those multitudinous microfolds that we cannot perceive, and that prickle us unawares. Then, given enough of these microperceptions and a macroperception, that is, something we really can take note of is going to make perceptible the process of deformation (Deleuze

1993: 87). Likewise, at the other end of the scale, the inconceivably large is not going to catch our attention either, even though its deformational effects will continue to haunt us. With this force that is given as apparently ungraspable, how exactly do we figure the virtual?

The virtual has been variously called the unseen, the invisible, the unthought, the unrepresentable, in Maurice Blanchot's *oeuvre* it is called the Outside, and so on. That which we can perceptually and conceptually grasp is the actual, and the real. More importantly, these are the states we are going to have more luck in manipulating or transforming. As Deleuze suggests when writing on Bergson, 'actualisation is creation', it is a process in which we can participate (Deleuze 1991: 98). Where actualisation pertains to the folds in the soul, those drapes that are writ large enough that we can make concepts of them, realisation is figured across the pleats of matter – for example, we could realise a material built form (Deleuze 1991: 26). The virtual is that which resists representation; the actual, on the other hand, punctures the threshold of the virtual and presents itself, but in no way does it resemble the writhing force of the virtual. This is very important. Though the actual and the real, the conceptual and the material, can only be framed or captured because of their relation with the virtual (though strictly speaking, the real relates more exactly to the possible), these states bear no resemblance whatsoever to the virtual. They are different in kind and their logic is one of relentless different/ciation.

The slash inserted in different/ciation denotes the dynamic threshold between the virtual and the actual. Paul Patton explains that where differentiation is the virtual content of a multiplicity of folds, differenciation is the actualisation of this multiplicity (Patton 2000: 38).[6] The virtual is unrepresentable, which is not to say that it does not constantly assail us, confronting us with effects that are less causal in their structure and rather like after-images, or effects of light that appear and disappear in a flash. The actual, or more exactly, the process of actualisation, is what we can grasp in order to make our creative moves. Still, the actual and the virtual are co-present, much in the same way that nonsense and sense are co-present, and co-productive. A dynamic threshold at the same time separates and articulates these two forces, but what exactly makes this threshold dynamic? Duration.

With our fifth concept, duration, we have a fold that draws the work of Deleuze alongside the work of the late nineteenth-century philosopher, Henri Bergson. Duration as a conception of time that confounds the chronological is exactly that which cannot be explained by way of spatial constructs and metaphors. It owns no such extensity; instead, it is intensive, a felt thought. It cannot be divided into discrete brackets, as we tend to do upon the circuits of the clockface, or in our time-tabled existences. It is made up not of juxtaposed, but of interpenetrating moments. It is the upsurge of unending novelty, despite our habits and ready-made opinions. Still, duration remains, irrespective of all this, intimately interconnected with space, entwined in a clinched embrace of indiscernibility, from which it, nonetheless, withdraws. And so an oscillation continues. Duration accounts for the folding, unfolding, and refolding of the plane of immanence and, as such, produces the paradox of a heterogeneous continuity. It continually manifests itself at the dynamic threshold between the virtual and the actual, states which are both fundamentally different in kind, and intimately related. There is duration and, simultaneously, there are multitudinous durations describing a schema composed of innumerable macrofolds and microfolds that are ever in motion.

Example One: Registering Duration

The architect, Greg Lynn, has set himself the task of reinserting the complications of the elusive force of duration into the field of architecture. He tells us that for too long we have been in the habit of assuming that architecture is 'timeless, motionless and static' (Lynn 1998: 165). Instead he wishes to affirm that there are innumerable forces that are brought to bear on the architectural form, which, he insists, is subject to space animated through the folds of duration, and not simply space conceived as a static condition or container. Lynn's tool of choice toward this experimentation in contact with duration is the computer. He is after what he calls 'the development of motion-based techniques' (Lynn 1996: 92).[7] Lynn champions a process of architectural design that employs 'temporal flows and shaping forces', through the use of computer-based animation techniques (Lynn 1996: 94). He describes a feedback between topological fields and animated forms, driven by temporal forces that are continuous as well as being differentiated by series of singularities, or innumerable folds. He writes, 'there are both stabilizing forms and fluctuating fields. Each is inflected by the other, yet they remain distinct' (Lynn 1996: 96). Architecture is being asked to join forces with the event, to produce a disjunctive synthesis between a fluctuating field and a form that erupts in its midst. For the most part Lynn's experiments remain lodged in the electronic space of the computer.

One cannot help but suspect that duration has only just been made available to us as a novel tool; that we have only now discovered the proper time to emancipate it from its former yoke to rigid space. Perhaps another way to address this new-found interest in the concept of duration is to consider how the architect as pickpocket might reinvest duration into her own disciplinary milieu. The challenge for the architect is how to consider duration not as an answer to her form-making activities, but as the medium within which she can continue to invent problems. From within the indeterminate, durational flux of the real, the architect must make her mark, even at the risk of oversimplification. With a few distinguishing marks, an 'ensemble opératoire des traits et des taches, des lignes et des zones, des traits [operative set of brushstrokes and daubs of colour, lines and areas]' (Deleuze 1994b: 66), as Deleuze writes of Francis Bacon's painterly technique, we breach the threshold of the virtual and install the actual. With this diagram, we can define a stretch of territory for the meanwhile.

The mode of operation of the diagram is our sixth concept. The diagram is constituted by a set of asignifying and non-representational operations, which can be as simple as a series of scratched lines, and zones of applied colour, or as complex as computer-aided digital techniques and experimentations with animation software. It is that which allows for the gestural deployment of material, but not in a habitual manner. The gesture particular to the diagram's activation is more crucial than what the developing marks represent, and the diagram itself is only ever the possibility of the fact of the painting, the building, not the painting or building as it is finally formed. The function of the diagram is to suggest an escape from figuration, illustration, and representation, or to find a way out of having to tell the same story over again. It is a tool that functions experimentally without making any claims on the 'semiotically formed', or a ready-made system of signs. Instead, the diagram deploys shapeless matter that is not yet 'physically formed' (Deleuze and Guattari 1987: 141). A little like automatic writing, the diagram attempts to ride the crest of the wave at the dynamic threshold between the virtual and the actual as it invents its line of flight and 'constructs a real that is yet to come, a new type of reality' (Deleuze and Guattari 1987: 142). As with the logic of different/ciation, which divides at the same time as sharing out the virtual and the actual, the diagram is different in kind from that which it finally produces. Deleuze tells us that, 'l'essentiel du diagramme, c'est qu'il est fait pour que quelque chose en *sorte*, et il rate si rien n'en sort [the essential thing about the diagram is that it is made in order for something to *emerge* from it, and if nothing emerges from it, it fails]' (Deleuze 1994b 102. Italics in original). Although it promises a future yet to come, in its application the diagram must be localised as a tool that contends with specific problems.

Deleuze tells us that the painter has many things in his head and many things that surround him, and that these ineluctable influences already dance across the canvas before he has lifted his brush (Deleuze 1994b: 57). The canvas is never a *tabula rasa*, but a noisy field of forces of habit, opinion, and cliché. The artist, and here we can also imagine the architect at the outset of the design process, approaches the canvas with a ready-made set of ideas, from which it is then a matter of disencumberment. The diagram can be applied as an interfering force. In the case of the artist, Francis Bacon, interference takes the form of a manual chaos of smears, smudges and blurs, most of which answer to chance. These manoeuvres (the hand is quite literally put to work) challenge pre-packaged codes, create surprises, and proffer the gift of the novel. The diagram forwards the possibility of a donation of sense transfigured.

Example Two: Eisenman draws some diagrams

Not only does Peter Eisenman compose what he calls his *Diagram Diaries* (1999), which map the progress of his architectural work to date, he also gives us quite clear instructions on how the architect can put the diagram to use. The first phase of the diagram describes a practice in which architects have almost always been adept. Taking the given brief for a proposed architectural project, the architect sets to work. First, the functions that the project will accommodate are specified. Second, these functions are arranged according to type. Third, the above arrangements according to type and function take into consideration a given site. The site is not simply made up of geographical, climatic, and other material conditions, but is inflected by minor histories, sentimental attachments, and the like. Finally, the architect discovers he has his container. Eisenman continues, 'the form of a container is clearly predetermined by its function as shelter and enclosure and because of this has its own meaning, whether intentional or not' (Eisenman 1997: 26). But the job does not finish here.

The second phase of the diagram is where Eisenman, having decided that the traditional process described above is insufficient, draws directly on the work of Deleuze and Guattari. The second diagram answers to a force that is preferably derived from outside the field of architecture so as to invest new possibilities into the architectural process. Take your pick – diagrams of solution waves, DNA structures, liquid crystals, geometric processes such as sine waves, fractals, morphing – it is up to you. These diagrams from the outside are then superimposed across the traditional diagram. The idea is to destroy one clarity with another clarity in order to create a blurriness, or what we might call a zone of obscurity, for, as Eisenman explains, 'two clarities equal a blur' (Eisenman 1997: 26), and with this blur battle can be done with the good and common sense of prevailing aesthetico-architectural techniques.

Eisenman has carried out his diagrammatic experiments in a series of architectural designs, many of which are documented in his *Diagram Diaries*. These diaries can be read as instructions for use. They explain how he has generated diagrams from the geometric patterns he has read across proposed architectural sites, from liquid crystals, from the wave patterns emitted by the human brain. Eisenman also describes how he has redeployed texts drawn from historical, narrative, and filmic sources, into his design process. Sometimes he suggests his diagrams are generated from conditions that are immanent to his given projects, sometimes he suggests his diagrams are rather more arbitrary. Finally, he tells us, 'the diagram attempts to unmotivate place, to find within place space as a void, as a negativity or nonpresence to be filled up with the new figuration of the sign' (Eisenman 1999: 215). The motivated architectural sign assumes the conflation of sign and signified, and makes a claim for the autonomy of architecture. By unmotivating the ground of architecture, a process that might be compared to Bacon's activities of blurring and smudging, Eisenman wishes to invent a series of novel figures for architecture.

Like the autistic children that people Deleuze's essay, 'What Children Say', architects 'never stop talking about what they are doing or trying to do: exploring milieus, by means of dynamic trajectories and drawing up maps of them' (Deleuze 1998: 61). We have seen just a glimpse of this activity above. Architects are already well-trained players with respect to the job of constructing diagrams. The biggest hole that they can fall into is the trap of representation, that is, when they attempt to make their buildings 'look like' the diagrams they invent or appropriate.

Example Three: Möbius strip as diagram

Take, for example, the geometrical model of the Möbius strip. The Möbius strip or loop is a geometrical diagram that illustrates a spatial

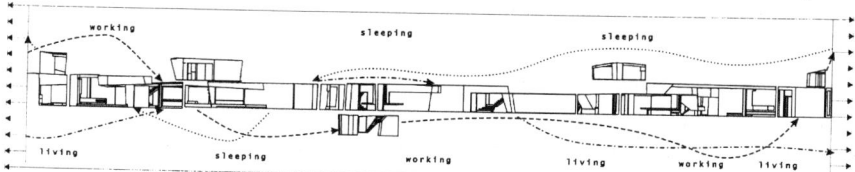

Figure 3.2 Möbius house diagram

paradox. One can build a Möbius strip by cutting a length of paper, twisting it once, and then attaching its ends together so that it forms a loop that confounds any distinction between interior and exterior. When we trace our finger along one surface of this construct we discover that its path is not only continuous, but that it traces the entire surface, both reverse and right sides of the loop. It is a ready-made conundrum, a three-dimensional diagram that speaks of many things, for instance, of ideas of surface, interiority and exteriority, space, time, and infinitude.

In the realm of contemporary architecture we discover a house that *is* a Möbius strip, that wants to be a diagram *and* a built form. The architects Ben van Berkal and Caroline Bos build a Möbius house as though it were simply a matter of building a concept. They suggest that the house's diagram 'liberates architecture from language, interpretation, and signification' (Riley 1999: 128). But by naming it a Möbius House and by confusing house with diagram, their gesture threatens to become recoded, to tell an old story. The architects are aware of these issues. Ben van Berkal claims that their design process has entered a cycle of text/project/text, so that conceptual diagrams and concrete constructions inflect each other in turn (Lynn 1995: 7). We could take the Möbius house in its own right, describe the way its materials follow the twisting inside-out of the form, the way the form is stretched so that its inhabitants occupy the interior-cum-exterior as though it were a choreographed promenade through the countryside in which the house is sited, but alongside these more concrete manifestations of the house there persists the exploratory diagram. What's more, the architects insist that the two are different in kind, that despite the fact that a ready-made geometrical diagram has been borrowed, the house does not become a mere illustration of its form, but responds instead to the virtual organisation of the chosen diagram so that a non-linear and deformative passage is traversed between the two.

In *The Logic of Sense*, Deleuze borrows the geometrical model of the Möbius strip and asks that we break it open so as to examine sense. He suggests that it is 'difficult to respond to those who wish to be satisfied with words, things, images, and ideas', for the process of constructing (architectural) sense neither exists in the mind nor in the things with which it contends (Deleuze 1990: 20). Unfolding the Möbius strip, the experience of sense must be stretched out so that we fall neither on the side of ideas nor of things, but walk the tightrope of the threshold between. Superadded to this tightrope act, the architect must set into action series that pertain to concepts, and series that pertain to the material of their built forms. It is how these series are finally conjoined, and there are so many ways of manifesting this conjunction, that locates the domain of problems with which architects and their many stated and silent collaborators must contend.

The diagram, after the logic of different/ciation, can become diluted in the endless process of folding, unfolding and refolding, or else it can make too much of a mess of things. How does the architect decide on a moment of capture, when should they say stop and decisively frame a little bit of the chaos that presses in all around? The diagram must be used as a tool of rarefaction; it must be selective, even exclusive. As Deleuze points out, we are obliged to 'favour this or that partial sequence at this or that time' (Deleuze 1993: 25). We can compose the chaos and produce what Deleuze calls a bloc of sensation. Art, following Deleuze's account, struggles with chaos in order to render it sensory, and architecture has a task that is similar. The architect, appreciating the combinatory of chance and necessity that circulates with every design project, must make an acrobatic leap and extract just a small, framed moment of difference.[8]

What do the above conceptual perambulations, lent to us by Deleuze, or poached from within the disciplinary field of philosophy, allow the architect? Now, rather than searching out its hidden meaning along both the false and the well-trodden trails, an attitude to the practice of architecture might instead be described as 'anything we like provided we make the whole thing work' (Deleuze 2000: 146). This is not a licence to get carried away. In order to make the whole thing work we must appreciate the interplay of chance and necessity that attends every problem. There will always be givens with which the architect must contend, there are precedents that we can choose to embrace or ignore, there is a context, and a client, and then there are all the accidents likely to happen along the way. What we can do is displace the anchor of meaning with the operative promise of sense, not the regulatory strictures of common and good sense, but a sense that is produced according to contingent, yet necessary circumstances. The threshold between architecture and its outside must be made trafficable in both directions, backwards and forwards, and it must be breached not once but every time a new set of material and immaterial factors is confronted. In order to become a successful pickpocket, the architect must learn about all the hidden nooks and crannies on both floors of Deleuze's Baroque house.

References

Bachelard, G. (1994), *The Poetics of Space*, trans. M. Jolas, Boston: Beacon Press.

Bogue, R. (1989), *Deleuze and Guattari*, London and New York: Routledge.

Cache, B. (1995), *Earth Moves: The Furnishing of Terrorism*, trans. A. Boyman, Cambridge: The MIT Press.

Deleuze, G. (1990), *The Logic of Sense*, trans. M. Lester, New York: Columbia University Press.

Deleuze, G. (1991), *Bergsonism*, trans. H. Tomlinson and B. Habberjam, New York: Zone Books.

Deleuze, G. (1993), *The Fold: Leibniz and the Baroque*, trans. and foreword T. Conley, Minneapolis: University of Minnesota Press.

Deleuze, G. (1994a), *Cinema Two: The Time Image*, trans. H. Tomlinson and R. Galeta, London: The Athlone Press.

Deleuze, G. (1994b), *Francis Bacon: Logique de la Sensation*, Paris: Editions de la Difference.

Deleuze, G. (1994c), *Difference and Repetition*, trans. P. Patton, New York: Columbia University Press.

Deleuze, G. (1998), 'What Children Say', *Essays Critical and Clinical*, trans. D. W. Smith and M. A. Greco, London and New York: Verso.

Deleuze, G. (2000), *Proust and Signs*, trans. R. Howard, Minneapolis: University of Minnesota Press.

Deleuze, G. and Guattari, F. (1987), *A Thousand Plateaus*, trans. B. Massumi, Minneapolis: University of Minnesota Press.

Deleuze, G. and Guattari, F. (1994), *What is Philosophy?*, trans. G. Burchell and H. Tomlinson, London and New York: Verso.

Deleuze, G. and Parnet, C. (1987), *Dialogues*, trans. H. Tomlinson and B. Habberjam, New York: Columbia University Press.

Eisenman, P. (1997), 'Processes of the Interstitial', *El Croquis* 83: 21–35.

Eisenman, P. (1999), *Diagram Diaries*, London: Thames and Hudson.

Grosz, E. (2001), *Architecture from the Outside*, Cambridge: The MIT Press.

Lynn, G. (1995), 'Conversation by Modem with Ben van Berkel', *El Croquis*: 6–15.

Lynn, G. (1996), 'Form and Field', in C. Davidson (ed.), *Anywise*, Cambridge and London: The MIT Press, pp. 92–9.

Lynn, G. (1998), 'Geometry in Time', in C. Davidson (ed.), *Anyhow*, Cambridge and London: The MIT Press, pp. 164–73.

Lynn, G. (1999), *Animate Form*, New York: Princeton Architectural Press.

Massumi, B. (1998a), 'Sensing the Virtual, Building the Insensible', *Architectural Design* 68 (5/6) (May–June): 16–25.

Massumi, B. (1998b), 'Line Parable for the Virtual (On the Superiority of the Analog)', in J. Beckman (ed.), *The Virtual Dimension: Architecture, Representation and Crash Culture*, New York: Princeton Architectural Press, pp. 304–21.

Nesbitt, K. (1996), *Theorizing a New Agenda for Architecture: An Anthology of Architectural Theory 1965–1995*, New York: Princeton Architectural Press.

Patton, P. (2000), *Deleuze and the Political*, London and New York: Routledge.

Proust, M. (1989), *Swann's Way*, trans. C. K. Scott Moncrieff and T. Kilmartin, London: Penguin Books.

Rajchman, J. (1998), *Constructions*, Cambridge and London: The MIT Press.

Rajchman, J. (1999), 'Time Out', in C. Davidson (ed.), *Anytime*, Cambridge and London: The MIT Press, pp. 152–7.

Riley, T. (1999), *The Un-Private House*, New York: The Museum of Modern Art.

Vidler, A. (2000), *Warped Space: Art, Architecture, and Anxiety in Modern Culture*, Cambridge and London: The MIT Press.

Notes

1. 'Less is a bore' is the glib response the postmodern architect, Robert Venturi, made to the modernist architect, Mies van der Rohe's dictum, 'less is more'.
2. By claiming that architecture is the first of all the arts, Deleuze and Guattari are, in fact, echoing the claim made by Vitruvius, a Roman architect of the first century BC, in his treatise, *Ten Books on Architecture*, that primitive man 'gradually advanced from the construction of buildings to the other arts and sciences'. Vitruvius is cited in the introduction to Nesbitt's anthology (1996: 18).
3. Deleuze writes, 'the surface and that which takes place at the surface is what "renders possible" – in other words, the event as that which is expressed' (Deleuze 1990: 186).
4. Rajchman writes of, 'the chance of new histories, new "possibilities of life"', and Grosz, in unison, suggests that, 'the future of each discipline requires that each open itself up to a reconsideration of the virtual and the promise it holds for newness, otherness and divergence from what currently prevails' (Rajchman 1999: 155). See also Grosz 2001: 113.
5. See also Deleuze 1994a: 46, for a lovely passage on the relationship between the actual and the virtual.
6. Deleuze insists that the 'greatest importance must be attached to the 'distinctive feature of the *t/c* as the symbol of difference: differen*t*iate and differen*c*iate' (Deleuze 1994c: 279).
7. Lynn develops these ideas in his book *Animate Form* (1999).
8. Massumi describes the role of the architect as a 'process tweaker and form flusher'. Confronted with innumerable possibilities each of which might lead to the fruitful resolution of a design problem, the architect, according to Massumi, 'becomes a prospector of formative continuity, a tracker in an elusive field of generative deformation'. (Massumi 1998a: 10, 16).

Chapter 4

Space: Extensive and Intensive, Actual and Virtual

Manuel DeLanda

There are at least two kinds of space relevant to our human identity. As biological organisms and as social agents we live our lives within spaces bounded by natural and artificial *extensive* boundaries, that is, within zones that extend in space up to a limit marked by a frontier. Whether we are talking about the frontiers of a country, a city, a neighbourhood or an ecosystem, inhabiting these extensive spaces is part of what defines our social and biological identities. There are, however, other well-defined spaces which we also inhabit but which are less familiar: these are *zones of intensity*, not only those zones of temperature that define different ecosystems (from hot jungles to cold tundras), but also the zones of high pressure explored by deep-sea divers, or the zones of low gravity explored by astronauts. These other spaces are also bounded but in a different way, the limits of one zone marked by *critical points* of temperature, pressure, gravity, density, tension, connectivity, points defining abrupt transitions in the state of the creatures inhabiting those zones. Although the weather maps that have become common in television news have made intensive spaces very tangible (zones of high and low pressure, cold or warm fronts defining sharp temperature transitions) the fact remains that most philosophers have hardly thought about the questions raised by the distinction between the extensive and the intensive.

An exception is the philosophy of Gilles Deleuze, where the distinction between intensive and extensive spaces is one of the two key distinctions grounding his ontology (the other is that between actual and virtual space). The concepts come from thermodynamics where they are defined not as a distinction between spaces but between magnitudes or quantities (which can then be used to define spaces). While extensive quantities (such as volume, area, length, amount of energy or entropy) are additive, intensive quantities are not. For example, if one adds two equal volumes of water one gets twice the amount of water. But if one adds two quantities of water at forty-five degrees of temperature one does not get a body of water at ninety degrees but one at the original temperature. Deleuze defines intensive quantities as 'indivisible', a definition which is simply another way of expressing the same point: a gallon of water at ninety degrees can be divided in extension, yielding, say, two half gallons, but the two parts will not each have half the temperature.[1]

Whatever way one chooses to define the terms what really matters is the reason for the lack of divisibility of intensive quantities: they are objective averages, and tend to preserve the same average value upon division. For two intensive quantities to produce a change, there must be a *difference*, or gradient, in their degree of intensity. And the change produced by a gradient of temperature (or pressure, density, speed) will not be a simple addition, but the emergence of a spontaneous flow or movement which will tend to cancel the difference in intensity, and restore equilibrium and average values. Yet, as Deleuze emphasises, despite the fact that it is the spontaneous cancellation of differences that explains indivisibility, the philosophical importance of intensive magnitudes can only be grasped prior to this cancellation. We can summarise what is philosophically relevant in this regard with the formula: *intensive differences are productive*. Indeed, it may be argued, wherever one finds an extensive frontier (for example, the skin which defines the extensive boundary of our bodies) there is always a process driven by intensive differences which produced such a boundary (for example, the embryological process which creates our bodies, driven by differences in chemical concentration, among other things).

This approach to intensive spaces, as the site of processes which yield as products the great diversity of extensive spaces, is key to Deleuze's ontology. In what is probably his most important book, *Difference and Repetition*, he writes:

> Difference is not diversity. Diversity is given, but difference is that by which the given is given . . . Difference is not phenomenon but the nuomenon closest to the phenomenon . . . Every phenomenon refers to an inequality by which it is conditioned . . . Everything which happens and everything which appears is correlated with orders of differences: differences of level, temperature, pressure, tension, potential, difference of intensity. (Deleuze 1994: 222)

It is traditional since Kant to distinguish between the world as it is given in experience to us humans, that is, the world of phenomena or appearances, and the world as it exists by itself, regardless of whether there is a human observer to interact with it. This world 'in itself' is the world of 'nuomena'. While most philosophers do not believe in nuomena Gilles Deleuze, as the quote above illustrates, certainly does. In other words, Deleuze's ontology is a *realist* ontology. But while most realist philosophers espouse one or another form of essentialism, the belief that what gives the contents of this mind-independent world their identity is the possession of an essence, for Deleuze the identity of any being can never be taken for granted and always needs explanation in terms of the historical process which produced it. If we characterise the identity of material beings as defined by extensities (not only by its spatial boundaries but also by the amounts of matter and energy contained within those boundaries) then the process that produces those beings will be defined by intensities. In this sense, human beings not only inhabit extensive spaces, they themselves are extensive spaces. Generalising this to include mental phenomena would involve defining psychological intensities (not only grief, joy, love, hate, but also beliefs and desires which also come in different intensities) as well as the corresponding extensities. In this essay I will avoid this important issue and stick to our bodily identities which do form extensive spaces in a straightforward sense.

Despite the fact that Deleuze takes the distinction between the extensive and the intensive from physics, in the page following the quote above he argues that nineteenth-century thermodynamics cannot provide the foundation he needs for his ontology. Why? Because that branch of physics became obsessed with the final equilibrium state (defined by its amount of entropy, an extensive quantity) at the expense of the difference-driven intensive process which gives rise to that state. Fortunately, this shortcoming of classical thermodynamics has now been fixed in the latest version of this field, appropriately labelled 'far-from-equilibrium thermodynamics', and the effect of this repair has been to make this discipline all the more interesting philosophically. In a nutshell, while equilibrium thermodynamics focusses on what happens once the intensive differences have been cancelled, far-from-equilibrium thermodynamics studies systems that are continuously traversed by a strong flow of energy or matter, a flow which does not allow the differences in intensity to be cancelled, that is, a flow that maintains these differences and keeps them from cancelling themselves out. In a sense, the new field studies systems in a *zone of higher intensity*, and it is only in this zone that difference-driven morphogenesis comes into its own, and that matter becomes an active agent, one which does not need form to come and impose itself from the outside, as is the case with essentialism. In short, only in this zone of intensity can we witness the birth of extensity and its identity-defining frontiers.

I said above that the distinction between extensive and intensive spaces is one of two distinctions which are fundamental in Deleuze's realist ontology. Far-from-equilibrium thermodynamics also throws light on the second distinction, that between *actual* and *virtual* space. Even in equilibrium thermodynamics scientists must face the fact that, given a system in which an intensive difference exists, the final state of equilibrium to which the system tends is somehow already 'present prior to its actualisation. That is, the final state acts as an 'attractor' for the process and explains the tendency of the intensive difference to cancel itself. But what ontological status does that final state have prior to its coming into actual existence? One may think that the category of 'the possible' is the ontological category one would need to describe this status, but this would be wrong. Despite what some essentialist modal logicians may argue, possibilities are not mind-independent entities, though they do possess psychological reality (no-one can deny that human beings can in fact entertain various possible scenarios in their heads). States acting as 'attractors', on the other hand, possess a certain objective efficacy even while not being fully actual, since they guide real processes towards a definite outcome prior to the latter's actualisation.

One way of approaching the ontological status of attractors would be to say that while they are not possibilities they do act as *the structure of a space of possibilities*. Of all the possible outcomes only one, or a few, become regularly actualised, a fact that suggests that the space of possible outcomes is greatly constrained, or in other words, that it has structure. While the possibilities making up this space are not real (other than in a purely psychological way) the structure of the space may be considered fully real and mind-independent. But if this reality is not actual (by definition) what is it? Deleuze's answer would be that it is virtual, not in the sense of a virtual reality (as exemplified by computer simulations, or even cinema) but in the sense of a *real virtuality*. In this regard, the contribution of the new thermodynamics is that only in the zone of intensity it explores do physical processes display the full repertoire of attractors. While in linear systems near equilibrium only steady-state attractors exist, non-linear far-from-equilibrium systems display steady-state, periodic and chaotic attractors. Moreover, instead of the single global equilibrium of the classical theory we now have multiple equilibria, which means that history matters. While with a single possible outcome the different paths followed by systems on their way there can be ignored, with multiple possible outcomes the details of the history followed do matter (this is what physicists call 'path dependence'). Why is all this important? Because once this rich structure is revealed it becomes harder for philosophers to ignore the ontological questions raised by it.

To tackle this ontological issue, however, we need to go beyond physics and into mathematics to define the status of virtual space. The mathematical distinction that we need is that between *metric and non-metric* spaces, that is, spaces in which the concept of 'length' is fundamental and spaces in which it is not. Mathematically a space is defined by a set of points and a definition of 'relations of proximity' between points, in other words, of the relations which define a given subset of the points as a neighbourhood. If proximity is defined via a minimum length (for example, all points less than a given distance away from a centre form a neighbourhood) the space is said to be metric (whether flat, as in Euclidean geometry, or curved, as in the non-Euclidean versions). If some other criterion is used the space is said to be non-metric (as in projective, differential or topological geometries). What other criterion of proximity could be used? In differential geometry, for example, one takes advantage of the fact that the calculus operates on equations expressing rates of change and that one of its operators (differentiation) gives as its output an instantaneous value for that rate of change. The points that form a space can then be defined not by rigid lengths from a fixed coordinate system (as in the metric case) but by the instantaneous rate at which *curvature* changes at that point. Some parts of the space will not be changing at all, other parts changing slowly, and others changing fast. A differential space, in effect, becomes *a field of rapidities and slownesses*, and via these infinitesimal relations one can specify neighbourhoods without having to use rigid lengths. Mathematicians refer to such a differential space as a 'manifold' or a 'multiplicity'.

To Deleuze this notion of 'multiplicity' has several important features. First of all, when Gauss and Riemann introduced the notion in the first half of the nineteenth century, they revolutionised the very way in which we can pose spatial problems. (Einstein and others would several decades later use these new problem-posing resources to, in turn, revolutionise our ideas of physical spacetime.) One feature of this revolution was to get rid of the idea that a space of a given number of dimensions (say, a two-dimensional folded sheet) must be inscribed within a space one dimension higher (a three-dimensional box) in order for it to be properly studied. The need for the extra dimension arises from the procedure of assigning Cartesian coordinates to every point of the sheet (via rigid lengths expressing the distance of each point to one of the three coordinates). But if the sheet can be studied using only local information (the rapidity or slowness at which curvature is changing at a given point) the need for such global embedding space is eliminated. This, Deleuze argues, also eliminates the extra dimension which relates to the space being studied as a transcendental dimension. As he puts it, 'In all cases the multiplicity is intrinsically defined, without external reference or recourse to a uniform space in which it would be submerged' (Deleuze 1994: 183).[2]

Eliminating a global embedding space and viewing all spaces in purely local terms is crucial for Deleuze because to him this is not a formal issue in the philosophy of mathematics but an ontological issue bearing directly on the status of the virtual. The virtual structure of possibility spaces must never be made into something transcendent but always conceived as *immanent* to the material world. A multiplicity, as Deleuze writes, 'however many dimensions it may have . . . never has a supplementary dimension to that which transpires upon it. This alone makes it natural and immanent' (Deleuze and Guattari 1987: 266).[3] But how, one may ask, can such a geometric object have ontological significance? In what sense can it act as the structure of a space of possibilities? The answer is that multiplicities or manifolds can be used to study a physical system if each of their dimensions is assigned values from one of the 'degrees of freedom' (or relevant ways of changing) of the system itself. That is, the multiplicity or manifold becomes the space of all the possible states which a given system can have. (This space of possible states is referred to as 'state space' or 'phase space'.)[4] And more importantly, while the points in the manifold represent all the possibilities for a given system, certain topological features of this space represent the invariant structure of that space. These *topological invariants* are what I referred to above as 'attractors'. While state spaces themselves are nothing but mathematical representations (and the possibilities they symbolise are not mind-independent realities) their topological invariants (their dimensions, their singularities or attractors) may indeed be interpreted as being fully real.

How one goes from a mathematical representation (a manifold) to a real non-actual entity (a virtual multiplicity) is a complex issue which I cannot tackle here, but which I have addressed in detail elsewhere.[5] But even if it were clear just how such an ontological move can be made that would take us only half way through an account of virtual space, the space formed by all multiplicities (the plane of consistency or plane of immanence). A full account needs to introduce yet another unfamiliar virtual entity (referred to by names such as 'abstract machine', 'line of flight', 'quasi-causal operator') whose job is continuously to extract multiplicities from the systems in which they are actualised and mesh them together without reducing their heterogeneity (that is, give them consistency as a space).[6] Again, just how these two operations are supposed to be performed cannot be discussed here but they are crucial if virtual space is to be truly immanent and not an eternal reservoir of fixed archetypes. In other words, philosophers cannot simply use the label 'immanent' and assume this is going to eliminate transcendence, they must give concrete mechanisms of immanence.[7]

Let's assume for a moment that one can give a full account of what virtual space is and how it is constantly being produced and reproduced. What materialist world view emerges from these ideas? In a nutshell, the world would consist of a topological (non-metric) space containing all the constraints which organise the physical, chemical, biological and social processes which produce the actual systems (planets, molecules, species, institutions) which inhabit our familiar Euclidean metric and extensive space. Non-metric and metric spaces would be connected via intermediate spaces which would be mostly intensive. Thus, the virtual, the intensive and the actual would constitute the three spheres of reality, with virtual multiplicities constraining and guiding intensive processes which in turn would yield specific actual entities. The opposite movement, from the actual to the intensive to the virtual, would also be constantly happening, guaranteeing the independence and immanence of multiplicities. Within this material world human thinkers of different types would follow one or the other movement, scientists tracking the actualisation of the virtual (and focussing on actual beings, as well as intensive processes), and philosophers tracking the opposite motion, that which reconstitutes virtual multiplicities (as ideal events) out of actual entities and gives them consistency as a space.

> It could be said that science and philosophy take opposed paths, because philosophical concepts have events for consistency whereas scientific functions have states of affairs or mixtures for reference: through concepts, philosophy continually extracts a consistent event from the states of affairs . . . whereas through functions, science continually actualizes the event in a state of affairs, thing, or body that can be referred to. (Deleuze and Guattari 1994: 126)

References

DeLanda, M. (2002), *Intensive Science and Virtual Philosophy*, London: Continuum Press.
Deleuze, G. (1988), *Bergsonism*, trans. H. Tomlinson and B. Habberjam, New York: Zone Books.

Deleuze, G. (1990), *The Logic of Sense*, trans. M. Lester with C. Stivale, New York: Columbia University Press.

Deleuze, G. (1994), *Difference and Repetition*, trans. P. Patton, New York: Columbia University Press.

Deleuze, G. and Guattari, F. (1987), *A Thousand Plateaus*, trans. B. Massumi, Minneapolis: University of Minnesota Press.

Deleuze, G. and Guattari, F. (1994), *What is Philosophy?*, trans. H. Tomlinson and G. Burchell, New York: Columbia University Press.

Notes

1. Actually Deleuze defines the intensive not as 'indivisible' but as 'what cannot be divided without changing nature', a definition that acknowledges the fact that critical points do subdivide an intensive line of values but only by marking the onset of an abrupt change of state. As he writes:

   > What is the significance of these indivisible distances that are ceaselessly transformed and cannot be divided or transformed without their elements changing in nature each time? Is it not the intensive character of this type of multiplicity's elements and the relations between them? Exactly like a speed or a temperature, which is not composed of other speeds or temperatures, but rather is enveloped in or envelops others, each of which marks a change in nature. The metrical principle of these multiplicities is not to be found in a homogeneous milieu but resides elsewhere, in forces at work within them, in physical phenomena inhabiting them . . . (Deleuze and Guattari 1987: 31)
   >
   > This quote uses the term 'distance' as if it were a non-metric property, though in its usual meaning it certainly denotes something metric. Deleuze takes this special intensive meaning of 'distance' from Bertrand Russell.

2. Elsewhere he writes:

   > Unity always operates in an empty dimension supplementary to that of the system considered (overcoding) . . . [But a] multiplicity never allows itself to be overcoded, never has available a supplementary dimension over and above its number of lines, that is, over and above the multiplicity of numbers attached to those lines. (Deleuze and Guattari 1987: 8–9)

3. This remark is made about the 'plane of consistency' not about multiplicities. But the former is nothing but the virtual space formed by the multiplicities themselves.

4. When Deleuze defines his multiplicities he always seems to be referring to manifolds whose dimensions are used to represent degrees of freedom (or independent variables) of some dynamic, and not to manifolds as mere geometric objects. Thus, in his first introduction of the term he says:

   > Riemann defined as 'multiplicities' those things that could be determined by their dimensions or their independent variables. He distinguished between discrete multiplicities and continuous multiplicities. The former contain the principle of their own metrics . . . The latter found a metrical principle in something else, even if only in phenomena unfolding in them or in the forces acting in them. (Deleuze 1988: 39)

   And elsewhere he says, using the word 'Idea' to refer to concrete universals or virtual multiplicities as replacements for essences:

An Idea is an n-dimensional, continuous, defined multiplicity. Colour – or rather, the Idea of colour – is a three-dimensional multiplicity. By dimensions, we mean the variables or co-ordinates upon which a phenomenon depends; by continuity, we mean the set of relations between changes in these variables . . . by definition, we mean the elements reciprocally determined by these relations, elements which cannot change unless the multiplicity changes its order and its metric. (Deleuze 1994: 182)

5. See DeLanda 2002: 30–8.
6. That Deleuze conceives of immanent virtual space in terms of both multiplicities and of an additional entity which weaves them together without homogenising them is clear from the following quote:

There was a first group of notions: the Body without Organs or destratified Plane of Consistency; the Matter of the Plane, that which occurs in the body or plane (singular, nonsegmented multiplicities composed of intensive continuums, emissions of particle-signs, conjunctions of flows); and the Abstract Machine, or Abstract Machines, in so far as they construct that body or draw the plane or 'diagram' [t]hat occurs (lines of flight, or absolute deterritorialisation). (Deleuze and Guattari 1987: 72)

7. The term 'mechanisms of immanence' does not, to my knowledge, occur in Deleuze's work, but he expresses himself in similar ways:

Many movements, *with a fragile and delicate mechanism*, intersect: that by means of which bodies, states of affairs, and mixtures, considered in their depth, succeed or fail in the production of ideal surfaces [the plane of consistency]; and conversely, that by means of which the events of the surface are actualized in the present of bodies (in accordance with complex rules) by imprisoning their singularities within the limits of worlds, individuals and persons. (Deleuze 1990: 167, my emphasis)

Chapter 5

'Genesis Eternal': After Paul Klee[1]

John David Dewsbury and Nigel Thrift

Resonances[2]

As geographers we are often seen as delegates and curators of 'space' by those who inhabit the humanities and social sciences. We are hemmed in by the three dominant ways in which space is rendered: (1) Space as a *Newtonian* conceptualisation where it is seen as a category equal to time, thus allying geography to history. Space here is the solution to the question: the interaction and integration of phenomena is explained in terms of space. In other words, space is the container for action – Kant's filing system for observation – an abstract frame of reference independent of matter; (2) More simply, and more commonly, space is understood as a *relative*, but active, term. Here space is a material reality dealing with questions of scale – space as a plane, as a distance, as something that acts as a weak actant and has effect; (3) More open to possibility but often just as constraining in how it is conceptualised, space is turned into something that is *relative to the transcendent*. Space is a product of society but also a factor in the production of the social becoming socially constructed, idealised and ideological (Crang and Thrift 2000).

But how does space fare when we set out onto the open seas of Deleuze's transcendental empiricism – that wilder sort of empiricism that emerges 'in contrast to everything that makes up the world of the subject and the object' (Deleuze 2001: 25)? For us, Deleuze turns space into a moving concept: so let's release it and ourselves into the storm.

We want to capture the movement of space in Deleuze's thought by seeing space in terms of an immanent spatiality. Whilst this chimes with the diagram of the late thought of Deleuze, and, in particular, that of 'Immanence: A Life . . .' (see Agamben 1999: 224), it haunts all his work. Indeed this sense of Deleuzian space is a kind of haunting, a world of phantoms, for, as we want to show, it speaks of space acting as a passage, without spatial movement, between a life and immanence. (It is not so much a movement between the two, for the actual world is one made out of the virtual chaos of immanence.) Thus, Deleuzian space is always real but not always actual; that will disappoint many geographers but to become an apprentice of Deleuzian space (a new type of geographer perhaps?) is to be firmly aware of being in a realm of virtualities, events and singularities. To act as an exemplar, we will address a particular realm, that of art in general and that of the work of Paul Klee in particular. It is through the incorporeality of Klee's work and its resonance with the intelligible materiality of the world that we seek ways to act out and address what Foucault (1998: 346) referred to as 'interior phantoms':

> interior phantoms that are quickly reabsorbed into other depths by the sense of smell, by the mouth, by the appetites, extremely thin membranes that detach themselves from the surfaces of the objects and proceed to impose colours and contours deep within our eyes (floating epiderm, visual idols); phantasms of fear and desire (cloud gods, the adorable face of the beloved, 'miserable hope transported by the wind').

It is our premise that an immanent spatiality can be apprehended in these interior phantoms, these affects of art, where above all this notion of an immanent spatiality comes to be about registering the world as a multi-linear complex which:

> can fold back on itself with intersections and inflections that interconnect philosophy, the history of philosophy, history in general, the sciences, and the arts. As though these are so many twists in the path of something moving through space like a whirlwind that can materialise at any point. (Deleuze 1995: 161)

The affect of art is like a materialisation that enables a reregistration of the world only discernible through the lens of philosophy, through philosophy's power to create concepts that alter meaning and 'impose a new set of divisions on things and actions' (Deleuze 1990b: 321). The new division that is achieved here is this immanent spatiality.

We are also going to use our notion of Deleuzian space to enter into an argument with Representation (brash rather than bare repetition of the same rather than of the different in itself). This is to recognise that Deleuzian thought is a thought for our times:

> Modern life is such that, confronted with the most mechanical, the most stereotypical repetitions, inside and outside ourselves, we endlessly extract from them little differences, variations and modifications. Conversely, secret, disguised and hidden repetitions, animated by the perpetual displace-

ment of a difference, restore bare, mechanical and stereotypical repetitions, within and without us. In simulacra, repetition already plays upon repetitions, and difference already plays upon differences. Repetitions repeat themselves, while the differenciator differenciates itself. The task of life is to make all these repetitions coexist in a space in which difference is distributed. (Deleuze 1994: xix)

For us, this is a call to embrace immanent space in order to find our place in a world where there is so much potential for differentiation in so many of the orbits of the social: from art to religion, from the life sciences to technological enhancements, from minor political movements to alternative communities, and from personal relationships to new configurations of our bodies. It is not a question of the existence of this world but of questioning its movements and intensities, 'so as once again to give birth to new modes of existence, closer to animals and rocks. It may be that believing in this world, in this life, becomes our most difficult task' (Deleuze and Guattari 1994: 75).

We want to signal here that in what follows the pathways or routes through Deleuze's texts form an open tracery: 'There is no heart, but only a problem – that is, a distribution of notable points; there is no centre but always decentring, series, from one to another, with the limp of a presence and a absence – of an excess, of a deficiency' (Foucault 1998: 343). And that within this open system we distribute this problem of immanent space and representation across three main terrains (there are, of course, many other pathways that could be taken); first, across the realm of art and the role of genesis in this practice, second, in the face of a politics of encountering the foreign, and, third, in the field of a science grappling with the nature within us and the role it played in Klee's programme of artistic expression.

Genesis Eternal: presenting the world anew[3]

Registering the world in different ways is something that we always do – it is just that representation designates a narrower realm of the possible interpretations available to us. Representation separates sense from its material expression – the distinction between recognition (through perception) and reminiscence (through representation) (Deleuze 1994: 141) – forcing us into a disturbing unfamiliarity with something we already know. Recognition loses its immanent munificence by way of representation for we are already instinctively delivered to the world by recognition alone, by encounters which can never fully be known, told or sighted. It is then not about understanding the world but about expressing it differently by taking on perceptions without representation. This is intimated more straightforwardly, if less philosophically, when Deleuze writes of language itself stuttering, thus in effect producing an affective and intensive presentation that has nothing to do with an affectation of the one who experiences it – the point being that such an affectation is already representationally scripted (see Deleuze 1998: 107).

Crucially, this problematisation of representation is indelibly linked to living in a world of multiplicities and to the notion of becoming; it is not possible to do space and Deleuze without accepting the kind of world that such a notion of space spaces out. It is therefore fundamental that, when constructing an appreciation of space with the difference engineering of Deleuze, you are aware of the kind of world that you are forced to believe in. Klee clearly belonged to the same church as Deleuze, seeing the world as the infinite, incessantly being created through a cosmic-earthly tension. Conceptually, Klee began in the right place resonating with a Deleuzian spatial awareness that asked, 'In the beginning what was?', answering in a way which immediately rebuffs the representational penchant for an origin and sending out an echo to Deleuze's later thought that there is only movement. Klee's full response was that there are only things as 'primordially mobile':

> Initially there is but one principle: to move. No law of motion, in other words, no special will, nothing specific, nothing partaking of order. Chaos and anarchy, a turbid jumble. The intangible – nothing is heavy, nothing light (light-heavy); nothing is white, nothing black, nothing red, nothing yellow, nothing blue, only an approximate grey . . . No here, no there, only everywhere. No long-short, only everywhere. No far-near, no yesterday, today, tomorrow, only tomorrow-yesterday. (Klee 1973: 13)

These words are perhaps some of the best with which to describe the world of which Deleuze writes; this world of genesis eternal. But how do we address an open world where finding one's orientation is so evidently antithetical? In this regard, in the argument of this chapter, geography is not the ideal place to search for a handle on space as it is apprehended in Deleuzian terms. Instead, so we will argue, the production of social scientific knowledge, and its demand for specific explications, requires a conceptual space which focuses on the Deleuzian event where the event itself, as a separate entity, is laid out on a prehistorical plane of 'duration', where duration is understood as a plane of immanence that has the power to separate itself into different fluxes and/or into single currents according to the nature of attention occurring (Deleuze 2000: 50).

Understood in this way, duration is not divisible in that it changes in nature in dividing itself:

> Many philosophers had already said that the whole was neither given nor giveable: they simply concluded from this that the whole was a meaningless notion. Bergson's conclusion is very different: if the whole is not giveable, it is because it is the Open, and because its nature is to change constantly, or to give rise to something new, in short, to endure. 'The duration of the universe must therefore be one with the latitude of creation which can find it in place'. So that each time we find ourselves confronted with a duration, or in a duration, we may conclude that there exists somewhere a whole which is changing, and which is open somewhere. (Deleuze 1986: 9; quoting Bergson, *Matter and Memory*)

This is a space, then, which haunts the actual world in which we find tangible expression of where we are via a sensation of the incorporeal, virtual immanence of the open whole of this world of movement.

What is fundamental is how we access this sensation, how we come to apprehend the resonances of this aspect of the world, how we traverse and make tangible/visible aspects of the real virtual world immanent to the real actual world in which we are placed. It is here that the way of registering the world in different ways through art, and in particular the conceptual apparatus underwriting the experimentation in the art of Klee, comes into its own, producing that quintessentially Deleuzian space between the virtual and the actual world. The artist's art acts as the conduit, translator and creator of the virtual, immanent and open, one and many (May 2004) world that has not yet found its expression but continues to unfold into actuality through the artist's forms that can register possible experience creating worlds in new ways.

> His sense of direction has brought order into the passing stream of image and experience. This sense of direction in nature and life, this branching and spreading array, I shall compare with the root of the tree. From the root the sap flows to the artist, flows through him, flows to his eye . . . and . . . he does nothing other than gather and pass on what comes to him from the depths. He neither serves nor rules – he transmits. (Klee 1966:13–15).

In this manner Deleuze's engagement with art operates on the level of general conceptions in the way that it creates an aperture onto the virtual, both in terms of thought and presentation. This engagement is illustrated by Deleuze's treatment of cinema that for Deleuze existed as a mode of thought produced by images of time, space and movement. Through this general art of thought, unfolding actualisations of signs, events, materials and concrete moments come to be referenced just as

Deleuze references individual works (films, paintings, novels) and particular intensities (images, sounds, phrases). Art, then, presents determinable but not determined affects that cast out both the world anew and us in our becoming otherwise within in it.

> The work of art is . . . *a bloc of sensations, that is to say, a compound of percepts and affects.* Percepts are no longer perceptions; they are independent of a state of those who experience them. Affects are no longer feelings or affections; they go beyond the strength of those that undergo them. Sensations, percepts, and affects are *beings* whose validity lies in themselves and exceeds any lived. (Deleuze and Guattari 1994: 164)

It is important to note that it is not just a question of any old art. Deleuze is acutely aware that in our times art is often drained of its full munificence for expressing and registering the world by the two dominant but mutually exclusive competing systems of representation: that of verbal sign and visual representation both of which tend to function towards ideological ends. In Klee we find an artist who restores art to the fullness of its potential:

> by showing the juxtaposition of shapes and the syntax of signs in an uncertain, reversible, floating space (simultaneously page and canvas, plane and volume, notebook graph and ground survey, map and chronicle). [Klee] produced both systems of representation in the interweaving of just one fabric. In so doing he overturned their common space and undertook to build a new one. (Foucault 1998: 1995)

This new space we here intimate as immanent space, but what comprises its dimension, and how does this entirely unexplored terrain furnish a different way of approaching the notion of life? (see Deleuze 1988b: 69; Agamben 1999: 221). Again Klee's passion for his work heralds him as a witness to this undiscovered country that immanently surrounds us:

> Art does not reproduce what is visible, but makes things visible. The nature of graphic art easily makes abstraction tempting, and rightly so. The imaginary character is both blurred and has a fairy-tale quality about it and at the same time expresses itself very precisely. The purer the graphic work, i.e. the greater the importance attached to the formal elements used in the graphic representation, the more inadequate the preparation for the realistic representation of visible things. (Klee 1920, *Creative Confession*; quoted in Partsch 2003: 54)

Stretching the fabric of our tangible world, the universes envisaged in art scatter 'themselves into nebulae or different stellar systems, in accordance with qualitative distances that are no longer those of space and time' (Deleuze and Guattari 1994: 196). Art here restores the infinite to us (Deleuze and Guattari 1994: 197). 'The world is enfolded in each soul, which unfolds this or that region of it according to the order of space and time (whence the overall harmony)' (Deleuze 1995: 154). It is never a completed world nor is it an indifferently cold open world of raw multiplicity for the actual world exists alongside the virtual world; the world of our particular region manifests and speaks to wider virtual harmonies. These harmonies are however better understood as a virtual chaosmos rather than as mutually exclusive worlds – 'hence it is chaos, after all, not chaos inconceivable, but chaos conceivable, as logos' (Klee 1973: 15). Famously, this is Klee's grey point which, 'leaps out of itself and generates a self-forming line, but only in order to wrest sensation from bodies, in order to form a "chaosmos", a composition of chaoid sensations that render chaos perceptible and make possible a passage through the finite to the infinite' (Bogue 2003: 176). In other words the artwork presents a leap from chaos to composition and from the virtual to the actual affecting us in a way that enables us to register the world anew (see Deleuze and Guattari 1994: 203). Art is therefore a realm that opens up the world, unfolding it towards that which we are unable to represent (in any form, not just in words but also in paint and image, for a representation is a static possession, a mastery: the world is captured, done and dusted which is not the Deleuzian world we are talking about here). For Klee, art both creates the world and attends to that hidden dimension, that interworld, that passage and passing of the world which exists beside communication and within which resonances of its presence, its reality, strike the fabric of our current ordinary actuality. Subtly recurring, such resonances of the virtual in the actual can take up a stronger presence in the ordinary as the world continues to unfold. Always, though, there is that extra-being that exceeds the experiential dimensions of the visible and in so doing suspends both affirmation and negation by making apparent the way the world is always somewhat beyond our mere representational understandings (see Deleuze 1990: 32). This translates directly into a manifestation of two further key Deleuzian notions that open the way for the realm of art to enter into the realm of general living (Deleuze 1995: 154); that of percepts and affects:

> Affects and percepts are thus the generic and immanent elements constitutive of *a* life . . . 'life' is constructed on *an immanent plane of consistency* that knows only relations between affects and percepts, and whose composition, through the creation of blocks of sensations, takes place in the indefinite and virtual time of the pure event (Aeon). (Smith 1998: xxxv)

The 'pure event' is the form under which the phenomenological or sensational datum is folded in a subject, being neither of the subject nor the object – the subject being the creation that is required to make sense of the obscurity of what it is our bodies connect with, of how the intelligible materialities of the world 'already attest to an activity of perception, discrimination and differentiation' (Deleuze 1993: 92). In the sensation of the intensity of colour in painting (affect), and in the provocative illustration of possible form and sign (percept), our bodies are taken to the interworld as affect and percept act through us as little glimmerings in the dark depths of a vast continuum of nature of which our bodies are just a part (Deleuze 1995). Life is thus enfolded and unfolded within our bodies, in particular here by the confrontation with the particular affects that are delivered to us in art – and from which we are delivered. In this sense is creation 'the genesis below the surface of a work' (Klee; quoted in Partsch 2003: 20). Thus Deleuze finds in art the being of Becoming, a sense of experimentation that 'is explicitly Nietzschean and not at all phenomenological or psychoanalytic. Art, like philosophy, has the capacity to renew itself continually because of its (un)grounding in a metaphysics of time as the being of Becoming is continually reasserted through eternal recurrence' (Rodowick 2001: 27). In other words, art attains a celestial state beyond the personal and the rational for the new space it presents in affect is four-dimensional and woven out of trajectories and becomings (Deleuze 1998: 65). To explain in more detail: a painting is an arrangement on a surface pointing towards this other, this fourth dimension. The surface shimmers with other meanings inclining thought to follow the will of the wispish, intensities that form and rise from the surface rather than pull thought down beneath the surface towards the depths of foundations, knowledge and more durable conceptions. Thus we do not ask, 'What does the content of the painting mean?' but rather confront the open pathway leading out of the painting's form, asking instead, 'What do these trajectories of registration show; where do they take us?' Trajectories are real in that they are the paths that we take next in scripting our inevitably onwards lives: go this way, go that way; think this, think that. 'What did I just think, it is gone.' Not to worry, this is natural for not only does the painting exhibit these trajectories, these places of passage, it also effervesces things of forgetting. Here, then, paintings are also about becomings, both as imaginary singularities of possibility and also as the incessantly ongoing process whereby discernibility and memory break down. These becomings, like silk woven into the fabric of a cloth, lace these trajectories with a virtual image unverified in the actual. So much is going on that it is not possible to register, let alone record it all. Thus, the space between art and philosophy is about creation; it is yet another provocation to think, wherein art and philosophy, each in their own domain, open up the world towards the different, opening us up towards the way the Deleuzian world is.

So where are we? We are not locatable since we are spaced out by these resonances of the unthought and the unseen visible that art makes tangible. But through art's novel registrations, and the affects that resonate upon us, we can gain an ability to see, even if this is an 'environment with which there are now only chance relations, of empty and disconnected any-space-whatevers replacing qualified space' (Deleuze 1989: 272). The vision here is like that of Tiresias: 'what speech utters is also the invisible that sight sees only through clairvoyance; and what sight sees is the unutterable uttered in speech' (Deleuze 1989: 260). Unphenomenal but real, imaginable but inaccessible – 'total love or absolute desire' – coextensive with the whole of the virtual from which it extracts itself, but adding to the virtual as it tears away (Deleuze 1989: 258).

In this necessarily growing world it is not enough to explore space, as geographers have traditionally been wont to do. Rather it is necessary to explore the dimensions that make space possible, to experiment whilst pushing knowledge to its nonsensical limits, stretching thought to the tune of this becoming world, creating registers by which we orientate ourselves as a different people and make the world anew. The registers are made up of concepts, or affects or percepts, and the different people that result are not revolutionaries, they are you and I; that one of me that paused in front of Klee's *She Cries, We Play* (in Partsch 2003: 60).

> What constitutes the unity of a work? What makes us 'communicate' with a work? What constitutes the unity of art, if there is such a thing? We have given up seeking a unity that would unify the parts, a whole that would totalise the fragments. For it is the character and nature of the parts or fragments to exclude the Logos both as logical unity and as organic totality. But there is, there must be a unity that is the unity *of* this very multiplicity, a whole that is the whole *of* just these fragments: a One and a Whole that would not be the principle but, on the contrary, 'the effect' of the multiplicity and of its disconnected parts. One and Whole that would function as effect, effect of machines, instead of as principles. (Deleuze 2000: 163)

The internal difference of life itself develops in divergent directions and it is through this divergence, or 'disassociations-of-itself', that virtuality comes to realise itself. Following Bergson's thought in reproaching the traditional and antecedent philosophical conceptualisations of being, Deleuze presents two aspects of being: the virtual and the actual. The unfolding of the virtual in the actual – in other words virtuality realising itself – is the process of differentiation, or, as Deleuze also refers to it, the process of actualisation.[4]

This relationship between the virtual and the actual opposes the machinery of thought produced through the representational belief in the relationship between the possible and the real. Deleuze uses this possible-real habit of representational thinking to make apparent the new directions in thought made viable through the virtual-actual connection by detailing 'that the transcendental term of each couple relates positively to the immanent term in the opposite couple' (Hardt 1993: 17). Several points follow. First, the virtual is to be distinguished from the possible. The possible is not real as it operates as a function of an Ideal such that the real is that which resembles, and not that which is, this 'possible-Ideal'. In this sense, the possible operates as an abstraction and as a limitation because conceptually it follows that there will always be 'possibles' that do not pass into the real. This is not to say that the possible, as a concept, does not have an actual existence; it can be actual in that it can have effects. In opposition to this the virtual is 'real without being actual, ideal without being abstract' (Deleuze, quoting Proust's formula 1988c: 96).

The virtual is part of the object of thought whereby 'every object is double without it being the case that the two halves resemble one another' (Deleuze 1994: 204). Therefore the object of thought has both a virtual and an actual side. For Badiou, the object in its entirety is a mere simulacrum. (One of the main disagreements with the 'philosophy-contra-Deleuze' that Badiou presents in *The Clamor of Being*, is that it is Badiou who argues that the virtual and actual are combined to both equal a simulacrum of a universal One, not Deleuze (May 2004: 67–76)). Not being fully actual the object can only be played out in an immanent theory of its double; in other words, it is possible to think of a plane of immanence when explicitly thinking through encounters with the concrete, empirical real. The encounter actually occurs but only as something achieved (actualised) through a duration (immanent). It is this relationship with duration that intimates the immanent virtuality of all things. The crucial point is that this immanent relation of the object, its transcendental quality if you like, is not located beyond its actuality, rather it is constituted *because of its actuality*. This transcendental quality is, for Deleuze, that which is beyond the human, but this 'beyond' does not denote the transcendent because it is still empirical. Deleuze puts this in another way, in terms of the Outside: 'something more distant than any external world. But it's also something closer than any inner world' (Deleuze 1995: 110). This reflects the clinical power of art to view the world from two perspectives at once: 'It is the peristaltic movements of the outside which serve to destratify fixed and stable identities and produce through doubling processes new possibilities for an intenser and more creative existence' (Ansell-Pearson 1999: 84).

In many ways Deleuze's philosophical journeys through Bergson set out the effects of thinking in two planes of thought at once – you have to think in 'two dissymmetrical jets, one of which makes all the present pass on, while the other preserves all the past' (Deleuze 1989: 81) – where the preservation of all the past is the virtual. This is the 'Open whole', the transcendental part of Deleuze's transcendental empiricism, where the present passing on is the realm of the empirical. It is also the ethical-practical motivation, or dream, of Deleuze's philosophy: the encouragement of 'the creation of new values and senses in the affirmative constitution of life and human existence' (Hayden 1998: 6).

This whole achieved is 'like a last localised brushstroke, not like a general varnishing' (Deleuze 2000: 165) just as 'a good picture seems incomplete until the last brush stroke' (Klee 1964: 235). In its unresolved state the painting exhibits, 'all the elements of a style-to-come that does not exist', intimating a means of creating a way of comprehending the world (Proust, quoted in Deleuze 2000: 165). Thus, style 'does not suggest, does not reflect: it explains, *explicates*' (Deleuze 2000: 165). Style unfolds the world, folding it into what it is as it goes: 'the creation lives as genesis beneath the visible surface of the work. All intelligent people see this after the fact, but only the creative see it before the fact (in the future)' (Klee 1968: 308). And thus, whatever the style of the painting, it is never completed. Rather it just stops being painted. The journey does not end. But this is not to say that it does not have meaning; it just loses its effect. Similarly, in language too, 'there is the risk of it falling silent, and non-style can easily come to resemble all the trademarks of an all too familiar style. The point, it seems, is to keep moving, that is, creating. The moment one stops, difference risks becoming uncreative, static, (non) Being' (Lambert 2002: 130). In painting, once the particular painting stops being painted, the 'Representationists' swoop in and attempt to fix its meaning firmly in our minds. What if Klee had stopped a few minutes earlier or an hour later? We could go on speculating – but you can't really stop with Deleuze:

> Reading does not consist in concluding from the idea of a preceding condition the idea of the following condition, but in grasping the effort or tendency by which the following condition itself ensues from the preceding 'by means of a natural force. (Deleuze 1993: 72)

Nor with Klee:

> An end one should allow to grow, like the natural process, as the result of form-determining activities. Here too it is the act of forming rather than form itself, form in the process of growth, as genesis, rather than as the ultimate appearance. (Klee 1973: 43)

What is effected is an explicative style wherein, in our individual monadic form, we can only ever be apprentices to, rather than knowers of, this becoming world. It is explicative in that it produces two effects: first of a partial object, here the artwork as that which is a tangible object accessible in a sensorial way; and second of resonance and forced movements wherein there is a minimum of objective description and associative suggestion. The material conditions of the artwork incarnate the artistic spiritual condition that speaks of that immanent harmonious whole; or at least a small region of it (see Deleuze 2000: 167). Thus the dimension that is the Deleuzian space we talk of here is a unity and totality established only for itself 'without unifying or totalising objects or subjects'; 'a dimension in time without common measure with the dimension they occupy in space' (Deleuze 2000: 169).[5] In embracing this sense of space, the geography we envisage is one that adds 'more spirit to the seen, making secret visions visible' (Klee 1966: 51).

Foreign territorialisations: encountering the politics within[6]

What kind of space are we trying to map, or, what are we talking about when we talk about space in a Deleuzian manner; and, further, what kind of space do we produce in that mapping? In formulating these questions, we are unfolding the world, creating a problem albeit one that is present with us every day in that it makes up the world. One thing is sure with Deleuze. It is that we are continually made aware of the beauty and dread of an incessantly open and becoming world. Beautiful because it is affirmative of the ongoing potential to create possible worlds anew, full of dread because nothing is certain and the created world might solicit unhappy encounters. The edge of this fear is a place where you are in touch with the raw energy of the world, of yourself as part of that world unfolding. Synonymous with this is an encounter with the unfamiliar. The beauty and dread of the new is available in every encounter but in the unfamiliar your guard is up, and you are more aware of your capacities (many or few) for negotiating ways on with the situation within which you find yourself. Of course, it is well known that Deleuze did not travel far. But this is not to say that he did not travel, for the unfamiliar and the foreign is everywhere; an encounter can even bring the foreign out of oneself. The foreign encounters in Klee's life are easier to understand as loci in traditional notions of travel – Bern, Munich, Rome, Tunisia, Weimar, Dusseldorf, Egypt, Locarno – but from them we can extract, in the registration of his paintings, those 'everywhere' syntactical operations of foreignness out of which we are scripted.

In conversation with geography, Deleuze's travelology, much like Kafka's imparting of knowledge as opposed to the importing of (arti)fact, is not one that charts places. Rather, it presents foreign encounters.[7] This is knowledge in a minor key, and as Deleuze and Guattari acknowledge, this is, 'experimentation without interpretation or significance resting instead only on tests of experience' (Deleuze and Guattari 1986: 7). Foreignness subjects us; it makes subjects out of us through the way in which we counter-actualise the encounters that we have with the other, the strange, the unique and the elsewhere and not known. In this space we experience without interpreting, thus we experiment, moulding what we do know with what is hitherto unknown to us. We experiment with experience, with actuality, actualising thus the ever new. There are spaces and times which contextualise this process and allow it to take place, but Deleuze turns neither to history nor geography to explain the impact of such happenings (say Klee's encounter with Tunisia); rather he always urges us through philosophy to go beyond what happened, to extract and create out of the munificence of all that could have been what can be. Whilst we live in the actual world we also have one foot in the virtual; thus we can travel without moving: 'History isn't experimentation, it's only the set of conditions, negative conditions almost, that make it possible to experience, experiment with, something beyond history . . . (E)xperimentation itself is philosophical rather than historical' (Deleuze 1995: 106).

Experimentation and travel lead one to the other – for Deleuze, experimenting in thought results in travel while, for Klee, travelling subsequently leads him to experiment in paint with the fresh sensations encountered thereby. Both practices are subjectified through their bodies. Through that subjecthood they grapple with the creation of new expressions of the world out of which the world can then be made to be. Whether it is through philosophy creating new conceptual connections within the world, or through art presenting new forms by which to comprehend the world, both cast the world in a new light. Thus, 'subjectification wasn't for Foucault a theoretical return to the subject but a practical search for another way of life, a new style' (Deleuze 1995: 106). One of the gifts of Deleuze's work comes from the sense that the ability to travel in this way is not natural to us either in the sense of our times (the point made earlier in relation to the contemporaneity of Deleuze's thought) or in the sense that inherently we are not all naturally predisposed to travelling (see Deleuze and Guattari 1994). The ability to search practically for different openings in the fabric of the world emerges out of dispositions (of materials, places, bodies, subjects, events) which we then augment in further investigations: 'That is not something you do in your head: but then where, these days, are the seeds of a new way of existing, communally or individually, beginning to appear; and are there any of these seeds in me?' (Deleuze 1995: 106). Tracing out the seeds of potential that we can manifest in our singular unfolding from within an event of an encounter is an obscure art but in Klee's many diary and notebook extracts such developments are discernible:

> I am now trying to render light simply as unfolding energy. And when I handle energy in black on a white surface, I ought to hit the mark again. I call to mind the entirely reasonable black made by light on photograhic negatives. Moreover, the lesser thing is always made special note of, so one imagines the situation of singling out a few highlights on a white surface by means of lines. To heap up an untold quantity of energy lines, because of these few highlights. That would be the real negative! (Klee 1968: 253)

Such abstractions exhibited here are neither artifice nor alien to our existence for they are an intrinsic, albeit perhaps obscure, part of the dramaturgy of the real. Sometimes the simple beauty and sheer line of the paint, seemingly coming from nowhere familiar, explicates from within our sensibilities a brief clutching hold of, tussle with or capture of something fast becoming now and here familiar and involving. Just because, 'we never say what we see and never see what we say', just because of this is it real; the virtual in the actual always more than what is possible; and for a brief moment we know it: 'The visible bursts out between two things. Intentionality gives way to a whole theatre; an endless interplay between the visible and the utterable' (Klee 1968: 107–8).

In this light, Klee's paintings are exemplars, existing as 'examples that convey not so much lessons to ponder as brief effects whose force fades almost at once' (Foucault 2000: 157). And yet the force affected us and stretched our conception of the world; it is the line outside that solicits a thinking, a thought-apprehension, that 'doesn't come from within, but nor is it something that happens in the external world. It comes from this Outside, and returns to it, it amounts to confronting it' (Deleuze 1995: 110). We are between worlds, folding the line between death and life, addressing us directly to the state of creation and becoming. Life is too strong and it is foreign in this sense: there is something beyond and outside what we are capable of withstanding in the space, given our current capacities.

> Whatever could have happened for things to have come to this? He [Fitzgerald] is the only one who has been able to carry this question to such a point of intensity . . . think of it as an affair of perception: you enter a room and perceive something as already there, as just having happened, even though it has not yet been done. Or you know that what is in the process of happening is happening for the last time, it's already over with. (Deleuze and Guattari 1988: 194).

The space that Deleuze deals with most, and to which he travels, is therefore an immanent one – immanent in terms of the intensity of the affect of being in this space. Being immanent, it is a space that is 'actualised at every moment in terms of the whole of one's "affections" (which are nonetheless in constant variation)' (Smith 2003: 62). Whilst immanent the thinking of this space is thoroughly grounded – being immanently in relation to the actual earth – and not contingent in that it is intimately bound up with the particular territory that affects the thought that acts as an actualisation of the virtual immanence (see Deleuze and Guattari 1994: 85).[8] Similarly, the composition of a Klee painting presses the outside of this immanent world and in this proximity the ensuing affects reveal to us the potential of the intangible effects of the virtual world upon the actual. This is not, then, to talk about the two-dimensional and representational space of the painting itself but of the immanent space that the affected thought spaces out in relation to the immanence of all that is currently possible: 'The earth is not one element among others but rather brings together all the elements within a single embrace while using one or another of them to deterritorialise territory' (Deleuze and Guattari 1994: 85).

Dialoguing with Nature: the science of instinct[9]

> The artist cannot do without his dialogue with nature, for he is a man, himself nature, a piece of nature and within the space of nature (Klee 1923, quoted in Klee 1973: 6).

It is clear that the politics solicited by Deleuze's thought is a call to attend to the effects produced by philosophy in promoting the creation of new principles and instincts that open up our social lives to the affirmative constitution of the world (Harrison, Pile and Thrift 2004). There is an obvious affinity for the natural world within Deleuze's work, arising out of Deleuze's transcendental empiricist concern for the immediate immanence of the energetic dynamism of the becoming world. Herein, thought conjoins with the diversity of the natural world and its real condition of immanent difference – its multiplicity, its diversity and its continuous becoming (see Deleuze 1990a: 261). We are immersed in a world of nature, and Klee understood that when he spoke of the nature's song as something that takes hold in both the mental constitution of the work and its physical execution, as Klee as artist grappled with his materials: 'Nature lured me onto paths which did not agree with the simple abstraction of the first successful works. These contained the germ of further works, which, for the time being, were not yet within the realm of the creatively possible' (Klee 1968: 147).

The germination not only of the work but of the world, us ourselves, 'nature, a piece of nature and within the space of nature', marries with Deleuze's Spinozist affiliation and his Epicurian-Lucretian naturalism (Deleuze 1990a: 266–79). Here everything that can be said about the world is pared down to nature's simplest entity, the atom: 'that which must be thought, and that which can only be thought' (Deleuze 1990a: 268). Nothing can be more total than this root conception, and thus neither atoms nor the world form a totality; their sum is infinite. There is no direction as such to this world since the basic relation underwriting it as it unfolds is the *clinamen,* a spontaneous, unpredictable deviation. As a result the world, as atoms, moves 'in a unique direction in a minimum of continuous time' (Deleuze 1990a: 269). It being Deleuze, this empiricism is connected directly to thought with the minimum of continuous time referring to the apprehension of thought. 'The atom moves as "swiftly as thought"' (Deleuze 1990a: 269). From this stance the manifestation of the world is neither contingent nor indeterminate but rather unassignable for what it manifests in its nature is 'the irreducible plurality of causes or causal series, and the impossibility of bringing causes together into a whole' (Deleuze 1990a: 270). Implicitly we are called on to protect the diversity of nature, not only in terms of conservation but in terms of experimentation; in other words to be open to the new forms that can be manifested in the infinite sum of the diverse.

That is the wider picture. But within the hands of the artist the very moment of conception is grasped and the apprehension of thought is almost tangible, as artist and material become together in the production of the new work, in the construction of a new register. At play here is cosmogony, for out of the seeming chaos of irreducible plurality comes a milieu, a rhythm; there emerges a block of space-time that is not homogeneous but heterogeneous, one communicating and differentiating with other such milieus. The communication is the rhythm, the line of flight through the chaos from one milieu to the next. This is apparent within paintings (colours encountering lines, other blocks of colour or other planes of composition), and across painters (painters communicating with their earlier selves or with the style of other painters). In sum:

> Every milieu is vibratory, in other words, a block of space-time constituted by the periodic repetition of the component. Thus the living thing has an exterior milieu of materials, an interior milieu of composing elements and composed substances, an intermediary milieu of membranes and limits and an annexed milieu of energy sources and actions-perceptions . . . The milieus are open to chaos, which threatens them to exhaustion or intrusion. Rhythm is the milieu's answer to chaos. What chaos and rhythm have in common is the in-between – between two milieus, rhythm-chaos or chaosmos. (Deleuze and Guattari 1988: 313)

Such rhythms are potential refrains for the future, in this they become a way of registering and understanding the world. The refrains territorialise and become expressive (see Deleuze and Guattari 1988: 315–17). Territories not made up out of land but still empirical territories nonetheless for they emerge out of apprehension-thoughts created out of nature's affirmative flux. We have to keep on reminding ourselves that with Deleuze and space we are mapping a becoming world; becoming in time as past selves fade, reform, and haunt, and becoming in space as our monadic perspective simultaneously vibrates with that of others.

> I cannot be grasped in the here and now
> For I live just as well with the dead
> As with the unborn
> Somewhat closer to the heart
> Of Creation than usual
> But far from close enough
>
> Paul Klee's epitaph (Partsch 2003: 84).

Concluding: of the Event. 'There is an exhibition tonight'[10]

> The most ordinary event casts us as visionaries, whereas the media turn us into mere passive onlookers, or worse still, voyeurs. (Deleuze 1995: 160).

Deleuzian space is not above and beyond nor is it inside or outside but rather self-referential in its time as an event. This is the space that the creation of a concept delivers us unto – consistent and absolute yet fragmentary (creative) and relative, infinite in its survey and speed but finite in the movement that traces that which comes into view (see Deleuze and Guattari 1994: 21–2). It is apparent in art in its pure state of colours, lines, songs. Herein art immanently spaces that interworld between the virtual and the actual, continually making the world 'outlandish' in a way that dis-accommodates the subject in its ongoing emission and production of signs (including spider's webs and wolf tracks; cf. Deleuze and Guattari 1988). The world that Deleuzian space speaks of is therefore one where we find ourselves in mutual immanence to *a* life (Deleuze 1997), wherein there is something that exists between a subject and an object, something incorporeal, something inherent within everything, such that everything is a virtue of the same substance. The events, captured in art by way of its different register, people this immanence and can be seen to be the effects of the interactions of bodies (organic or non-organic) as combinations of action, passion and circumstance that have no 'origin in the consciousness of the knowing subject' (Hayden 1995: 292). The encounter with art takes us forward by using the spaces and spacings it opens up to construct a new vocabulary for presenting that which cannot presently be said. This grammar connects us to the immanence of our organic matter, to the immanence in the effect of material spaces to our immaterial sense of them, and to a syntactical appreciation that the particular is immanent to a more general nature. The relation of Deleuze and space is therefore one that adds to the corpus of spatial theory through the way that it addresses an immanent and becoming world. It maps a world of events not places and in this:

> It is almost a question of faith. Either you side with deconstruction: the event as always already constituted, determined by the scene of the event. Or you get a little more religious: the event as something genuinely unexpected. Importantly, this need not involve a transcendent aesthetic. In fact there may be a way of reconfiguring the event as *immanent* to this world, as not arriving from any transcendent plane but as emerging from the realm of the *virtual*. In the realm of the virtual, art – art *work* – is no longer an object as such, or not only an object, but rather a space, a zone, or what Alain Badiou might call an 'event site': 'a point of exile where it is possible that something, finally, might happen'. At any rate art is a place where one might encounter the affect. (O'Sullivan 2001: 127)

It is of course up to you what space you create and whether you believe in this particular world of immanent spatiality. And it is, of course, possible to map out many different spatialities within the work of Deleuze, for the many conceptual personae he addresses run into each another and get mixed up so that the theory he offers is always incomplete at the edges, complete only when you stop reading. 'A good picture seems incomplete until the last brush stroke' (Klee 1964: 235). Or perhaps, 'it would be better to talk about what I want to do next' (Deleuze 1995: 137). Genesis eternal!

References

Agamben, G. (1999), *Potentialities*, Stanford: Stanford University Press.

Ansell-Pearson, K. (1999), *Germinal Life: The Difference and Repetition of Deleuze*, London: Routledge.

Badiou, A. (2000), *Deleuze: The Clamor of Being*, trans. L. Burchill, Minneapolis: University of Minnesota Press.

Bogue, R. (1996), 'Gilles Deleuze: The Aesthetics of Force', in P. Patton (ed.), *Deleuze: A Critical Reader*, Oxford: Blackwell Publishers, pp. 257–69.

Bogue, R. (2003), *Deleuze on Music, Painting and the Arts*, London: Routledge.

Crang, M. and N. J. Thrift (eds), *Thinking Space*, London: Routledge.

Deleuze, G. (1986), *Cinema 1: The Movement Image*, trans. H. Tomlinson and B. Habberjam, London: The Athlone Press.

Deleuze, G. (1988a), *Spinoza: Practical Philosophy*, trans. R. Hurley, San Francisco: City Lights Books.

Deleuze, G. (1988b), *Foucault*, trans. S. Hand, London: The Athlone Press.

Deleuze, G. (1988c), *Bergsonism*, trans. H. Tomlinson and B. Habberjam, New York: Zone Books.

Deleuze, G. (1989), *Cinema 2: The Time-Image*, trans. H. Tomlinson and R. Galeta, London: The Athlone Press.

Deleuze, G. (1990), *The Logic of Sense*, trans. M. Lester with C. Stivale, London: The Athlone Press.

Deleuze, G. (1991), *Empiricism and Subjectivity: An Essay on Hume's Theory of Human Nature*, trans. C. Boundas, New York: Columbia University Press.

Deleuze, G. (1993), *The Fold: Leibniz and the Baroque*, trans. T. Conley, London: The Athlone Press.

Deleuze, G. (1994), *Difference and Repetition*, trans. P. Patton, London: The Athlone Press.

Deleuze, G. (1995), *Negotiations: 1972–1990*, trans. M. Joughin, New York: Columbia University Press.

Deleuze, G. (1997), 'Immanence: A Life . . .', *Theory, Culture and Society*, 14(2): 3–7.

Deleuze, G. (1998), *Critical and Clinical*, trans. D. W. Smith, London: Verso.

Deleuze, G. (2000), *Proust and Signs*, trans. R. Howard, London: The Athlone Press.

Deleuze, G. (2001), *Pure Immanence*, trans. J. Rajchman, New York: Zone Books.

Deleuze, G. (2004), *Desert Islands and Other Texts*, trans. M. Taormina, Brooklyn: Semiotext(e).

Deleuze, G. and Guattari, F. (1986), *Kafka: Towards a Minor Literature*, trans. D. Polan, Minneapolis: University of Minnesota Press.

Deleuze, G. and Guattari, F. (1988), *A Thousand Plateaus: Capitalism and Schizophrenia*, trans. B. Massumi, London: The Athlone Press.

Deleuze. G. and Guattari, F. (1994), *What is Philosophy?*, trans. H. Tomlinson and G. Burchell, London: Verso.

Foucault, M. (1998), *Michel Foucault: Aesthetics, Method and Epistemology: Essential Works of Foucault 1954–1984 – Volume 2*, trans. R. Hurley et al., New York: The New Press.

Foucault, M. (2000), *Michel Foucault: Power: Essential Works of Foucault 1954–1984 – Volume 3*, trans. R. Hurley et al., New York: The New Press.

Hardt, M. (1993), *Gilles Deleuze: An Apprenticeship in Philosophy*, London: University College London Press.

Harrison, S., Pile, S. and Thrift, N. J. (eds) (2004), *Patterned Ground*, London: Reaktion.

Hayden, P. (1995), 'From Relations to Practice in the Empiricism of Gilles Deleuze', *Man and World: An International Philosophical Review* 28: 283–302.

Hayden, P. (1998), *Multiplicity and Becoming: The Pluralist Empiricism of Gilles Deleuze*, New York: Peter Lang Publishing.

Klee, P. (1966), *Paul Klee on Modern Art*, London: Faber and Faber.

Klee, P. (1968), *The Diaries of Paul Klee 1898–1918*, Berkeley: University of California Press.

Klee, P. (1973), *Notebooks Volume 2: The Nature of Nature*, London: Lund Humphries.

Lambert, G. (2002), *The Non-Philosophy of Gilles Deleuze*, London: Continuum.

May, T. (2004), 'Badiou and Deleuze on the One and Many', in P. Hallward (ed.) *Think Again*, London: Continuum, pp. 67–76.

O'Sullivan, P. (2001), 'The Aesthetics of Affect: Thinking Art beyond Representation', *Angelaki* 6(3): 125–35.

Partsch, S. (2003), *Klee*, London: Taschen.

Rodowick, D. N. (2001), *Reading the Figural, or, Philosophy after the New Media*, London: Duke University Press.

Serres, M. (2003), 'The Science of Relations: In Interview', *Angelaki* 8(2): 227–38.

Smith, D. M. (1998), 'A Life of Pure Immanence: Deleuze's "Critique et Clinique" Project', in Gilles Deleuze, *Critical and Clinical*, trans. D. W. Smith, London: Verso, pp xi–liii.

Smith, D. M. (2003), 'Deleuze and Derrida, Immanence and Transcendence: Two Directions in Recent French Thought', in P. Patton and J. Protevi (eds), *Between Deleuze and Derrida*, London: Continuum, pp. 46–66.

Williams, J. (2003), *Gilles Deleuze's Difference and Repetition: A Critical Introduction and Guide*, London: Routledge.

Notes

1. View *High Spirits*, 1939 (Partsch 2003: 82). All paintings referenced are by Paul Klee, and the instruction to view is for affect only: no explanations will be given here.
2. View *Battle Scene from the Comic-Fantastic Opera* The Seafarer, 1923 (Partsch 2003: 2).
3. View *Separation in the Evening*, 1922 (Partsch 2003: 57).
4. In another direction, the virtual is, in the burgeoning number of works on Deleuze, something of a signature concept: note that pages of commentary have been given to the conceptualisation of the virtual and the actual: for example Badiou (2000, 42–52) and Hardt (1993: 14–22).
5. See Badiou 2000 and Serres 2003 for critiques of the presence of a transcendence within Deleuze's thought countering this with the explication of May 2004 and the passages in Deleuze and Guattari 1994: 47–8.
6. View *Moonrise (St Germain)*, 1915 (Partsch 2003: 22).
7. 'I am not appealing for any man's verdict, I am only imparting knowledge, I am only making a report' (Kafka 1971: 259).
8. As James Williams observes: 'Deleuze does not seek universal phenomena through a process of reduction – he seeks universal conditions on the ground of sensations of individuals' (Williams 2003: 110).
9. View *Colourful Lightning*, 1927 (Partsch 2003: 61).
10. View *Vegetal-strange*, 1929 (Partsch 2003: 68).

Chapter 6

After Informatic Striation: The Resignification of Disc Numbers in Contemporary Inuit Popular Culture

Gary Genosko and Adam Bryx

It is interesting to note that until 1967 all Eskimos in the Yukon and Northwest Territories were identified by numbers imprinted on tags worn around the neck. Not surprisingly the Eskimos objected to the system and, in preparation for its abandonment, during the four years from 1967 to 1971 the Eskimos selected their own surnames which are now used in lieu of numbers. Neither the old disc-number files nor the new registry of names contain data other than that normally recorded at birth.

Government of Canada, *Privacy and Computers*

The early 1970s in Canada marked a, perhaps not the, beginning of the privacy debate as we know it today. Under the sway of technological innovation, especially computerisation of records and the spectre of dataveillance, the federal government sought to investigate administrative practices pertaining to the handling of personal information. One of the formative documents remains the report *Privacy and Computers*, established by two federal governmental departments, Communications and Justice. The above quotation represents a moment of historical reflection on past governmental practices as they pertain to the administration of the lives of First Nations peoples in Canada.

What is remarkable about this passage is that the few, rather vague, details provide for a dramatic tension between rejection and remedy, from the alleged perspective of the Inuit themselves: they 'rejected' the disc numbering system (and the 'dog tag' technology) and then 'selected' a new system that permitted the choice of surnames. The sense of empowerment is undeniable, if illusory, and is at least as strong as the government's desire to exonerate its past practices.

Although this is not a history paper, as our title suggests, it is worth revisiting, in the form of an outline of events, the use of disc numbers as a system for the identification of Inuit. Indeed, this is not a privacy paper either for the issue at stake, again flagged conceptually in the title, is about social categorisation and not individual rights; in fact, the matter concerns the organisation of an entire population for the purpose of individuating identification. Sociologists tend to distinguish between privacy and sorting, a key metaphor of the entire discourse of surveillance, as a social issue in the classification and management of groups and populations within risk society (Lyon 2003: 19). Within this tendency, we also want to take up the conceptual terms of striation and smoothness as viable sociological concepts for an investigation of a phenomenon called informatic striation and its aftermath. Sociologists like William Bogard (1998: 68) have already used Deleuze and Guattari's work on these concepts to enrich inherited socio-theoretical senses of stratification, especially toward the complexification of segmentarities.

Informatic striation is a concept that identifies a complex communication between two kinds of spaces: smooth and striated (Deleuze and Guattari 1987: 474). Generally, we want to describe the use of informatic means (administrative coding) as the translation of a smooth cultural practice considered ambiguously heterogeneous or 'non-formal' into a formally organised, manageable collection of distinct yet homogeneously coded data. Our working hypothesis is that there are elements of smoothness in Inuit culture that are an affront to bureaucrats, culturecrats, and sundry administrators. Although this hypothesis remains problematic in many of its details, as we will demonstrate below, it is less an attempt to name an originary element than an effort to find a starting point that can adequately explain the conditions to which the disc number system and related redrawings of the Arctic from the perspective of a sorting, classifying, and ordering national bureaucracy responded. Striation 'captures' through the imposition of criterial discernment; whereas a striated space may be smoothed over or 'dissolved' by the discontinuation of a certain coding or by the reintroduction of smooth elements resisting containment or evading certain subordinations. What we are introducing into the discussion of the smooth-striated relation is an informatic model of social sorting as it pertains to Inuit experience and, more generally, to First Nations experience in Canada. The smooth-striated pair is malleable and this makes it attractive for our purposes. The history of disc numbers and their replacement by another naming system alluded to above ('Project Surname'), in addition to the perspective on contemporary redeployments of older, out-of-official-use systems in contemporary Inuit popular culture, centred on Iqaluit, involves passages between, mixtures of, fixing and unfixing smooth and striated informatic sortings.

Students of culture will be familiar with questions of resignification or the relaunching in new contexts to other ends of signs culled from different historical moments and symbolic economies, which is the point on which we will conclude. The issue of 'rejection' or even of the replacement of one striating governmental practice for another does not reach far enough into the reappearance and myriad reuses of disc numbers and the disc themselves, although it has been flagged by some of those directly involved in its justification. For instance, a longtime Arctic researcher, John MacDonald, Director of the Igloolik Research Centre, has maintained that, 'A more practical employment of disc numbers recently came to my attention. There's a man in Igloolik . . . who always uses his E-number on combination locks and even on his banking access card because . . . it's the only number he'll remember all his life' (Alia 1994: 30–1). The question here concerns not only the long-lasting effects of striations but whether everyday redeployments of them after the life of the disc number programme are in fact smoothings and, if so, do these have a softly subversive (without ever 'sufficing to save us', as Deleuze and Guattari remind their readers (1987: 500)) rather than a simple adaptive dimension?

The context of the transformation of striated to smooth capital is central to the analysis of Deleuze and Guattari (1987: 492) and is, as they put it, the 'essential thing'. The resignification of striations like the disc numbers in a 'post-classical' smoothed space of integration and control, a smooth capitalist space, seems on the one hand a moot point considering the inevitability of the conclusion: reuses of disc numbers after the fact of the program merely participate in the new networked relations whose transversal flows are smooth. Yet the interesting question concerns the 'necessity and uncertainty' (Deleuze and Guattari 1987: 493) of such passages. And in our case, the refloating of disc numbers in such a smooth space of computer assisted mediation suggests that no amount of bureaucratic striation could contain the smooth elements of Inuit culture that survive and, in fact, counter the renaming regime of old by reinvention or resmoothing.

As a final introductory qualification, we remain fascinated by the examples in the Deleuze and Guattari formulations of smooth igloos and nomads and Eskimo ice space drawn from cultural anthropologist Edmund Carpenter (Genosko 1999: 110–11). For us what is at issue is less a space than a set of cultural practices in relation to striations and smoothings sponsored by federal and territorial governments (and crossing into personal security and systems security in commercial transactions) in dynamic centrifugal movement from centre to periphery, finally sufficiently smoothed to translate and engage the flows of the information economy (circulation in remote and anonymous systems of verification), and partially refloated in creative productions (conversely, under which conditions they are not refloatable).

The debts of Deleuze and Guattari to Carpenter, while not counting among their 'models' (technological, musical, maritime, mathematical, physical, aesthetic) are sufficient to ask after, among the many anthropological source materials in *A Thousand Plateaus*, since they help give definition to nomad thought. Unlike Christopher L. Miller (2001: 1117) who reads the anthropological source materials of nomad thought as 'foreign to nomadology itself', while skipping over the material borrowed from Carpenter, we want to recast the issue of 'Eskimo space' (Deleuze and Guattari 1987: 494) (the use of this term 'Eskimo' already signals acceptance of a depreciatory label used by outsiders, including anthropologists, and seems quite period-bound).[1] This is not to criticise either Carpenter's McLuhanatic enthusiasms for so-called 'Eskimo Realities' (his praise of 'great' documentary filmmaker Robert Flaherty, director of *Nanook of the North* (1922), rekindles a kind of prototypical act of cinematic primitivism – noble, happy subjects in an ethnographically thin drama set in the cinematographic present) or his omissions (such as disc numbers despite an acute sensitivity to the inauthenticity of governmental policies and the effects of the welfare state especially in the influence of James Houston and sundry aesthetic missionaries, notably Jack Molson's Canadian Guild of Crafts and the Hudson's Bay Company in the brokering of cashless exchanges of goods for carvings and in the production of 'souvenir art' (Carpenter 1973:192). Indeed, Carpenter's role as founding editor of what would become McLuhan's famous journal of the 1950s, *Explorations*, the final instalment of the original series of which (1959) featured a special issue, 'Eskimo', by Carpenter, Flaherty and Frederick Varley, makes clear that the decisive influence of McLuhan on Carpenter's vision of Eskimo society is implosive, an individual, auditory-tactile, haptic-close, non-optical, non-linear, non-nominal – in short, smooth. Deleuze and Guattari's (1987: 574, n. 28) heavily ellipsised quotation from Carpenter runs together paragraphs from pages 20 and 25 on orientation and igloos creating an 'intricated aggregate' in words perhaps adequate to Carpenter's (1973: 78) descriptions of Eskimo language as consisting of independent 'tight conglomerates, like twisted knots'. A language of felt. We are not prepared simply to discard these examples of poetic anthropology for they all settle on the same point: that there is something smooth about Inuit life that keeps issuing challenges to the self-appointed bestowers of names and number crunchers in Ottawa and elsewhere.

One of the oddities of Inuit art in Canada is that art historians and curators are perhaps most familiar with disc numbers since they work with them every day. Most museum and gallery collections hold sculptures and prints 'signed' with disc numbers, often but not always in lieu of names. The compilation of a given Inuit artist's biography is a complex affair involving up to six different names: commonly known name; its various spellings; a surname (if one of the above is not such); nickname; baptismal name; and disc number (Roch 1974: 20). Names, then, multiply and bureaucrats lose their bearings. Drift was arrested by the 'decisive striation' of the disc number, but not even it could hold the incipient smoothness that would escape from it. So the bureaucrats asked again: how do we contain Inuit names in the little spaces on our forms and documents? By 1970 a new plan of attack called 'Project Surname' was launched. This was a sponsored (Northwest Territories Commissioner) census-like, self-identification project in which Inuit could 'choose' surnames, even though they had not used them before; they could also have first names as long as these 'could be written in Roman Script or English letters'. (DIAND 1993: 24) like the 'southern readers' for schoolchildren introduced into the government schools for Inuit in the 1950s (Diubaldo 1985: 111). First and last names are ordered in the standard last-name-first-first-name-last routine and semiologically subjected by Imperial language, linking the requirement of the form-fillable response to another national project, the issuing of Social Insurance Numbers to all citizens, including Inuit, who were not yet included when the programme was introduced in 1964, but who would be issued the springboard for dataveillance that is the Canadian SIN.

The issue of contemporary 'Eskimo space' poses a problem of how to study its informatic striation and (re)smoothing and, despite severe criticisms, remains relevant. For example, in many far northern communities such as the aforementioned Igloolik, at one time houses had no street numbers: 'One occupies without counting', to refocus a musical example from Deleuze and Guattari (1987: 477). This is quite common in small communities in rural and remote Canada (that is, what we call unorganised municipalities). What happens when populations diversify and grow and new services appear such as taxi cabs and other delivery vehicles? Then, 'one counts in order to occupy', if you will, so that deliveries can be made. Which numbering system is used? In some instances, it isn't a system at all but a matter of personal choice. Some houses in Igloolik bear the disc numbers of their inhabitants (MacDonald and Bryx 2003). This is a good example of 'melding' smooth and striated, of an impure intermixture, a Brownian address. The challenge here is to grasp the 'tone' of the example. In which register is it to be understood: parody of street numbers? Probably. We will return to this because understanding the tone is key to what resignification communicates.

Administrative Convenience as Endocolonialist Violence

The imposition of disc numbers, sometimes referred to misleadingly and unintentionally ironically as E-numbers (just why will be easy to appreciate shortly), dates from the 1940s. The first date of note is 1941, which was a census year in Canada. National census taking occurred during this period every ten years. One of the typical methodological challenges facing census statisticians was the under-enumeration of First Nations peoples, as well as inaccuracies in the collection of personal information about them, that skewed the official data. Mid-way between census years, then, government bureaucrats in the Departments of Indian Affairs and Natural Resources began to initiate changes that would address a variety of issues around identification and enumeration of First Nations peoples. The need for this had been developing throughout the 1930s through parallel and complementary identificatory acts of 'cultural inscription' (Marcus 1995: 33) aimed at Inuit, that ranged from standardisation of spelling of names adapted with difficulty for English pronunciation (above and beyond a missionary naming regime inscribed in baptismal certificates that reproduced redundancy in the proliferating Johns and Marys), fingerprinting, imposition of surnames, discussions of the appropriate model for the disc numbers systems (that is, military dog tags bearing individual and unit numbers), and a range of related issues driven forward by the collection of reliable vital statistics as well as policing issues in what was then known as the Northwest Territories. It was the responsibility of the Royal Canadian Mounted Police (RCMP) to update the lists, who thereby made their presence felt in outlying communities, and which allowed them to identify individuals, especially in order to place them under arrest (DIAND 1993: 23). In a sense striation is precisely the practice of identifying individuals for the dual purposes of enabling and constraining them.

This general situation was exacerbated in the case of Inuit because of cultural naming practices in which many persons might very well have the same name, of a great hunter, for instance; all of those bearing the name would be connected with the ancestor and embody the soul of their namesake, a condition for his/her resting in peace, even though not everyone bearing the name would have the same intimacy with the deceased (Alia 1994: 14). The fact that Inuit names were genderless and without surnames, and that many persons had the same name, even Christian names, not to mention that there could be a different spelling and pronunciation of the same name in every colonial institution present in the north, defined a local smoothness based on intensities of spiritual affiliations that aggravated the search for viable models of striation. Even animals could temporarily hold a name until a new human birth occurred.

Our interest is in personal names. It is easy to appreciate the politics of naming as it relates to toponymy, at least, by considering that the place known since 1987 as Iqaluit, an Inuktitut word meaning the 'place of fish [arctic char]', had been known since the late sixteenth century as Frobisher Bay, after its so-called 'discoverer' Martin Frobisher. The Department of Natural Resources has authority over the Geographical Names of Canada system of authorisation and assigns its own imprimatur – Unique Identifier codes – to official names. Dating from the late nineteenth century, the Canadian 'Names Board' is a state apparatus of capture, a machinic enslavement to official geography and cartography and it consolidates endocolonial assertion of sovereignty over the territory it appropriates in its names (containing the name 'Iqaluit' in brackets on older maps below Frobisher Bay), but also entails a social subjection of Inuit to an 'exterior object' (Deleuze and Guattari 1987: 456–7), that is, entering processes of statistical subjectification. Indeed, the process of endocolonialisation, which turns processes of colonialist domination inward on targeted groups of a given state's population within its national boundaries, makes a 'subject' (loyal, beholden, captured) who is a part of an inverted colonial machine (hence we can speak of national-imperial subjectification). Resistance to the imposition of external over indigenous names has gained immense ground since the 1980s. A strong example of southern academic and Inuit collaboration towards regaining place names is found in the work of geographer Ludger Müller-Wille (1987) on Nunavik. The rich gazetteer of place names that he produced in collaboration with Inuit elders reveals the uniqueness and subtlety of naming within oral tradition. Müller-Wille's project not only countered the erasure of cultural tradition carried out by machinic enslavement with the reinstatement of such names, whose specificity right down to the shore, dune, point and line was remarkable, but provided energy for renewing bonds with the land.

Machinic enslavement has been, however, advancing and mutating with computerisation in the society of surveillance; this generalised, networked enslavement (Williams 1992: 55; Hardt 1998: 139–52) accelerated in the years of the Second World War before passing into the postmodern forms of control with their distinct textures of modulation and flexibility. The 'list-form' catches up Inuit peoples in Canada through the disc numbers scheme, but this is not unique for First Nations have been since the mid-nineteenth century in Canada subjected to regimes of registration for the purposes of the construction of 'Status' as Indians in the Indian Register. The register is maintained by DIAND, and subject to shifts in policy (dominated at one time by the principle of assimilation, then amended by expanding entitlement through reintroduction of hitherto excluded categories of persons determined through political positions taken on lines of descent) and thus in legislation defining conditions of inclusion or exclusion (known during the assimilationist period as 'enfranchisement', doublespeak for disenfranchisement from status or forced integration) for the sake of registration. The Indian Register, and the Band Lists comprising it, intersects with another Register – Reserve Land entitlements administered through Location Tickets (until 1951) and thereafter Certificates of Occupation. These dense machinic striations of identity and location are linked to exterior objects, as they are in the case of the Inuit, because 'Status' confers rights to federally administered benefit programmes (specific tax exemptions, and so on). The Certificates of Indian Status or 'Status Cards' are no-tech paper identity cards produced by the Bands themselves and include a registration number with vital statistics (date of birth, height, weight, eye colour, sex, band name and number) and a photograph (see Reiter 1991: 14; Imai 1998: 26). 'Status' is the product of a history of superfine bureaucratic striations of the welfare state in concert with crude endocolonialist racism still active today in the constructions of health knowledge about First Nations peoples (diabetes 'epidemic' studied by Poudrier (2003)).

The politics of the erasure of personal names and their renumbering for official purposes has been described as an exercise in 'administrative convenience' (Alia 1994: 40). Wearing fibre discs that hang around the neck or that are attached to the wrist produced individually identifiable bodies ('tagged') through a process of animalisation. As Alan Rudolph Marcus (1995: 32) describes it, this 'taxonomic' strategy was done in the interest of 'good administration', thereby 'transform[ing] Inuit society into a more manageable entity'. The discs themselves were rich in semiotic overcoding. Small, circular and fibrous, they bore the stamp of the Crown on the centre of one side around which the words 'Eskimo Identification Canada' turned (an icon of semiotic enslavement). All lettering was in English (national or official languages are one of the examples Guattari used to illustrate the semiological economies of power that set the parameters of competence and set the means for comportment and communication (Guattari 1996: 143–5) and syllabics were disre-

garded. The reverse side held a sequence of letters and numbers. The disc
was not a unanimous choice of interested state representatives but it was
preferred to identity cards. (Alia 1994: 32). The initial programme of disc
design and their distribution in the early 1940s used individual identification numbers on each disc of up to four digits. In addition to semiological subjection through the symbol of state authority, official language,
and numerical code, there was a social subjection initiated through taxonomic capture and classification. Importantly, this social subjection
merely meant that classification could reproduce itself in experimentation or, as Marcus put it, 'classification preceded experimentation'
(Marcus 1995: 33).

The subjection to an exterior object was renewed, this time in 1944 to
1945 with the introduction of the Family Allowance Program, then a
universal system of monthly payments to families with children under the
age of 16 years. This was the occasion for the revision of the disc number
protocol to include geographic identifiers prior to the personal identifiers: twelve districts and two regions segmented the Arctic – initially nine
in the East and three in the West; they grew to fourteen in the 1950s
(DIAND 1993: 23). These identification districts were represented in the
form of E or W – dash – 1 – 12 before personal identifiers indicating place
of birth ('E' is neither electronic nor Eskimo). The aforementioned
Frobisher Bay was E7. The geographic striation caused by registration
districts created manipulable categories open to experimental combina-
torics that accelerated during the 1950s: actual population relocations to
bleak areas being the most severe; these were subjections to disciplinary
calculations of federal welfare expenditures – rising – in relation to
alleged sites of employment opportunities – falling – conceived with
complex references to Cold War technological development; and earlier,
such as the landing strip at Frobisher Bay built in 1941 as a stopover
point for US military flights to Europe. And further: Distant Early
Warning Systems installations in Canada's Arctic, opportunities for
resource extraction and geological surveys, livestock raising schemes (a
steady stream of sheep and pigs went north in the 1950s, but livestock
farming simply didn't work in the Arctic), art commodification programmes, sovereignty jitters in Canada's north, and estimations of fluctuating game reserves, to name only a few (Marcus 1995: 23). The salient
point is that the technical machines of the state shift enslavement to subjection (Deleuze and Guattari 1987: 457). Inuit were subjected to the
technical machines of capitalist expansion in the north, with humanist
apologies provided by the state's welfare policies and 'well-intentioned'
experiments (during the 1920s 'confusion' reigned about who was

responsible for the Inuit, as Duffy observes (1988: 10); it was in 1939 that the federal government assumed 'responsibility' for the Inuit, a Supreme Court decision that did not go down well, and in the 1951 and 1970 Indian Acts the Inuit were excluded (Diubaldo 1985:4, 51). Even today, the pollution from the Second World War and Cold War militarisation is bringing federal government 'remediation' money and short-term employment to the Arctic. It is not unusual to peer into the waters around Iqaluit and see a submerged parking lot of military vehicles.

The militarisation of the Arctic in the 1940s and 1950s by the US Air Force and Royal Canadian Air Force was the most important factor in the introduction of a historic striation, the temporary wage economy. Deleuze and Guattari (1987: 491) explicitly link work to military organisation, both through the appropriation of the war machine and the 'nullification of smooth space' but also through the state organisation of armies and the production of surpluses in the form of stockpiles – weapons industries. In the case of the Inuit the link is strong but incomplete. On top of traditional range patterns of Inuit groups (not strictly nomadic but structured by base camps and trap lines and shifting hunting groups), the clusterings produced by the locations of missions and trade posts, free or forced adjustments to trapline patterns and locations, not to mention the centralising influences of earlier whaling stations, the military installations created significant 'contractions' that were at odds with existing policies of population dispersal advocated by the Hudson's Bay Company at least from the 1920s to the 1950s, before forced relocation became a government policy where state welfare could be thus administered (further, the residential school system was created as well as vocational training programmes for the minting of new proletarians). Pressures from federal welfare programmes such as the Old Age Pension Act (1927) were not felt in the Arctic until decades later due to uneven distribution of funds. The overwhelming evidence is of a policy cluster against the settlement of Inuit, despite the pressures for 'in-gathering' that had been building for decades. Paternal visions of 'native life', supported by epidemiological worries about Inuit health amid the squalor around the bases (Duffy 1988: 28–9), as well as the spectre of post-construction unemployment in settlements around military and other installations, and RCMP concerns about social instabilities, continued to 'discourage aggregations', despite the effects of the wage economy at such places as Frobisher, Cambridge Bay and elsewhere and, by the 1960s, the centralisations of populations produced by government welfare, loans, housing (the DEW Line brought subsidised housing with it, even if the housing consisted of styrofoam igloos, that is, simulated igloos; see Duffy 1988: 31–2), health programmes and resource extraction of the so-called 'Diefenbaker [Canadian Prime Minister from 1957 to 1963] vision' (Damas 2002: 112). Aggregation was necessary for population surveillance and efficient programme delivery and administration. Aggregation, one might say, is space-time striation on its way to generalised machinic enslavement whose perfection and 'absolute speed', in turn, is to be reconstituted as smooth capitalist space.

De- and Recoded Flows

All apparatuses of capture release 'decoded flows'. Such flows are overflows or escape-flows appearing beside and beyond the codes that give rise to them (Deleuze and Guattari 1987: 449). But the flows do not simply escape for they are knotted together (conjoined, recoded, netted, determinate), and then in turn escape once more out of the holes in the nets. The distinction between the conjoining of topical becomings and an abstract, generalised conjunction – *a general axiomatic of decoded flows* that is capitalism (Deleuze and Guattari 1987: 453) – is decisive for a 'new threshold' and is thus reached.

This process is evident in the case of disc numbers: the subordination of Inuit cultural naming practices to administrative overcodings – capturing them by making naming functional, that is, regularising naming, for bureaucratic sorts – in the form of the disc numbering and related systems that synthesise identity in new and bizarre connections (for example, personal numbers with their geographic striations were connected with estimates of shrinking caribou populations and thus groups were forcibly relocated from one place to another regardless of other considerations). What we have been calling resignification slips through the nets of overcoding. Resignifications of disc numbers arose because the codes that created them could no longer contain them. The overcodings that gave rise to disc numbers were displaced by a new overcoding called 'Project Surname', and this was a scattering force because no collection for disposal of discs was undertaken; anyway, a molar injustice of the disc system was that the number (and not necessarily the material signifier) remained in the memories of each and circulated with them, finding new referential materials with which to attach freely. Some call the power of resignification cultural reappropriation (Alia 1994: 102). The issue is that decoding is already in resignification linked to new recodings. The examples we have in mind are all from the 1990s and after. The decodings that undoubtedly arose prior to this time are less vivid than those that are available for, largely because the latter are tied to material recodings that circulate widely as commodities. The question of the 'rarity' of such recodings cannot be definitively solved by our current study.

An example is in order. In 1991 a promotional activity was staged in Iqaluit as a fund raising event for the Elders' Society, that featured the issuing of mock discs – Q-numbers and registration certificates – aimed at *Qallunaat* (white people with bushy eyebrows) and signed by Abe Okpik, the Inuk originally hired to undertake Project Surname (Alia 1995: 102–6). The parodic tone of these mock discs constitute smoothings that communicate new values of cultural becoming. Hence, decoding attaches to mimetic recoding in parodic mode that issues from the Inuit-initiated *Qallunaat* Registry. This Registry, unlike the DIAND controlled and maintained Indian Registry, does not transform the identity of the white celebrities (hockey players, media stars) who participated in it, except inasmuch as it occurs in a different space, that of becoming – temporary, semiotically disruptive, less an exact value that commands the tools of the informatics revolution in a countervailing fashion than a refloating of hand-inscribed artifacts embedded in a site-dependent locale where the stakes have been reconstituted and redirected.

Decoded flows are rather quickly attached to recodings. The touristic artifact is a good example. The Q-certificate is politically pointed, quite unlike most tourist art. Some recodings succumb more readily to imposed forms, and thus to a limiting 'practicality', than others. There are music industry product recodings. In 1999 and 2002, two songs of note appeared on compact discs: Susan Aglukark's 'E186' and Lucie Idlout's 'E5–770, My Mother's Name'. Both CDs graphically reproduce original discs and run strings of E-numbers as borders or frames around the artwork and lyric sheets. Both Aglukark and Idlout have family roots in Nunavut and are well-known, but neither lives there today, pursuing careers elsewhere. Both singers make disc numbers the subject of songs and deliver criticisms of E-numbers as theft. However, the fury with which Idlout delivers her message of animalisation ('cattled E') in a clanking machinic redundancy of the government 'farming' of 'name numbers' – the same background recitation of strings of E-numbers is used by Aglukark – is dismissed in some quarters as 'youthful radicalism', since she was not old enough to have received a disc number, unlike Aglukark, for example (Shirley and Bryx 2003).

In music, storytelling, cultural geography reporting, the sculptural arts, and documentary filmmaking, the reclaiming of disc numbers is under way. Surely, this is an effect of the optimism and pride in the success of the land claims process that led to the creation of the territory of Nunavut in 1999. The most significant shift is that disc numbers have become integrated into the subject matters of various works. In addition to song titles, film titles, sculptures bearing the disc numbers of their sculptors, but not as signatures, have been noted (McCann 2003: 29). These artistic recodings only tell part of the story, even if they are far from the overcodings that separated 'right' from 'wrong' names and used numbers in lieu of names. This phenomenon and its alleged corrections in Project Surname have also become a subject of interest for the Nunavut Law Review Commission's attempt to correct the corrections of Project Surname in 'Project Correction': not only misspellings, but missed registrations that snarl due bureaucratic processes (for example, ineligibility for old age pension benefits due to lingering uses of disc numbers on birth certificates as a result of being overlooked during Project Surname), incorrect birthdates, and mismatches between pieces of ID (Spitzer 2000). Compared with a use of substitute names in legal discourse in, for example, the famous adoption case 'Deborah E4–789', the work of the current Law Commission is confronting head on the obstacles of the intensive violence of the past. Resmoothings have the salutary effect of exposing lingering effects of striations.

The problem with which we are grappling is the emission of smoothings from striations. That is, the release of decoded flows beside and beyond the imprisoning striations and overcodings of informatic impositions, and the recoding of these. The decoded flows are not free in the sense that when Inuit regain cultural naming practices and in the process resignify disc numbers, new attachments to cultural products and informations systems are made and hence new subjugations arise (to commodity forms, to music product formats, and so on). Yet there is an indeterminacy to the flight of decodings. When an Inuk uses a disc number on a snowmobile bib, as an email address, as a PIN number at the cash machine, as a house number, as part of the subject of a work of art, in short, when such a number is deployed in any instance requiring a personal identifier (but not exclusively since a personal identifier, which is partially striating, is not necessary in many potential reuses of disc numbers such as in the purchase of lottery tickets), there is a positive and enabling engagement existing between flight and (re)capture. This is precisely how surveillance resembles stratification: both are enabling and restrictive, beneficial and unfortunate, as Deleuze and Guattari state (1987: 40). When informatic striations are embedded in the memories of individuals and intersect with cultural naming practices, disc numbers are externalised and find new attachments. If Inuit names are points of transition that carry some values (inspiration, fear) while erasing other specificities (holding in abeyance the recipient's gender specificity until puberty while carrying that of the previous owner), and disc numbers, despite their 'functional' and unfortunate histories, are regained in the field of this cultural practice, they, too, communicate and constellate and connect, often with the values of irony and parody, enabling the transit of individuals into informatic matrices (MacDonald-Bryx 2003). After all, as Guattari (1989: 104) reminds us, transits-transformations between striated registers consitute smoothing operations par excellence and possess the power to effect 'ontological conversions' (my translation, G. G.). In our study, however, we began with a hypothesis of a smoothness that was then striated by disc numbers and further resmoothed with qualifications. The punchline, as one Inuk put it in terms of a redundancy full of irony, is this: 'I am seeking the right government agency to apply to renew my disk!' exclaimed Jaipiti Nungak, E9–1956 (2002). So often laughter accompanies the contemporary mentions of disc numbers – the humour having a local inflection such as the person who was an 'E1' – 'only 1' – or had an 'E6' but attended school in a differently numbered region and was out of sorts. Although many of the discs themselves have been lost over time to all but memory, today surviving discs are reappearing as personal accessories, affixed to hats and coats as pendants, and worn with pride as a kind of jewellery.

In a time of cultural renewal and innovation, resignification of disc numbers is itself a cultural smoothing marking transits, real changes of direction, intensities of tradition and its multiple interruptions, into the new social flows of integrated world capitalism. As these transits proliferate, smoothness homogenetically emerges. The question is no longer or so much that of intergenerational resurrection through names, but a general, largely passive process in which the striations of discontinued disc numbers find new manifestations through resignifying attachments as linear strings of identifying letters and numbers, that is, as individual or personal identifiers for the purpose of engaging pervasive machinic networks of computer-mediated communication, which are retained and reproduced and compared in ways not so far removed from their original usage. This is largely passive because it is not a question of development or intensification in the fields of possibility, as the pure potential of decoded flows pass into actual recodings but, rather, it is more a matter of their reinsertion for pragmatic purposes in everyday transactions and activities, a point underlined by Inuit today. Still, even here there are subtle explorations of fields of possibility in parody and humour, and in the laughter they can still elicit in interpersonal communication among Inuit (it is, after all, still quite laughter-provoking to refer to someone by their disc number), indeed, in the injustices they revisit in protest, even in the small acts of experimenting with disc and number in different contexts. The resignification of disc numbers in contemporary Inuit popular culture effects displacements, not a global overcoming, of semiotic subjections and machinic enslavements, and is not a coherent subcultural, oppositional practice. Rather, today, disc numbers are viable and concrete subject matters for creative adventures of cultural self-reference.

Acknowledgements

The bulk of the on-site research for this project in Iqaluit was undertaken by Adam Bryx during the summer of 2003. We are greatly appreciative of the financial assistance received from the Northern Studies Committee of Lakehead University and for permission to conduct our project granted by the Nunavut Research Institute under Scientific Research Licence # 0100303N-A. We would in addition like to thank CBC Radio Iqaluit for permitting us to explain our project and make a public call for comment in June 2003. All those who came forward with information remain anonymous with the exception of the two persons listed in the references section, John MacDonald (Igloolik Research Centre) and Jim Shirley (*Nunatsiaq News*). We are also grateful for the insightful comments on this paper provided by Valerie Alia, University of Sunderland (UK). An earlier version of this paper was presented at the 'Experimenting with Intensities: Science, Philosophy, Politics and the Arts ' conference at Trent University in May 2004.

References

Alia, V. (1994), *Names, Numbers, and Northern Policy: Inuit, Project Surname, and the Politics of Identity*, Halifax: Fernwood.

Bogard, W. (1998), 'Sense and Segmentarity: Some Markers of a Deleuzian-Guattarian Sociology', *Sociological Theory* 16(1): 52–74.

Carpenter, E. (1973), *Eskimo Realities*, New York: Holt, Rinehart and Winston.

Damas, D. (2002), *Arctic Migrants/Arctic Villagers: The Transformation of Inuit Settlement in the Central Arctic*, Montreal and Kingston: McGill-Queen's University Press.

Deleuze, G. and Guattari, F. (1987), *A Thousand Plateaus*, trans. B. Massumi, Minneapolis: University of Minnesota Press.

Department of Communications and Department of Justice, Government of Canada (1972), *Privacy and Computers: A Report of a Task Force*, Ottawa: Government of Canada.

Department of Indian Affairs and Northern Development (1993), *Identification and Registration of Indian and Inuit People*, Ottawa: DIAND.

Department of Natural Resources Canada, 'Geographical Names of Canada', www.geonames.nrcan.gc.ca

Diubaldo, R. (1985), *The Government of Canada and the Inuit: 1900–1967*, Ottawa: Research Branch and Corporate Policy, Indian and Northern Affairs Canada.

Duffy, R. Q. (1988), *The Road to Nunavut: The Progress of the Eastern Arctic Inuit since the Second World War*, Montreal-Kingston: McGill-Queen's University Press.

Everett-Green, R. (2003), 'On Top of the World', 11 Jan., *The Globe & Mail*.

Genosko, G. (1999), *McLuhan and Baudrillard: The Masters of Implosion*, London: Routledge.

Guattari, F. (1989), *Cartographies Schizoanalytiques*, Paris: Galilée.

Guattari, F. (1996), 'Semiological Subjection, Semiotic Enslavement', in G. Genosko (ed.), *The Guattari Reader*, Oxford: Blackwell, pp. 141–7.

Hardt, M. (1998), 'The Global Society of Control', *Discourse* 20(3):139–52.

Houston, J. (1995), *Confessions of an Igloo Dweller*, Toronto: M&S.

Imai, S. (1998), *The 1999 Annotated Indian Act and Aboriginal Constitutional Provisions*, Toronto: Carswell.

Lyon, D. (2003), 'Social Sorting', in D. Lyon (ed.), *Surveillance as Social Sorting: Privacy, Risk, and Digital Discrimination*, London: Routledge, pp. 13–30.

MacDonald, J. and Bryx, A. (2003), telephone interview, 17 July.

Marcus, A. R. (1995), *Relocating Eden: The Image and Politics of Inuit Exile in the Canadian Arctic*, Hanover and London: University Press of New England.

McCann, J. (2003), 'Reclaiming Inuit Tags', *Canadian Geographic Magazine*, Sept./Oct.: 29.

Miller, C. L. (2001), 'The Postidentitarian Predicament in the Footnotes of *A Thousand Plateaus*: Nomadology, Anthology, and Authority', in G. Genosko (ed.), *Deleuze and Guattari: Critical Assessments*, vol. 3, London: Routledge, pp. 1,113–49.

Müller-Wille, L. (1987), *Gazetteer of Inuit Place Names in Nunavik*, Inukjuak: Avataq Cultural Institute.

Nungak, J. (2002), 'E9–1956', Canadian Film Centre's Great Canadian Story Engine, http://www.storyengine.ca/serlet/ReadAStory?story=90. Accessed June.

Poudrier, J. (2003), 'Racial Categories and Health Risks: Epidemiological Surveillance among Canadian First Nations', in D. Lyon (ed.), *Surveillance as Social Sorting*, London: Routledge, pp. 111–34.

Reiter, R. A. (1991), *The Fundamental Principles of Indian Law*, Edmonton: First Nations Resource Council.

Roch, E. (1974) (ed.), *Arts of the Eskimo: Prints*, Montreal: Signum Press.

Shirley, J. and Bryx, A. (2003), Personal communication.

Spitzer, A. (2000), 'Getting the Names Right – Finally', *Nunatsiaq News*, http://www.nunatsiaq.com

Tucktoo, R. and Kitchooalik, D. (1972), 27 D.L.R. (3d): 225.

Williams, J. (1992), 'Monitoring vs Metaphysical Modeling: Or, How to Predict the Future of the Postmodern Condition', *Warwick Journal of Philosophy* 4: 41–65.

Other Media

Aglukark, S. (1999), *Unsung Heroes*, Toronto: EMI Canada.

Idlout, L. (2002), *E5–770: My Mother's Name*, Ottawa: Heart Wreck Records. http://www.lucieidlout.com

Note

1. The term's survival in *A Thousand Plateaus*, originally published in 1980, suggests that the authors were not aware that it went out of use in the mid-1970s and was replaced by 'Inuit'.

Chapter 7

Thinking Leaving

Branka Arsic

> There are some intervals to which I would migrate; to which, methinks, I am already acclimated.
>
> Thoreau, *Walden and Other Writings*

Gilles Deleuze is among those rare philosophers who poses the question of a thinking that would not be conditioned by time. He asks whether it is possible not only to criticise Kant in order to offer a theory of thought fractured by time in a non-Kantian way, but also to think a radically different thought that would be neither temporal, historical, reflexive nor active, and instead geographical, inorganic, passive and vegetal. As is well known, in order to develop the possibility of such a thought Deleuze introduced a highly elaborated terminological apparatus at whose core was the thought of multiplicity or, more precisely, thought as multiplicity. Multiplicity is not simply a multiple thing or body (something, somebody, someone) for the multiple is only the effect of the multiplication of the one (it is the difference within the one introduced by time as the force of production of change or of temporal differences). Multiplicity escapes the difference between the one and the multiple:

> Principle of multiplicity: it is only when the multiple is effectively treated as a substantive, 'multiplicity' ceases to have any relation to the One as subject or object, natural or spiritual reality, image and world . . . There is no unity to serve as a pivot in the object, or to divide in the subject. There is not even the unity to abort in the object or 'return' in the subject. A multiplicity has neither subject nor object, only determinations, magnitudes, and dimensions that cannot increase in number without the multiplicity changing in nature. (Deleuze and Guattari 1987: 8)

To the extent that it has neither subject nor object multiplicity does not belong to any 'I' and is not temporal (it is not the effect of the relation of the subject and object within time). Rather, it is made of relations in such a way that they produce relates (as so many different relations) and not vice versa. A thought that would be a multiplicity could therefore be only an impersonal thought made of lines of relations that can, but do not necessarily, intersect and that extend in various directions (Deleuze never got tired of repeating that its image is grass and not the tree with its roots). To the extent that such a thought is made of different relations (without relates) it always delineates a new space. Or, more precisely, it *is* a new space. It is a thought that has become space, a spatial thought. That is why for Deleuze to think space is to think thinking.

Deleuze always insisted that in his effort to think the possibility of a spatial thought he was guided by a certain line of 'underground' philosophers (Lucretius, Spinoza, Hume, Bergson) and, above all, by American literature. For American writers, he says, invented a possibility of leaving, of betraying without becoming traitors, of crossing the horizon without, however – and that is the point – falling back into the traps of the imaginary (regaining the lost world through sentimental images of a better one or by mythologising it). It is thus the question of leaving that in the end leaves itself and falls into oblivion. An absolute leaving or an absolute self-abandonment, therefore, that Deleuze called the 'clean-break:' 'A clean break is something you cannot come back from; that is irretrievable because it makes the past cease to exist' (Deleuze and Parnet 1987: 38).

In what follows I will suggest an interpretation of the clean break or of spatial thinking that does not, however, refer to Deleuze's favourite examples (Melville, Henry James, F. Scott Fitzgerald) but proposes instead a reading of the experiment in thinking undertaken by Thoreau. Connecting Thoreau with Deleuze is anything but strange. It is true that Deleuze did not often mention Thoreau, but the context in which he mentioned him is nothing if not illuminating. For Deleuze precisely mentioned Thoreau several times in his essay on Melville's *Bartleby, The Scrivener*. Disregarding (as he should have) anecdotes about Melville's private reserve toward transcendentalism or, differently, refusing to read literature as the symptom or confession of the private preferences or tastes of this or that author (for example, what it is that Melville said to Hawthorne about Thoreau during their conversations at Arrowhead and can we detect that in certain of his writings), Deleuze claimed that Melville sketched out and extended the traits of a thinking already posed by Thoreau and Emerson, a thinking that conceives the world as an archipelago (as multiplicity). As Deleuze put it, that thought is:

first of all the affirmation of a world in *process*, an *archipelago*. Not even a puzzle, whose pieces when fitted together would constitute a whole, but rather a wall of loose, uncemented stones, where every element has a value in itself but also in relation to others: isolated and floating relations, islands and straits, immobile points and sinuous lines. (Deleuze, 1997: 86)

Deleuze states here that Thoreau (and Emerson) invented a thought that thought time (or process) as the distribution of spatial points (archipelago) thus translating time into space. It is this insight that instigates the analysis that follows. I will try to read Thoreau's work as the attempt to invent a thought of loose, uncemented stones. This is but another way of saying that Emerson's thesis from *Fate*, that 'each spirit makes its house; but afterwards the house confines the spirit', was a persistent obsession motivating Thoreau's thinking. Reading Thoreau in the light of this thesis should allow us to conclude nothing less than that Thoreau's thinking was the most radical experiment in spatial thinking ever undertaken, an experiment to whose lesson we are still not sufficiently acclimatised.

House, Walls, Ceilings

At first sight the strategy of reading Thoreau as an experimenter in breaking down walls is strange. For was it not Thoreau who enforced the petty little desire of humans to be protected by building wall after wall after wall? Was he not precisely the one who withdrew himself into solitude, placed himself in a forest near a lake and there built a house in order to isolate himself, thus merely multiplying the layers and envelopes of self-identity (the forest as the house of the house which is the house of the self which is the house of the body and its affections, sensations and perceptions)? In short, did he not try to conquer space and place it in the service of the self-constitution of temporal thought? In this way, far from exploring the possibility of spatial thought (that is, not the thought that thinks space but the thought that is itself made of spatial relations in a single 'now') Thoreau's effort would work toward its subversion: space should be organised in such a way as to provide the continuity of temporal thinking. That is how quite a few critics read his enterprise. It is true that he talked about spaces, places and spatial relations; it is true that he was obsessed with going out of himself and becoming a thing, preferably inorganic, or becoming a vegetable (corn or beans); but he did it only in order to return to himself 'richer' for what he appropriated on his excursions, and illuminated by it. Thus, he wasn't doing anything other than expanding consciousness and its temporality. However, that something is wrong with this interpretation is already suggested by

Stanley Cavell when, in his reading of *Walden,* he asks a simple question: why would anybody build a house only in order to leave it after it was built? How can anybody's consciousness and its gesture of appropriation be enriched and reaffirmed by this abandoning of what it was, an abandoning with no dialectical return to the abandoned?

Obviously, and in spite of the mainstream interpretations of Thoreau's gesture, nothing is less obvious than the thesis according to which he was preoccupied with occupying himself. Let us therefore recapitulate Thoreau's gesture in order to highlight its strangeness. A man leaves a town for a forest, cuts the pines, worrying all the time if the pines will understand him and forgive him for cutting them, builds a house in which he writes about cutting the pines and building the house and then, one fine day, opens the pine door of the house, goes for a walk through the forest as he would every day, only this day he does not return to the house. His walk outlines a line of flight that could be traced all the way to the interval where he finally disappears in the forest, disappearing beyond the horizon into imperceptibility. A whole forest of questions, important not only for thinking itself but also for its politics, immediately appears. Is the house that Thoreau left still and forever his? Whose property is it? Who has the right to move into it? Could the abandoned house still be called a house? Are the things in the abandoned house still Thoreau's (are Thoreau's writings his writings)? Where did he disappear to and what does he do now that he is imperceptible? How can we track him down, identify him and call him by his name again? At stake here is the whole politics of identification (naming, appropriation and propriety), the whole tactics of motion (leaving, coming, departing, arriving). However, if leaving means leaving the house, the space of *heimlichkeit,* then such a leaving is always a gesture of radical deappropriation of what is most my own or most at home in me: name and identity. The question then is not only 'why leave?' but 'how?' How one leaves one's name and house thus translates into how one leaves one's own self?

In *Anti-Oedipus* (a title that could be read as *Anti-House*), Deleuze and Guattari remark that the whole effort of new spatial thinking does not reside in finally teaching us how to die (how to think time differently), but in enabling us to leave and thus to come.

Such a thinking, which, as is well known, they call 'the schizo' (needless to say, one should not hasten to identify it with schizophrenia), is the thinking that knows something about leaving, about intensities and about joy:

> The schizo knows how to leave: he has made departure into something as simple as being born or dying. But at the same time his journey is strangely stationary, in place . . . These men of desire – or do they not yet exist? – are like Zarathustra. They know incredible sufferings, vertigos, and sicknesses. They have their specters. They must reinvent each gesture. But such a man produces himself as a free man, irresponsible, solitary, and joyous, finally able to say and do something simple in his own name, without asking permission. (Deleuze and Guattari 1983: 131)

The question is thus how to make of leaving something as simple and joyous as dying. But to make of leaving something light and simple requires nothing less than a turn in thinking, its stepping out of time. For if leaving is joyous it is because we do not mourn what we have left, which is possible only if by leaving it we did not lose it. Not to lose what we have left is, for its part, possible only if by leaving whatever we are leaving we also leave our self in the place we abandoned and arrive at another self. What is at stake here is the radical discontinuity between two selves; instead of the temporal synthesis of the two selves performed by mourning, their spatial separation. The trick is to leave one's self in some place and to emerge in another space as a newly-born self. Which is why this innocent self has to start from the beginning time and again. It has to invent and learn new motions, emotions, thoughts, languages and (even if for a day only) how to build a new house. The house of those who 'know' how to leave it is thus radically different from the house of those who learn how to die (in it). There are differences among the houses. The question is which house did Thoreau leave?

There is no text of Thoreau that is not marked by his insistence on the possibility of a new thought as the possibility of a different house. He reminds us that the Goddess of wisdom watches over the old world house. Minerva builds the rooted house (which stands for the stability of interiority, sobriety of reason and reliability of the soul). However, when it comes to the house it would be wise not to rely on wisdom but to listen instead to Momus whose objection to Minerva shows that wisdom (divine or human) is not always very wise. It is that objection that Thoreau reiterates and reinforces:

> As I understand it, that was a valid objection urged by Momus against the house which Minerva made, that 'she had not made it movable, by which means a bad neighbourhood might be avoided;' and it may still be urged, for our houses are such unwieldy property that we are often imprisoned rather than housed in them; and the bad neighbourhood to be avoided is our own scurvy selves. (Thoreau 1962: 47)

According to a well-known interpretation, whose heirs we are, Minerva's owl flies out in the dusk to identify the forms produced by the labour of the day and to determine what was as what is and what will be. Or, more to the point, she builds the immovable house of the self that it then cannot leave. Entrapped within the heavy walls of its past the self is forced to live what it once was and what it is no longer. The self thus lives by mourning its own death. Every house built becomes no more than a grave bearing witness to the fact that the life of identity is possible only as the life of a dead identity. Or, to put it in Thoreau's words, the self is thus nothing other than the carpenter of the coffin embedded in a house built according to the architecture of the grave:

> Much it concerns a man, forsooth, how a few sticks are slanted over him or under him, and what colours are daubed upon his box. It would signify somewhat, if, in any earnest sense, *he* slanted them and daubed it; but the spirit having departed out of the tenant, it is of a piece with constructing his own coffin – the architecture of the grave – and 'carpenter' is but another name for 'coffin maker'. (Thoreau 1962: 57)

Nothing can free the self from itself but death. We emancipate ourselves from our identity and from our houses only by dying:

> I know one or two families at least, in this town, who, for nearly a genera-tion, have been wishing to sell their houses in the outskirts and move into the village, but have not been able to accomplish it, and only death will set them free. (Thoreau 1962: 47)

Imprisoned in history, genealogy and origin, we stand still waiting for death. And in a certain sense, as Thoreau half-jokingly remarked, the grave is more of a house than the house, there is more life in it than in the house, for in it one dies 'more lively' than in the house: 'Better are the physically dead, for they more lively rot' (Thoreau 1929: 82).

The whole experiment undertaken in Walden had as its single goal to explore the possibility of building a house that one could joyously leave. Thoreau describes the house he tried to build as the house without a clear distinction between its interiority and exteriority, as a house without a stable form. If painted, such a house would correspond more to a 'picture in outlines' than to the calculated plans of architects. It is a house that gave up on figuration (a house therefore such as Jackson Pollock might paint it):

> It was suggestive somewhat as the picture in outlines. I did not need to go outdoors to take the air, for the atmosphere within had lost none of its fresh-ness. It was not so much within-doors as behind door where I sat, even in the rainiest weather. (Thoreau 1962: 85)

In other words, to sit in the house is never to be enclosed, but to sit behind which is always behind some interiority. Wherever one sits 'in' such a house one always sits in the freshness of the outside, in the outside of what is within. If such a house is only a suggestion (a guessing) of the house (if it is only an outline), it is because it embodies the paradox of a non-framed frame that changes each time we look at it, open the door, close the window or move the chair. Every motion changes the house, because the house is, to use Thoreau's metaphor, light as a cloud, and reacts to the motions of things and people in it: 'This frame so slightly clad, was a sort of crystallization around me, and reacted on the builder' (Thoreau 1962: 85). The encounter (re-action) is what constitutes (for a moment) both dweller and house. It is the atmosphere or the mood that cuts and fractures the 'insideness' of every space.

We can already hear an objection: a house light as a cloud? A flying house? A house that is a mood, an atmosphere, an aura, a passage? Well, that is all nice and fine, in a strange way it is even seductive, *but what does it mean?*

House, Thought, Atmosphere

Which comes down to the question: what does it mean to live 'out-houses', to think 'out-houses?'

We are familiar with Deleuze's reading of the Baroque house and Baroque architecture in general as architecture of the Baroque mind. According to him the Baroque house had two storeys. The first floor with the living space is the floor with all the windows and doors. Light, sound, odours and tastes come through them. They are like eyes and fingers, mouth and lips; they are the body exposed to the waves and flows of sensations. The first floor is thus the floor of the pleats of matter or the floor of the body which in its receptivity receives the sensations (the outside) that then resonate within it. Hence the equation between the reception room and the receptive body. The windows and doors through which the sensations enter the house make of its interiority a floating atmosphere. It is to them that the body owes its elasticity and plasticity.

Elasticity means that changeability is not absolute. The atmosphere changes but the house remains the same thanks to the frames of its walls. But how do the walls remain the same? They retain their 'stability' thanks not to the foundations but to the second floor.

The second floor is a different story. There are no exits on the second floor: 'It is the upper floor that has no windows. It is a dark room or chamber . . .' (Deleuze 1993: 4). Needless to say, the soul (or the monad) resides there. It is not directly connected to the outside (its room is dark) but neither is it absolutely withdrawn from it. Its way out is the first floor for it always looks at the life that is taking place there. Perspectival space emerges: 'To the degree it [the changeable life of the first floor, the body] represents variation or inflection, it can be called *point of view*. Such is the basis of perspectivism.' However, the subject, the one who 'lives' on the upper floor is not, as the word suggests, subjected to what it sees. Rather, it oversees the body of the living room. It is thus sur-jected into that space:

> The subject is not a sub-ject but, as Whitehead says, a 'superject' . . . The point of view is not what varies with the subject, *at least in the first instance*; it is, to the contrary, the condition in which an eventual subject apprehends a variation (metamorphosis), or: something = x (anamorphosis). For Leibniz, for Nietzsche, for William and Henry James, and for Whitehead as well, perspectivism amounts to a relativism, but not the relativism we take for granted. It is not a variation of truth according to the subject, but the condition in which the truth of a variation *appears to the subject*. That is the very idea of Baroque perspective. (Deleuze 1993: 20)

At first sight one would think that by insisting on anamorphosis the James brothers, together with Leibniz and Whitehead, introduced a significant change in Cartesian 'heavy-Baroque' perspective. For it is true that since the 'object' is but a variation, the point of view of the subject is made of relations among variations, which is why the subject cannot fix himself in a stable position (that explains why there are so many secrets in Henry James where one sees only on condition that one sees obliquely). However, as Deleuze made clear, this is so only in the first instance. For since the subject is still on the floor above he is the one who gathers together the variety of what he is superjected to in order to arrange his own room. In other words, he is the one who represents sensations and paints his room by those representations. The dark chamber is therefore the space for the decorator and his activity of mastering form. Thus we slide from the first instance (first level or floor) where the point of view is the condition in which an eventual subject apprehends a variation, to the upper floor where the representation is 'not the variation of the truth according to the subject' but the 'condition in which the truth of variation appears to the subject'. There is no truth other than the truth of paintings. Only a little 'trick' was needed for anamorphosis to fall into geometrical perspective: *what* appears to the subject may be conditioned by the happenings in the living room, but *how* it appears to him is conditioned by him in such a way that 'how' determines (shapes, forms) the 'what'. We end up with focussed gazes, rigid subjects and fixed hierarchies (the dialectics developed in almost all of James' novels).

That is not all. For the first and second floor are connected by the 'low and curved stairs that push into space' (Deleuze 1993: 4). In the Baroque architecture (of the mind) sensations travel to the upper floor by the curved path of the stairs. The stairs are the space where sensations are not yet represented and apprehended but no longer purely bodily. They are the fold in the proper sense: neither inside nor outside, neither body nor thought, but something that emerges when both body and mind leave themselves; neither the light of the day nor the night of the dark chamber, but the dawn. If the stairs are both of those things at the same time it is because they are in between them: they are the space or the embodiment within a space of a pure relation. They are the space of verbs or motions in indeterminate form; the space of walking, waiting, leaving, making (love); one does not eat on the stairs, one does not seat one's guests on them, one does not write on them. Nothing substantive or substantial can take shape on them. Only the happening itself, the 'going on' itself.

This location of the stairs brings us closer to Thoreau's house built on a different thought. Far from being a variation of the Baroque house (a variation visible in the town houses that Thoreau could have seen, with curved stairs that push the space all the way to the upper floor), Thoreau's house is the announcement of a new house that I will call the 'American house' or the 'house of the beyond'. However, the ruse of the American house is that it cannot be conceptualised. One does not know in advance what an American house will be since it must be a house that is not built from any plans, projections or calculations. The best one could say is that the American house is the very process of building it – what Thoreau calls 'deliberate building' – the process that, since it does not rely on anything, is the process of the pure experimentation of building the house. To the extent that this process affects the builder, building becomes the process of experimentation with one's own self. To build is thus to think in a new way, which is why the most urgent architectural question is: what is it to think? What is it to think for Thoreau?

We could begin to answer this question by looking at the characteristics of his house. It is a house without a cellar, basement or foundation. The architecture of the substance or support is unnecessary for those 'who have no olives nor wines in the cellar' (Thoreau 1962: 57), in other words, no roots or anything that needs time (or history) to taste good. And it is a house without ornaments. The architecture of ornaments presupposes the play of background and foreground, optical space and perspective:

True, there are architects so called in this country, and I have heard of one at least possessed with the idea of making architectural ornaments have a core of truth, a necessity, and hence a beauty, as if it were a revelation to him. All very well perhaps from his point of view, but only a little better than the common dilettantism. (Deleuze 1993: 56)

This raises another question: in a house without basement and cellar, in a house without a proper foundation, what could be called a foundation? It cannot be, as was the case with the Baroque house, the second floor that gathered together the multiplicity of the first, because, and this is of utmost importance, Thoreau's house does not have an upper floor. No basement, no upper floor, no ornaments, only flatness with windows on all sides. And if this house is the image of thinking what are we then to think about that thinking? Obviously, the absence of the upper floor is the absence of self-surveillance and self-mirroring. But what is less obvious is that the absence of the upper floor does not suggest a 'thought' naïvely reduced to an 'objectivity', objective truth with no intervention of the subject, and so on. Still less does it suggest a 'structure' in which the second floor would be substituted for the first so that there would be only the self absorbed in itself, the pure 'I' withdrawn from the world, a naïve solipsism.

The radicality of Thoreau's experimentation with thinking is that he located it in the space of the stairs and then made of that space the only floor there is. In other words, if the upper floor has fallen and become one with the first it is only because both of them have fallen into the stairs, become the stairs. To say that Thoreau's house is a house made of stairs is to suggest that the whole house has become the floating space 'in between', or that thought has become sensation which, for its part, and to the extent that it is also thought, is not 'mere' sensation any more, but an affect. Thoreau uses a very precise term to refer to this kind of thought. He calls it contemplation.

Several points should be immediately made clear. First, Thoreau uses the term contemplation systematically and always referring to the specific form it took in the Oriental praxis of thinking (in Walden, for example: 'I realized what the Orientals mean by contemplating soul') thus announcing that the term does not have the status of a metaphor for thinking in general. Or, to put it differently, to contemplate is not another vague term for the vague action we call 'to think' but a very specific praxis of thinking. Second, Thoreau insists that thinking as contemplation aims at subversion of the Western metaphysical tradition that rejects it in favour of the appropriation of the object of thought through its representation in time: 'Western philosophers have not conceived of the significance of

Contemplation . . .' (Thoreau 1929: 143). He thus makes it manifest that he is quite aware of his resistance to the dominant (Cartesian) 'model' of thinking. Third, to the extent that it escapes representation, contemplation is neither reflexive thinking nor pure 'sensing', which is why it cannot be reduced to the analogy or to the resemblance (to the object of thought).

And that is how the story of contemplation begins; by announcing, precisely that the mind is not at a distance from the body and that, by the same token, the body is at no distance from the mind but that they become one, forming the oneness he defined and Emerson endorsed, as 'mental ecstasy never to be interrupted'. The absence of distance, however, is the absence of translation or of representation and the presence of language without metaphor, the language of affects spoken by things and events. As Thoreau puts it in *Walden*, the forgetting of that language is the danger to which we are exposed: 'We are in a danger of forgetting the language which all things and events speak without metaphor, which alone is copious and standard' (Thoreau 1962: 105). We are in a danger of forgetting the mute nothingness, the vast void that nevertheless speaks. But how is it possible to understand anything without the labour of the metaphor and translation? What kind of understanding is it that is not related to reason?

In 'Sounds,' Thoreau gave a rather elaborate description of this process of 'understanding':

> I did not read books the first summer; I hoed beans. Nay, I often did better than this. There were times when I could not afford to sacrifice the present moment to any work, whether of the head or hands . . . Sometimes, in a summer morning, having taken my accustomed bath, I sat in my sunny doorway from sunrise till noon. (Thoreau 1962: 105)

Thus, assuming the pure stillness that employs neither mind nor body Thoreau becomes a passive 'plate', as it were, on which there can be inscribed, directly, the 'speaking of the event without metaphor'. But what is this event to which he is exposed? Strictly speaking, he is exposed to the repetition of the habits of animals and birds. The birds fly, the flies enter the spider's web, the rain rains, and so on. And that happens with such a regularity that it becomes more precise than a clock, and firm as the firmest habit: 'They would begin to sing almost with as much precision as a clock, within five minutes of a particular time, referred to the setting of the sun' (Thoreau 1962: 114). Sitting thus for hours and days exposed to the repetition of the same Thoreau grows into the habit of following the habit of birds (or beans or corn); his habit becomes the habit of the anonymous sound and his time becomes its time. But those repetitive sounds are multiple. The owl, for example, releases and repeats the sound 'gl, gl, gl . . .' (the repetition of instants) which is, in Thoreau's words, 'expressive of a mind which has reached the gelatinous mildewy stage in the mortification of all healthy and courageous thought' (Thoreau 1962: 115). The symbol of wisdom speaks the language of idiots and repeats it until when? Until another owl responds to the repetitions of gl's: 'But now one answers from far woods in a strain made really melodious by distance – Hoo hoo hoo, hoorer hoo' (Thoreau 1962: 115). We have, therefore, a series of gl's that strangely enough ends up in the series 'Hoo'. In other words, the repetition of the cases AB, AB, changes into A . . . B or B or A. This slight change does not change the state of affairs among owls but it changes everything for the soul that contemplates it. For the contemplative soul this change is nothing less than its being affected by the new quality; it is thus affected by something different. As Deleuze made clear in his analysis of contemplation, 'the repetition changes nothing in the object or the state of affairs AB. On the other hand, a change is produced in the mind which contemplates it: a difference, something new in the mind' (Deleuze 1994: 70).

But how does the mind function here if it does not translate the cases? The answer to this question leads us to the 'core' of contemplation. For, as Deleuze suggested, contemplation is precisely the mind or the soul that functions as:

> contractile power: like a sensitive plate, it retains one case when the other appears. It contracts cases, elements, agitations or homogeneous instants and grounds these in an internal *qualitative* impression endowed with a certain weight. When A appears, we expect B with a force corresponding to the qualitative impression of all the contracted ABs. (Deleuze 1994: 70)

The sensitive (or contemplative) plate contracts the repetition of sounds in such a way that the repetition with its habitual rhythm is contracted each time with a 'different intensity'. The repetition of the same (of the same boring sounds) thus becomes the intense difference. This new 'thing' or affect is the event.

Both space and time are affected by the repetition of contractions. For the contraction does not take place in time but produces time as the synthesis of a spatial encounter between two instants. What is contracted, the intensity, constitutes as Deleuze put it:

> the lived or living, present. It is in this present that time is deployed. To it belong both the past and the future: the past in so far as the preceding instants are retained in the contraction; the future because its expectation is anticipated in this same contraction. The past and the present do not

designate instants distinct from a supposed present instant, but rather the dimensions of the present itself in so far as it is a contraction of instants. (Deleuze 1994: 71).

Thoreau insists on the same thing. Since both the past and the present are the representations of what is not they cannot be *presented*, they are not affects or contractions: 'The past cannot be *presented*; we cannot know what we are not' (Thoreau 1929: 97). Similarly, in the passage quoted from *Walden*, when Thoreau says that he would sit in his doorway in order not to sacrifice 'the present moment', he was referring to the contraction of time, to the contraction of days or weeks into the 'living present'. At the beginning of 'Sounds' he explicitly refers to contemplation as the synthesis of affects into the 'now':

> My days were not the days of the week, bearing the stamp of any heathen deity, nor were they minced into hours and fretted by the ticking of a clock; for I lived like the Puri Indians, of whom it is said that 'for yesterday, today, and tomorrow they have only one word, and they express the variety of meaning by pointing backward for yesterday forward for tomorrow, and overhead for the passing day. (Thoreau 1962: 106)

In other words, he did not live in a time that was the condition of all possible times (time as an *a priori* category) nor did he live in chronometric time (his days were not fretted by the ticking of a clock). He lived in a present without past or future, both past and future having become merely points in space (for past one points backward, for future forward).

To the extent that this contraction (the synthesis of the present) does not happen in time but constitutes it, it is not performed by the mind. If it were the mind that performed it we would have but another version of reflexive thought: the mind would just gather the affects into a framed image and instead of contemplation there would be yet another form of representation. But instead of carrying the contraction or actively performing the synthesis the mind is only exposed to it; the synthesis occurs in it not by means of it but by means of the motion of the instants.

Deleuze thought that this synthesis must be given a name: 'In any case, this synthesis must be given a name: passive synthesis. Although it is constitutive it is not, for all that active. It is not carried out by the mind, but occurs *in* the mind which contemplates' (Deleuze 1994: 71). As is immediately clear, this passiveness is not simply the opposite of the active. For such a synthesis is not passive because it is inert, immobile or frozen, that is to say because it is 'purely' receptive, for in that case it would not be a synthesis at all. Passive synthesis refers to the receptiveness that 'works', that synthesises itself through its own movement, motion, 'fever' or restlessness. If it is passive, therefore, it is because it is not the effect of the mind's active synthesis of representation. Passive synthesis is involuntary motion without the power of self-appropriation, which is why in trying to explain contemplation Thoreau quoted Kreeshna's thesis that 'every man is involuntarily urged to act' (Thoreau 1929: 87), his action being the outcome of the force to which he is exposed and which he cannot appropriate. In the moment in which it occurs (the occurrence that constitutes the moment) the I and the body fall into one, they become a single plate of contraction or affection, a single space (of stairs).

We can therefore understand not only why Thoreau's house does not have an upper floor (the dark chamber) but also why there are no walls on the only floor there is, which would separate it into different chambers and rooms (and which would in turn separate sensations from perceptions and perceptions from affections). Thoreau's ideal house, as he himself described it, is thus one space where everything falls into the multiplicity of the one (the body has become the mind that has become the body or the mind without the I):

> Such a shelter as you would be glad to reach in a tempestuous night, containing all the essentials of the house and nothing for the house-keeping; where you can see all the treasures of the house at one view, and everything hangs upon its peg that a man should use; at once kitchen, pantry, parlour, chamber, storehouse, and garret. (Thoreau 1962: 202)

Such a shelter is precisely the contemplative plate of the mind-body on which various contractions occur. Or, differently, such a shelter is at the same time speculation and action, speculation that takes place as action (of contraction). As Thoreau insisted (again quoting Oriental sources): 'Children only, and not the learned, speak of the speculative and the practical doctrines as two. They are but one' (Thoreau 1929: 144).

However, Thoreau himself tried to avoid the term 'passivity' probably out of fear that he would be 'accused' (as he only too often was) of advocating immobility, mere receptivity and non-labour, or passivity as understood by common sense (the very same common sense he accused of dullness). It was precisely in order to avoid such a misunderstanding that he gave us the 'complementary verses' to the chapter on economy in *Walden*: 'We not require the dull society/ Of your necessitated temperance, / Or that unnatural stupidity / That knows nor joy nor sorrow; / nor your forc'd / Falsely exalted passive fortitude / Above the active.' Thus 'strategically' avoiding the term 'passivity' he tried to explain the contemplative state of mind/body by using terms such as unconsciousness or the 'state of reverie' or, sometimes, simply absent-mindedness. But the unconsciousness he refers to here does not resemble anything that psychoanalysis will discover (the primary process of desire released from the leash of the ego) nor is absent-mindedness the laziness of a mind that is not ready to work. Furthermore, the terms that Thoreau uses to explain the 'passive synthesis' of contemplation should not be read synonymously but in such a way that each refers to the other and explains it: contemplation is unconscious because the mind is absent from it, because the mind has abandoned itself through self-abandoning, thus leaving its own self behind itself. This makes of it a state of restless reverie, which is neither the immobility of death nor the appropriating activity of representation but an interval between two contractions which Thoreau wants to enter as soon as he is acclimatised enough for it.

It is only now that we can understand the process of Thoreau's walking and what it means to become a walker. 'To walk' is not to employ the body in senseless and boring exercise while enabling the mind to 'observe' objects; it is also not enough that while walking the mind thinks walking. To put it simply, if 'to walk' is a task for thinking, a task worthy of being addressed by a:

> new thought, it is not because walking opens up the possibility of thinking but because walking is thinking: 'I am alarmed when it happens that I have walked a mile into the woods bodily, without getting there in spirit . . . The thought of some work will run in my head and I am not where my body is, – *I am out of my senses*. In my walks I would fain return to my senses. (Thoreau 2000: 632)

What Thoreau says in this notorious paragraph is not that his mind or his 'I' would simply fall into his body but rather that it would fall into where the body is. For the body itself is never simply where it was. By walking, it is moved from where it was (wherever it was) to where it is while walking. It has abandoned the 'depth' of its organs, it has come out on its surface, to the senses (such as perform the role of the stairs in the house of the body), as the plates of the motion of sensations, as involuntary contractile powers. By walking the body abandons itself and its own form and becomes the formless rhythm of migrations of affects (which is what Thoreau calls the 'cultivation of senses'). Now, to move the 'I' is to move it to that space (of the interval) into which the body has already migrated (what Thoreau calls to 'think deliberately' or the 'cultivation of thought'). When that happens both mind and body fall into one. In other words, it is only then that they come to the 'truth' or to themselves. But one should not fail to register here that both mind and body come to themselves by abandoning or leaving themselves and going to their meeting place which is the state of contemplation: neither the wind of sensations nor the frost of pure thought but the breeze of contracted affects. And the repetition of the each time different contraction is the language of events and encounters, a language outside of the time of the metaphor. Spatial thought.

It is when this encounter takes place that 'a walk' or 'to walk' becomes 'walking'. In a sense, nineteenth-century critics (such as James Russell Lowell) were right to claim that *Walden* was the chaos of fragments and as such the result of its author's discontinuous mind. What they unmistakenly sensed (for common sense is always on guard) is that an attack on modern logic was at stake there. The only thing they failed to notice is that such an attack resulted in the invention of a logic of the event that happened as the reinvention of a very old logic, namely that of the Stoics (the fact that Thoreau was 'trained' in classical studies should never be underestimated). For, as is well known, modern logic allows for the existence of a quality (or of the attribute) only insofar as there is a subject (the substance) to which that attribute can be attributed. Quality is always the quality of something or somebody (and that subject is what provides the continuity of thought). As Deleuze (another reinventer of Stoic logic) reminded us, 'the scheme' of modern logic is 'subject-copula-attribute: I am writing, I am travelling', so that it can always be (and must be) reduced to 'I am a travelling being.' However, in the logic of the Stoics the predicate is not attributive, is not reducible to the copula:

> The Stoics accomplished this by making the event neither an attribute nor a quality, but the incorporeal predicate of a subject of the proposition (not 'the tree is green', but 'the tree greens . . .'). They conclude that the proposition stated a 'manner of being' of the thing, an 'aspect' that exceeded the Aristotelian alternative, essence-accident: for the verb 'to be' they substitute 'to follow', and they put manner in the place of essence. (Deleuze 1993: 53)

Thoreau provided the second step: he put manner in the place of existence as well. Thus the existence/essence became the manner, the atmosphere, the mood, or, to borrow another word dear to Thoreau, the charm. 'I am a walking being' became 'walking' and 'walking' became thinking because 'I am a thinking being' became thinking without the 'I' (since the self is beside itself) thus becoming leaving (through this abandoning of the self). To put it quite simply, being became passing: 'Transiting all day . . . It is only a *transjectus*, a transitory voyage, like life itself' (Thoreau 1929: 121).

Thoreau was careful enough to remark that this being beside itself is not insanity but a new thought (needless to say, one can always claim that any form of 'insanity' is nothing other than the proposition of a new thinking):

> With thinking we may be beside ourselves in a sane sense. I *may* be affected by a theatrical exhibition; on the other hand I *may not* be affected by an actual event, which appears to concern me much more. I only know myself as a human entity; the scene, so to speak, of thoughts and affections; and am sensible of a certain doubleness by which I can stand as remote from myself as from another. However intense my experience I am conscious of the presence and criticism of a part of me which, as it were, is not a part of me, but spectator, sharing no experience, but taking note of it, and that is no more I than it is you. (Thoreau 1962: 122)

Thinking takes place beside the self; it is the process of leaving the self and becoming a strange 'entity', strange insofar as that entity is not identifiable or is not the substance but an always changeable scene of thoughts and affections, a scene made of affections. The 'I' that could give it a support or constancy is 'remote' from it and since it is not exposed to the affections, since it is not on stage, as it were, it is not part of (the selfless) me. The notes it takes are, therefore, not notes about the stage; the stage, the bundle of affections, thinking itself is not representable, it cannot be thought; it is a sub-representative thinking which is why the reflexive self, playing the role of the spectator, cannot reach it; or, differently, it is why there is no spectator. The spectator is 'no more I than it is you', it is neither 'I' nor 'you' but an empty shell of representation 'signifying nothing'. On the one hand, therefore, there exists the ruined house of the reflexive self, a dead limit reduced to nothingness, and on the other hand, there is a thinking that now goes in all directions, as it were, but does not belong to anybody, a selfless 'me', an impersonal life. This life is then a 'manner', an atmosphere, a mood or a charm. Neither mind nor body but a contractile soul and probably green: 'Methinks my own soul must be a bright invisible green' (Thoreau 1929: 250). It is a soul that greens. That is the radical meaning of leaving (thinking or walking): thinking or walking is leaving one's own self behind. Walking is thus the practice that exercises what is most difficult, the practice of *radical disidentification*. It is not that I do not possess this or that thing; it is that I do not possess anything whatsoever; nothing is ever mine, because I do not possess myself, because there is no 'me'. Instead there is just the 'greening' soul, the soul that *is* the 'greening'; there is always and only the 'greening'. Such was the main 'task' of the performance performed in *Walden*: to transgress oneself, to abandon the limits of the self: 'We need to witness our own limits transgressed, and some life pasturing freely where we never wonder' (Thoreau 1962: 255). Once the limits of the self are transgressed, life becomes not my life, but some life, a life. An impersonal life. However, and precisely because impersonal life cannot be witnessed, what must be done cannot be done: we will never witness the transgression. For transgression occurs as the transgression of witnessing.

References

Deleuze, G. (1993), *The Fold, Leibniz and the Baroque*, trans. T. Conley, Minneapolis: University of Minnesota Press.

Deleuze, G. (1994), *Difference and Repetition*, trans. P. Patton, New York: Columbia University Press.

Deleuze, G. (1997), *Essays Critical and Clinical*, trans. D. W. Smith and M. A. Greco, Minneapolis: University of Minnesota Press.

Deleuze, G. and Guattari, F. (1983), *Anti-Oedipus*, trans. R. Hurley, M. Seem and H. R. Lane, Minneapolis: University of Minnesota Press.

Deleuze, G. and Guattari, F. (1987), *A Thousand Plateaus: Capitalism and Schizophrenia*, trans. B. Massumi, Minneapolis: University of Minnesota Press.

Deleuze, G. and Parnet, C. (1987), *Dialogues*, trans. H. Tomlinson and B. Habberjam, New York: Columbia University Press.

Thoreau, H. D. (1929), *A Week on the Concord and Merrimack Rivers*, Boston: The Concord Edition.

Thoreau, H. D. (1962), *The Variorum Walden*, annotated and introduction by W. Harding, New York: Twayne Publishers.

Thoreau, H. D. (2000), 'Walking', in Brooks Atkinson (ed.), *Walden and Other Writings*, New York: Modern Library.

Chapter 8

On the 'Spiritual Automaton', Space and Time in Modern Cinema According to Gilles Deleuze

Réda Bensmaïa

The unifying thread of this article is the 'spiritual automaton', a 'concept' that appears relatively late in Gilles Deleuze's work, in *Cinema 1. The Movement-Image* (1986) and *Cinema 2. The Time-Image* (1989), but one that nonetheless plays a crucial role in the general economy of the Deleuzian conception of the way(s) space and time are produced and negotiated in cinema.

A certain familiarity with the work of Deleuze makes readily apparent both that the concepts he creates need not appear in the title of a book or a chapter to play an important role in his analysis, and that any examination of these concepts must be taken up in light of the theoretical problematic in which he reworks and re-evaluates them. Apart from the very rare exception, a Deleuzian concept cannot be read as such, or as left to posterity by a given philosophical 'tradition'. The originality with which Deleuze practises the history of philosophy and the broad versatility with which he uses his 'canonical' concepts have been noted by a number of critics, and in the two books on film he wrote one just after the other, Deleuze does not break with this practice. By detaching concepts from their original theoretical contexts, he is able to reactivate them, to re-evaluate their tenor and make them play new roles – in a word, he is able to transform them into 'conceptual personae'.[1] In this way, philosophical concepts are never, for Deleuze, static entities fixed once and for all, but are, rather, matter to be further worked through and reconnected, ever called into crisis and reinvented. The 'spiritual automaton' is, in this sense, one of the finest examples of a philosophico-conceptual 'persona' that film theory has ever invented to account for its 'object'.

The thought process animating the creation of such personae is exemplified by the notion of the 'Body without Organs'. Introduced for the first time in *The Logic of Sense* (1990), Deleuze, we recall, presented it as borrowed from Antonin Artaud (a poet) and from Gisela Pankow (a psychiatrist). Some years later while working with Félix Guattari, Deleuze would again take up this figure, this time giving it a crucial role to play, in *Anti-Oedipus* (1983). By means of this transfer, the nature and definition of the concept would completely change: no longer drawing its valence and effect solely from the work of the authors who had originally fostered it as an intuition, the BwO would draw from at least two new systems of thought, themselves referring to two new theoretical regimes. Indeed, as André Pierre Colombat has aptly shown in his excellent article on the concepts at work, like 'tools,' in *A Thousand Plateaus* (Colombat 1991: 10–24), the concept of the BwO, articulated around the idea of non-sense as developed by Artaud and Lewis Carroll, is presented *at once* 'as an egg' (that is, as a biological metaphor) *and* as a 'Spinozist substance' (this time, as a properly philosophical concept). Inevitably, the juxtaposition of these two apparently 'incompatible' fields of explanation creates nonsense or, if you will, an 'excess of meaning' that sets the reader's intellect and imagination in movement: 'The concept of the "Body without Organs" will therefore be *defined in between* two heterogeneous series, thanks to a never-ending *to-and-fro motion* between Deleuze's conception of the egg, borrowed from François Dalcq, and his conception of the Spinozist substance' (Colombat 1991: 14), which he derived this time from his own interpretation of Spinoza's *Ethics* (Deleuze 1990). In *A Thousand Plateaus* (1987), the BwO re-emerges to play a still more complex role, or more exactly, it crisscrosses and is crisscrossed by new determinations: here, the BwO still remembers having been an egg and a Spinozist substance, but it also reveals itself to be an 'intensive and unshaped matter' (Colombat 1991: 14), the 'plane of consistency specific to desire' of Spinoza's *Ethics*, Heliogabalus, *Logos Spermaticos*, and so on (Deleuze and Guattari 1987: 149–66). As a 'rigorous and inexact concept', the BwO is in constant metamorphosis, 'occupying the in between space that allows intensities and desiring flows to circulate before actualizing themselves in different shapes of thought and in living organisms, on a physical or a metaphysical plane' (Colombat 1991: 14).

With the concept of the 'spiritual automaton', we observe the same kind of thought process with respect to film. Although initially taken from Spinoza's *Treatise on the Emendation of the Intellect* (Spinoza 1992: 255–6), the 'spiritual automaton' would soon be transformed into a concept of the Jabberwocky, Snark, or BwO type. That is to say, we have once more to grapple with one of the 'inexact and rigorous' concepts traversing Deleuze's work and making for the richness of the theoretical and practical effects he draws from them.

The 'spiritual automaton' is first and foremost an 'inexact' concept, because it is difficult if not impossible to assign to it a singular and stable origin. Indeed, Deleuze does not hesitate to bring its use and effectiveness to bear on writers, artists, historians, creators, and theorists as different as Élie Faure, Jean Epstein, and S. M. Eisenstein, to name but a few, whom he immediately associates and connects in a complex and contradictory way to an author like Artaud and filmmakers like Pier Paolo Pasolini and Jean-Luc Godard, only to arrive at (and thus to take up the question anew) a poet like Paul Valéry or philosophers like Spinoza and Heidegger.

At the same time, the concept of the 'spiritual automaton' can still be called 'rigorous' in that, as suggested above, what are clearly the 'transference' and 'translation' undergone by the concept are neither gratuitous nor improvised; on the contrary, they obey the most consistent thought process. Yet, according to what criteria are we to judge this consistency? How can we say of a concept that it is at once 'inexact' and 'rigorous'? Why the re-creation and re-activation of a concept on the particular occasion of a reflection on cinema? And finally: in what way does this 'concept' affect time in film?

Deleuze's interest in the Spinozist concept of the 'spiritual automaton' is not so much in any 'automatic' or 'mechanical' aspect – Spinoza is in no way a 'mechanistic' philosopher – but, rather, in what has since Spinoza been referred to as a 'method' that, although borrowing its starting point from geometry, nonetheless only finds its intrinsic form of action in the thought process that makes it exceed its own ordinary limits, raising it to an essence as the 'genetic reason of all knowable properties' (Deleuze 1990: 115). For Deleuze, interest in the Spinozist 'spiritual automaton' stems from at least two indissociable factors: the immanence of thought and the theory of parallelism. 'Spiritual automaton,' Deleuze writes, 'means first of all that an idea, being a mode of thought, has its (efficient and formal) cause nowhere but in the attribute of Thought. Equally, any object whatever has its efficient and formal cause only in the attribute of which it is a mode and whose concept it involves' (Deleuze 1990: 115).

These definitions may seem rather 'abstract' when thus formulated out of context, but they become much more effective and concrete once we understand that, for Spinoza, they implied none other than the *power* of parallelism: to say that an idea or an object finds its efficient and formal cause 'only in the attribute of which it is the mode' is to affirm that 'all efficient or formal (and even more, material and final) causality is *excluded between ideas and things, things and ideas*' (my emphasis).

What holds Deleuze's attention in Spinoza's 'automatism', then, is the multiple consequences he infers from Spinoza's first axioms: the affirmation of the independence of two series, the series of things from the series of ideas; and immediately thereafter, the independence of the series of images from the series of objects, things, or bodies – series of words from images, and so on. Deleuze would focus especially on the 'autonomy' and 'automatism' of thought.[2]

Like Spinoza's, Deleuze's method in *Cinema 1* and *2* includes (at least) three great moments, each narrowly implicated in the others: a first moment in which the apprehension of movement and the 'objects' it carries is granted to intuition or to the 'immediate contents of consciousness', also the moment of film analysis as simple 'image-movement' or 'image-representation';[3] a moment when it is no longer movement as such, but the dislocation of movement that precedes analysis, and thus, the eruption of image-time and 'image-figure'; and finally, a third moment, one of synthesis, albeit disjunctive, when it is an 'unthinkable' Outside that takes on the order of thought – the thought of the unthinkable: 'spiritual automaton'.

Such is, schematically drawn, the 'programme' laid out by the reactivation of the concept of the 'spiritual automaton'. From this, everything else unfolds because, as suggested above, in bringing this concept to bear, it was never a question for Deleuze of 'applying' it as such to cinema; on the contrary, it was a matter of using cinema to transform an 'exact' concept – too 'exact' in the work of Spinoza – into an *operator of analysis* or an accelerator of concepts, or even an 'inexact and rigorous' concept that would allow it to 'give rise' in us to a new way of thinking cinema. In other words, the 'spiritual automaton' acts as a 'transformer' of the regime of concepts and images in film. As Deleuze writes: '*Automatic movement* gives rise to a *spiritual automaton* in us, which reacts in turn on movement.' Furthermore, from the moment of its confrontation with the disjunctive logic at work in cinema, the concept of the:

> [s]piritual automaton no longer designates – as it does in classical philosophy – the [merely] logical or abstract possibility of formally deducing thoughts from each other, but the circuit into which they enter with the movement-image, the shared power of what forces thinking and what thinks under the shock: a *nooshock*. (Deleuze 1989: 156–7)

Thus, the effect of displacing the 'automaton' from one given theoretical field to another is two-fold: *at the same time* that it unyokes Spinozist philosophy – and perhaps all philosophy – from its latent 'formalism', it tears cinema from its patent 'mechanism' (the simple 'shock') to reveal therein what forces us to think (beyond the opposition of movement-image and action-image). As soon as the nature of the spiritual automaton's intervention in film is understood, it 'is as if cinema were telling us: with me, with the image-movement, you can't escape the shock *which arouses the thinker in you*. A subjective and collective automaton for an automatic movement: the art of the "masses"' (Deleuze 1989: 156–7, my emphasis).

As long as they had available to them only a formal conception of movement and of the production of ideas in cinema – ideas that still remained *representative* – filmmakers and film theorists inevitably missed its *noetic* dimension, for they confused the 'shock' with the 'nooshock' and thereby reduced the vibrations of the movement-image to the 'figurative violence of the represented'. Such a 'reduction,' intensified by a *confusion,* would quickly and unduly assimilate cinema as 'spiritual automaton' with cinema as the 'art of propaganda' or the reproduction of reality! According to Deleuze, even a filmmaker with the genius of S. M. Eisenstein, with all his theoretical vigilance, could let himself be taken in by an entirely mechanical conception of the noetic dimension of cinematographic 'automatism'.

If Eisenstein did indeed locate the 'movement' in cinema that goes from the shock of two images to the thought or, as he himself said, to the 'concept'; if he had indeed exposed the twisted dialectic that turns the first movement upside down so as to pass from the 'concept' to the 'affect' and from the 'organic' to the 'pathetic', he never managed to produce an adequate idea of the nature of the 'automatism' at work in cinema. As Deleuze aptly put it, with Eisenstein, 'we no longer go from the movement-image to the clear thinking of the whole that it expresses; we *go from thinking of the whole which is presupposed and obscure to the agitated, mixed-up images which express it*' (Deleuze 1989: 159, my emphasis). In this sense, Eisenstein managed to intuit the complex nature of the cinematographic 'shock' 'in the form of opposition', as well as the thought that it engaged 'in the form of opposition overcome, or of the transformation of opposites' (Deleuze 1989: 158). But in order to be 'dialectical', this transformation could not renounce the idea of a totality as a harmonic 'synthesis' of parts ('shots') that pre-existed them in a 'Subject' or a 'World'. If he clearly signals the (dialectical) passage of a Logos that 'unifies the parts' to a Pathos that 'bathes them and spreads out in them', that is, the shock rebounding from the unconscious concept (of a whole) to the matter-image – 'fountains of cream, fountains of luminous water, spurting fires, zig-zags forming numbers, as in the famous sequence in *The General Line*', for example – Eisenstein could still believe in cinema as a 'device' that allowed him to go back to images and string them together according to the demands of an 'interior monologue' that he could reduce 'to the course of thought of a man'.

To rid himself of a conception of cinema tending to close off the rhetorical dimension that determined it in logical and grammatical dimensions, Eisenstein would have had to appreciate the more purely *noetic*[4] range of cinema. For although cinema was awakened, with him, to the power of the 'figure-image', that is, to the formal play, 'that [in cinema] gives the image an affective charge that will intensify the sensory shock', he did not take account of what, again in cinema, can refer to an 'outside' that is neither reducible to an 'interiority' as subjectivity nor to an 'exteriority' as *res extensa* or 'exterior' world. We must therefore envision a third 'moment' that no longer consists in going from image to thought (percept to concept) or from concept to affect (thought to image), but which surpasses this dialectic to create a movement *in which concept and image are one*: 'The concept is in itself in the image, and the image is for itself in the concept. This is no longer organic and pathetic *but dramatic, pragmatic, praxis, or action-thought*' (Deleuze 1989: 161, my emphasis). In this sense, for Deleuze, Eisenstein would have been the theorist-filmmaker to detach 'Narrative-Representative' cinema from its imperatives and who, following this, would have embarked on the course of a *cinematographic noetic* – except that everything happens as if he had reduced it too quickly to an 'automatism', an instrument in the service of the historical revolution or of dialectical reason. With Eisenstein, the 'spiritual automaton' became 'revolutionary Man', as for Leni Riefenstahl it would become (the instrument of) 'fascist Man'. In both cases, the 'audio-visual battle' ended in a belief that led them to abandon their prey to go chasing after shadows: in spite of everything, the audio-visual battle became a powerful instrument for capturing the exterior world – 'our world'! – without knowing that it drew from the original forces of an 'unformable and unformed Outside'.[5]

At this level, what we willingly call the 'Spiritual Automaton-Transformer'[6] reveals its full effect because instead of leading to an impasse, this last acknowledgement participates in a revival of the *problems*. Indeed, thanks to the veritable 'transformer' of concepts that is the 'spiritual automaton', Deleuze is able to point out that the failure of the movement-image and the action-image in cinema, as well as the gross mediocrity that lies in wait for its most commercial productions, can be attributed neither to the poverty of ideologies nor to the 'fascism of production' (Deleuze 1989: 165) – after all, Riefenstahl made 'beautiful' films – but more pointedly, to a thought that did not always know how to raise itself to the height of the cinematographic automatism's intrinsic power. Everything happens for Deleuze as if cinema had failed to take account of and to play out fully its potentialities, not because of an *excess* of 'automatism' but because of a lack of radicalism. It is at this level that the work of a writer like Artaud plays such an important role.

With Artaud, the S-A-T would be invested with new valence, allowing the renewed thinking of the economy of such key concepts as *montage* and *a whole* in cinema. Indeed, no longer conceived of as 'the [simple] logical possibility of a thought which would formally deduce its ideas from each other' (for example, Eisenstein's 'montage-king'), and even less as 'the physical power of a thought that would be placed in a circuit with the automatic image' (for example, the Expressionist 'shock-image', (Deleuze 1989: 166, translation modified), the S-A-T would instead be conceived of as a 'Mummy' that would no longer serve as a caution to endeavours,[7] like those still played out in the Eisenstein aesthetic, that undertake to recentre the Subject (as 'People', 'History', 'Reason', and so on). Henceforth, cinema could finally be thought of not as a dialectical or logical instrument of referral to a 'world' and a 'subject' always already given, but as the indicator of a virtual world and subject (to come). With Eisenstein, the 'automaton' allowed going from the image to the thought, having provoked the shock or the vibration that was supposed to give rise to 'thought in thought' (Deleuze 1989: 166); but from thought to image, there was still the self-incarnating figure in the interior monologue 'capable of giving us the shock again': 'dialectical' automaton!

With Artaud, we witness an altogether different regime of thought, as well as the actuation of an otherwise more complex dialectic:

> What cinema [henceforth] advances is not the power of thought but its 'unpower', which will no longer be conceived of in terms of a 'simple inhibition that the cinema would bring to us from the outside, but of this central inhibition, of this internal collapse and fossilization, of this 'theft of thoughts' of which thought is a constant agent and victim. (Deleuze 1989: 166).

Once raised to the height of 'spiritual automatism', cinema would no longer be conceived of as an instrument serving to reproduce thought or represent the real, but would instead be understood as a machine of a superior order, one that sets thought in relation to an Outside that cannot be reduced to a world said to be 'exterior'. Cinema as spiritual automaton is this 'machine' that puts thought into contact with an Outside that

itself comes to subvert the nature of the relations of representation existing in cinema between image and reality. We might say that for Deleuze,
cinema becomes the producer of an original composition of space-time
that metamorphoses the real. Faced with such an Outside, given to us by
cinema like an 'offering', the represented reality appears as a fallout
effect of cinematographic virtualities.

By way of illustration, I will take a specific example analysed by
Deleuze: that of the *Whole*, the idea of the whole in cinema. The Whole,
Deleuze tells us, is a poetic notion that can be traced back to Rilke but is
also a philosophical notion elaborated by Bergson. It is, therefore, also a
'rigorous and inexact' concept. As Deleuze points out, however, it is
important not to confuse the Whole – the idea of a whole in cinema –
with the idea of a set. In fact, for all that a set unites very diverse elements, its structure must remain no less closed or sealed off. It may refer
to or be included in a larger set, but this latter will in its turn wish for
closure, and so on to infinity. But the Whole, Deleuze tells us, is of
another nature entirely; it cannot be assimilated to a set because it 'is of
the order of Time' (Deleuze 1983: 40). To quote Deleuze: '[The Whole]
traverses all sets and is precisely what prevents them from fully realizing
their proper tendency, which is to say, from completely closing themselves off' (Deleuze 1983: 40).

Following Bergson, Deleuze says in his turn: 'Time is the open, it is
what changes and keeps changing its nature in each instant'. (Deleuze
1983: 40).[8] We can translate this thesis by saying that Time is the Open,
it is what changes all things, not ceasing to change the nature of things
in each instant. Time in cinema is this Whole, which is precisely not a set
but is, rather, the perpetual passage from one set to another, the transformation of one set into another. My working hypothesis therefore
becomes the following: Deleuze created the notion of the spiritual
automaton in an attempt to think about the relation *time-whole-open*.
He does not say that only cinema thinks this relation; he merely says that
'it is cinema that makes it easier for us to think it'. In this sense, there is,
for Deleuze, something like a 'pedagogical' dimension proper to cinema.
And in fact, its demonstration is relatively simple once cinema is used as
an operator of analysis for intuiting such a singular phenomenon. To
'illustrate' his point of view, Deleuze takes as a 'model' the following
three levels of organising and articulating the image: framing, cutting,
and movement.

I quote: 'Framing is the determination of an artificially closed provisional set' that to all appearances does not exhaust what is at stake in a
cinematographic image; yet it is constantly traversed by cutting, which

is, 'the determination of movement or movements distributed in the elements of the set; but movement in its turn also expresses a change or variation in the whole, which is the job of montage' (Deleuze 1989: 40). In this sense, the Whole is the 'power', the *Dunamis* that cuts across all sets and specifically prevents them from being 'totally' closed off. To illustrate his 'case', Deleuze takes the example of the notion of 'off-camera' that refers, according to him, to two distinct realities. On one hand, he indicates that any given set is part of a greater set of two or three dimensions (there are objects found on this side of the door and objects that are 'out-of-field', on the other side. *The secret beyond the door!*). On the other hand, he indicates that all sets, 'plunge into a whole of another nature, that *of a fourth and fifth dimension*, that keeps changing through the sets it traverses, no matter how vast they are. In the one case, it is a spatial and material extension, while in the other, it is spiritual determination' (Deleuze 1989: 40 my emphasis, R. B.). Among the numerous 'examples' Deleuze specifically analyses are, of course, the works of Dreyer and Bresson, whose films show just how difficult it is to separate the two types of 'dimensions': the material and the spiritual, the spatial and the temporal. Each filmmaker must recreate from the ground up the relation or relations to the Whole that will traverse the sets. For, as Deleuze says, in a great film as in all works of art, 'there is always something open' (Deleuze 1989: 40). And anyone seeking to know what it is will discover it is time, it is the whole, produced as they are by the 'automaton'; because the automaton is none other than the 'machine' that allows the adding of n dimensions to the first and the second dimensions of the image: 'shot-reverse shot'.

Here, then, is the idea of the Whole severed from any idea of organic or dialectic totality. But this is not the complete story, for the S-A-T also enables Deleuze to foreground the differences between a 'theorematic' and a 'problematic' regime of film thought,[9] leading him to rethink completely cinema's relation to its language and its objects. Indeed, armed with the S-A-T, Deleuze easily shows that the cinema of Eisenstein or Godard, for example, refers not only to an ideological or aesthetic difference but more pointedly to a prior difference of position vis-à-vis the nature of the 'problems' posed by cinema and its way of resolving them. Thus, from one filmmaker to another, from one aesthetic to another, there exist not only two confronting or opposing aesthetics, but two new signifying regimes and two new regimes of thought: the problematic regime and the theorematic regime – two regimes that affect the way we treat time and the way time affects us.

This analysis also reveals – thanks again to the S-A-T – the fundamental aspect of 'new cinema' as being not necessarily linked (only) to some technical or historical particularity, but as linked to a 'formal' characteristic of cinema in general, which alone can 'make (a) difference': what is the nature of the existing link between the film-image or better, the film-*thought*, and the world? Deleuze discovers that separating them is not so much any particular *worldly disagreement* as a 'break in the *sensory-motor link* (action-image) and *more profoundly* in the link between man and the world (great organic composition)' (Deleuze 1989: 173, my emphasis). We have here an archaeological or even a 'transcendental' discovery that 'makes a difference' because it is no longer a question now of negotiating the relationship of cinema to the world in psychological or practical terms, but is one of opening up a new field of thought: a pure 'psychic' field and situation and the specific modes of agency of op-signs and son-signs that must be mobilised by filmmakers if they are to be up to the task of facing a vision that will carry them off into an indefinite, like a becoming that is too powerful for them: the unthinkable![10] 'It's too beautiful! Too hard to take!' (Rossellini). 'Impossible to say! To formulate!' (Godard). Cinema of the seer.

In such conditions – and this is the contribution of the S-A-T – the work of an Eisenstein is characterised less by any formal 'tic' or 'ideologeme' than by the primacy he grants to a thought in which 'the internal relationships from principle to consequences' (Deleuze 1989: 174) would prevail. By contrast, the work of a Godard or a Pasolini is characterised by the 'problematic' character of the encounter of images (op-signs) and sounds (son-signs) with the 'world' that is to be privileged. This is brought about by the intervention of 'an event [this time] from the outside – removal, addition, cutting – which constitutes its own conditions and determines . . . the cases' (Deleuze 1989: 174). Thus cinema is no longer conceived of as a 'device' or an 'apparatus' allowing us to represent the world in a more or less realist or adequate way, but as an 'automaton' – in this it is called 'spiritual' – that allows us to 'bring the *unconscious mechanisms of thought* to consciousness' (Deleuze 1989: 160, my emphasis). These premises result in the radically different 'forms' or 'types' achieved according to the orientation – or 'choice' – one makes. A multiplicity of 'forms' corresponding to a variety of new 'beliefs' are presented, not necessarily in opposition to, but in addition to the Eisensteinian 'types': the *'unsummonable'* of Welles, the *'inexplicable'* of Robbegrillet, the *'undecidable'* of Resnais, the *'impossible'* of Duras, or again, the *'incommensurable'* of Godard, each accompanied by its own sensitivity to time (Deleuze 1989: 182, my emphasis). So many variations would have been impossible to bring to light as Deleuze likes to put it – without the *scanning* that made the S-A-T possible. They now appear as the *forms* or the effects of the intrinsic noetic *power* of cinema as 'spiritual automaton'.

Thanks to his operator, Deleuze would subsequently be able to show that the theoretical demand to ascribe a new status to the image in modern cinema corresponds to the necessity of reworking or re-evaluating the *rhetoric* that had prevailed in film theory before the discovery of the S-A-T. Indeed, at the same time that he tears the cinematographic image from the 'Narrative-Representative' field that held it the prisoner of an abstract or simply 'logical' thought, Deleuze discovers that what connects cinema to the outside of all representation could not have been intuited had not the logic presiding at the production of its objects remained unaffected.

If the *first aspect* of the revolution that altered cinema was the break in the 'sensory-motor link' and that between 'man and the world', the *second aspect* of this break, 'is the *abandoning of figures, metonymy as much as metaphor, and at a deeper level the dislocation of the internal monologue as descriptive material of the cinema*' (Deleuze 1989: 173, my emphasis). No more metaphors, no more metonymies, and still fewer 'interior monologues', not only because cinema would have become amorphous or undifferentiated or even insensible to 'poetry', but more profoundly, 'because the necessity which belongs to relations of thought in the image has replaced the contiguity of relations of images (shot–reverse shot)'. For example, the shot-reverse shot of classical cinema would henceforth be replaced by depth of field, the high-angle or low-angle shots of Welles or Astruc, the 'model' of Bresson, or the 'irrational cuts' of Godard or Pasolini, or even by the 'hyper-spatial figures' that no longer refer cinematic images to the allegedly 'familiar' representation of the world, but that refer instead to 'an outside which makes them pass into each other, like conical projections or metamorphoses' (Deleuze 1989: 173).

When perception is made up of pure op-signs and sounds, it no longer enters into relation with simple movement or action alone, but with a virtual image, 'a mental or mirror image', says Deleuze. The new 'automatism' would make the actual image and the virtual image blend to produce the 'crystal-image', always double, always intensified such as we find it in Renoir, Ophüls, Fellini. As Maurizio Grande has aptly shown in the fine study he devoted to Deleuze's work on cinema (1992), 'the crystal-image is a kind of *mirror-time*. In it, the real is always a present, but the present is the real image with, *in addition*, its own past rendered contemporaneous.' As 'spiritual automaton', cinema gives us an image that will no longer be 'cut off only from the thing and the body', 'not only *something else* with respect to representation, memory, and recognition, which maintain a physical relation to the sensory-motor schemes of action', but an image – 'hallucinatory' if you will – 'grasped in the very instant of its dissolution, in the instant of its crystallization in an immediate temporality, directed and without connection to any other thing having to do with the image formed in crystal-time' (Grande 1992: 61). This means that only the 'automatism' can enable us to think of cinema's contribution to our apprehension of time as the 'unhinging of images from the body and from reality', or 'time as *immediate image without possible body*, which translates as *Seeing* and as *Hallucination*' (Grande 1992: 61, my emphasis). The mode of crystallisation changes in each instance, but in each instance a new quality of Time and its layeredness [*nappé*] is experienced (R. Barthes). Deleuze situates the revolution that touched modern cinema in its essence in this 'unhinging' related to the body and to consciousness – as the 'originally synthetic apperception' of an I-Me-present-to-itself. For ever since it was raised to the power of the 'spiritual automaton', cinema reversed the relation of the subject to its body – in particular to its 'vision' – and its memory, because 'the image no longer derives from a perceiving (sleeping, memorizing . . .) body, nor from a brain-archive of data; the image sets the subject adrift, *sucking it into a trans-perceptive and "falsifying world"* ' (Grande 1992: 60, my emphasis).

Having become 'spiritual automaton' (non-dialectical 'machine'), cinema must also conquer a new force, one that will still make it an 'automaton', but this time, as an a-grammatical and a-rhetorical machine, a machine with the power to 'carry the image to the point where it becomes deductive and automatic, to substitute the formal linkages of thought for sensory-motor representative or figurative linkages' (Deleuze 1989: 174). For Deleuze, modern cinema is (or became) henceforth 'spiritual automaton' in that it can make the unrolling of film a true *theorem* instead of merely a pure association of images – 'it makes thought immanent to the image' (Deleuze 1989: 173). A direct product of the new 'automatism' traversing cinema, only this 'immanence' actually permits an understanding of the veritable 'mutation' that would come to affect other concepts in cinema and to change its economy.

Depth of field, for example, would no longer be situated in relation 'to obstacles or concealed things' – a still entirely 'mechanical' conception that reduces it to a technical feat or a simple aesthetic feature – 'but in relation to a light which makes us see beings and objects according to their opacity' (Deleuze 1989: 176). Because depth of field is an integral part of an open 'totality', it also has the 'mental effect of a theorem, it makes the unrolling of the film a theorem rather than an association of images, it makes thought immanent to the image'. Similarly, the sequence shot would no longer be merely one instrument among others for producing an action-image dominated by movement and the displacement of objects and beings in neutral space, but the 'instance' or 'viewpoint' of a *problem*. It is again due to the S-A-T that the notions of 'out-of-field' and 'false continuity' can be seen to adjust their new status in relation to a 'whole' that likewise undergoes a mutation, 'because it has ceased to be the One-Being, in order to become the constitutive "and" of things, the constitutive between-two of images'. Henceforth, the material automatism of images and sounds would no longer refer to the given world nor to a preformed psychological interiority, but would provoke from *outside* – an outside no longer homogeneous to exteriority – 'a thought which it imposes, as the unthinkable in our intellectual automatism'. The Whole would no longer be confused with a flat structure or 'model', but with what, referring to Blanchot, Deleuze calls 'the force of "dispersal of the Outside"' or 'the vertigo of spacing': cinema as the generator of a new 'chaosmos' and of half-actual, half-virtual crystal-images capable of letting us see once more a world that had itself become a 'hallucination'.

In the end, the S-A-T enables us to understand better the nature of the mutations that condition the eruption of an image and a thought no longer having anything to do with actual things or beings, but that relate, rather, to a purely optical and sonorous world that refers to virtual things and beings: a world to come, a world where the actual image and the virtual image have fused, giving birth to 'crystals' of unified time and space. In mobilising the noetic force of the S-A-T, these are the different *modes of the crystallisation of time* that Gilles Deleuze gave us to rethink so that we might better understand and better see (through) cinema. Yet, what we can 'see' thanks to the S-A-T – or thanks to 'the Mind's Eye,' to cite Deleuze once more – 'is Time, layers of time, a direct time-image that makes us able to grasp the mechanisms of thought' and thereby establish new links with the world – and to believe again in this world (Deleuze 1983: 38).

But 'to believe' here is not to rediscover the virtues of faith; no, it is, rather, to 'return discourse back to the body and thereby to reach the body before discourse, before words, before the naming of things' (Deleuze 1983: 38).

Translated by Denise L. Davis

References

Colombat, A. P. (1991), 'A Thousand Trails to Work with Deleuze', *SubStance. A Review of Theory and Literary Criticism*, 66: 10–24.

Couchot, E. (1988), *Image, de l'optique au numérique*, Paris: Hermes.

Couchot, E. (1998), *La technologie dans l'art. De la photographie à la réalité virtuelle*, Paris: editions Jacqueline Chambon.

Deleuze, G. (1983), 'La photographie est déjà tirée dans les choses', interview with P. Bonitzer and J. Narboni in *Cahiers du cinéma* 352, October: 38–40.

Deleuze, G. (1986a), *Cinéma 1*, trans. H. Tomlinson and B. Habberjam, Minneapolis: University of Minnesota Press.

Deleuze, G. (1986b), *Foucault*, trans. S. Hand, Minneapolis: University of Minnesota Press.

Deleuze, G. (1989), *Cinéma 2 (The Time-Image)*, trans. H. Tomlinson and R. Galeta, Minneapolis: University of Minnesota Press.

Deleuze, G. (1990), *Expressionism in Philosophy. Spinoza*, trans. M. Joughlin, New York: Zone Books.

Deleuze, G. and Guattari, F. (1987), *A Thousand Plateaus*, trans. B. Massumi, Minneapolis: University of Minnesota Press.

Deleuze, G. and Guattari, F. (1994), *What is Philosophy?*, trans. H. Tomlinson and G. Burchell, New York: Columbia University Press.

Dyens, O. (2001), *Metal and Flesh: The Evolution of Man-Technology Takes Over*, trans. E. J. Bibbee, Cambridge: MIT Press.

Grande, M. (1992), 'Le temps au miroir', in R. di Gaetano (ed.), *Deleuze. Penser le cinéma*, Rome: Quaderni di Cinema/Studio 1, Bulzoni Editore.

Rodowick, D. (1990), 'Reading the Figural, *Camera Obscura. A Journal of Feminism and Film Theory*, September.

Spinoza, B. (1992), *Ethics. Treatise on the Emendation of the Intellect, and Selected Letters*, trans. S. Shirley, ed. S. Feldman, Indianapolis: Hackett Publishing Company.

Notes

1. [The conceptual persona has nothing to do with an abstract personification, a symbol, or an allegory, because it lives, it insists.] The philosopher is the idiosyncrasy of his conceptual personae. The destiny of the philosopher is to become his conceptual persona or personae, at the same time that these personae themselves become something other than what they are historically, mythologically, or commonly (the Socrates of Plato, the Dionysus of Nietzsche, the idiot of Cusa). The conceptual persona is the becoming or the subject of a philosophy, on a par with the philosopher . . .'. (Deleuze and Guattari 1994: 64, my emphasis R. B.)

2. [W]hen he shows that our ideas are causes one of another, he deduces from this that all have as cause our power of knowing or thinking. It is above all the term 'spiritual automaton' that testifies to this unity. The soul is a kind of spiritual automaton, which is to say: In thinking we obey only the laws of thought, laws that determine both the form and the content of true ideas, and that make us produce ideas in sequence according to their own causes and through our own power, so that in knowing our power of understanding we know through their causes all the things that fall within this power. (Deleuze 1990: 140)

3. This 'moment' occupies the greatest part of the analyses in the first book and is presented as a rereading of Bergson as a philosopher of movement.

4. Which means, for Deleuze, as we will see below, non-dialectical, non-grammatical, and non-rhetorical.
5. I refer here to the fine analysis Deleuze proposed of the audio-visual complex as it works in Michel Foucault's thought. See Deleuze 1986: 94–123. David Rodowick shows the importance of the theoretical stakes for film theory of the confrontation between the regime of 'visibilities' and the regime of 'énoncés' in Foucault:

> Rather than closing in on itself, enunciation now obeys a centripetal force derived from the accelerated orbit of the expressible with respect to the increasing density of the visible. The velocity of regimes agitates énoncés like atoms in a particle accelerator. But what new elements – as concepts or possibilities of thought and imagination – will be created? What possibilities of liberation or alienation will they herald? (Rodowick 1990: 33)

Olivier Dyens' papers on 'cyberspace' and 'morphism' (2001) and Edmond Couchot's work on the 'virtual' image (1988 and 1998) give us an adequate idea of the new possibilities offered to cinema for thinking the relation of cinematographic images to the 'real'.
6. I will henceforth write S-A-T in order to keep its operative, that is 'machinic', dimension in mind: The 'spiritual automaton' as 'accelerator'. . . of concepts!
7. Or as this 'dismantled, paralyzed, petrified, frozen instance which testifies "the impossibility of thinking that is thought"' (Deleuze 1986b: 166).
8. In *The Time-Image*, we find another formula: 'The Whole can only be thought, because *it is the indirect representation of time which follows from movement*' (Deleuze 1989: 158, my emphasis, R. B.).
9. For a theoretically pointed discussion of these two regimes, see Deleuze 1989: 173f. and here, on page 174:

> The problematic is distinguished from the theorematic (or constructivism from the axiomatic) in that the theorem develops internal relationships from principle to consequences, while the problem introduces an event from the outside – removal, addition, cutting – which constitutes its own conditions and determines the 'case' or cases.

10. 'It is the material automatism of images,' writes Deleuze, 'which produces from the outside a thought which it imposes, as the unthinkable in our intellectual automatism' (Deleuze 1989: 178–9).

Chapter 9

Ahab and Becoming-Whale: The Nomadic Subject in Smooth Space

Tamsin Lorraine

The work of Gilles Deleuze develops a way of conceiving reality in terms of dynamic process that privileges difference rather than identity, movement rather than stasis, and change rather than what remains the same. This way of thinking challenges not only traditional ontologies focussed on the underlying essences of shifting appearances, but theories of space and time related to those ontologies. On Deleuze's view, common sense notions of space and time as totalised wholes within which everything can be either spatially or chronologically related with respect to everything else are no more than retrospective constructs. The movements of life are related to one another in heterogeneous blocks of space-time that defy such representation. Of course we can and do locate ourselves with respect to spatial constructs (grids of miles or metres, for example) or time-lines that we can coordinate with the spatial and temporal constructs of others. But on Deleuze's view, conscious experience, informed as it is by the spatial and temporal orientation of individuals as well as the coordination of individual experiences into a collective experience of a socially shared space and time, are the emergent effect of mostly imperceptible processes.

The normative subject of contemporary culture orients herself with respect to conventional notions of space and time. The 'nomadic' subject that appears in the work of Deleuze, and Deleuze's work with Félix Guattari, experiences and thinks space and time in terms of blocks of space-time that are not necessarily linked into a rational whole of measurable units. The transformation of the paranoid subject of contemporary culture into a schizo subject able to evolve creatively in interdependent communion with others requires not only relinquishing normative conceptions of self; it also requires rethinking the space-time coordinates of the conventional reality through which normative subjects orient themselves.

I explore the alternative conception of space that emerges in the concepts of heterogeneous blocks of space-time and smooth space developed by Deleuze and Guattari in *A Thousand Plateaus* (1987). Like Deleuze's concepts of the time-image in *Cinema 2* (1989) or the non-pulsed time of Aion in *The Logic of Sense* (1990), the concepts of blocks of space-time and smooth space challenge the reader not only to think but experience reality differently. In particular, they foster sensitivity to the spaces that might disrupt processes of what Deleuze and Guattari call 'territorialisation' that homogenise heterogeneous blocks of space-time into the regulated units of social space, thus opening up new possibilities in living. The nomadic subject open to unconventional spatial orientations can make new connections in keeping with the movement of life as it unfolds. I will consider the case of Ahab – the sea captain obsessed with chasing the great white whale, Moby-Dick – in order to explore the opportunities as well as the risks such experiments in living can entail.

Territories and the Refrain

Deleuze conceives of a body (be it physical or conceptual) as a set of habitually patterned forces that sustains itself through its powers to affect and be affected by the forces surrounding it. The non-personal powers to affect and be affected of the myriad processes of a human subject sustain patterns of the past in keeping with the conditions of the present. Conscious awareness – including the spatial orientation that inflects it – is the emergent effect of processes that are imperceptible as well as perceptible. Physical and symbolic processes comprise events or singularities – points at which critical thresholds are reached that result in a set of elements moving from one kind of state into another. Each state in the series of states that comprises the subject is a convergence of habitual patterns of these processes, relations of movement and rest, and capacities to affect and be affected that are either actual or potential. These states of relative equilibrium are always on the verge of shifting in keeping with shifting conditions that bring the elements of its patterns to thresholds that constitute shifts in patterns. These processes take place at levels below as well as above the threshold of awareness.

Painting, like other art forms, can alert us to the fragility of our spatial orientations. Artists can create monuments that evoke imperceptible forces that affect the body at a level typically below the threshold of normative consciousness. Thus, the brush-strokes of painters like Van Gogh and Francis Bacon bring our attention to micro-perceptions of the flesh that defy conventional notions of objects and their boundaries, including our own bodies as physical things occupying definite positions in space. In *What is Philosophy?* (1994) Deleuze and Guattari suggest that such painters depict the body as flesh that is opened onto a surrounding space – the 'house' (Deleuze and Guattari 1994: 179–81). This space or territory is a space of intimate exchange of the body with its immediate surroundings that allows the self-regulation of the organism that sustains its continued existence. This territory, in turn, opens onto the 'cosmos-universe' or the universe as whole. Opening the flesh to the cosmos-universe without the protective space of a house or personal territory would lead to the demise of the individual. Refusing any connection to the cosmos-universe except those permitted by one's territory can lead to deadening repetition. Art can 'think' our relationship to the universe in a way that can open us up to a reality beneath the threshold of conventional experience without completely destroying our spatial orientation in the process.

In *A Thousand Plateaus*, Deleuze and Guattari characterise territorial animals as natural artists who establish relations to imperceptible as well as perceptible forces through the refrains of song (birds) or movements and markings (wolves, rabbits) that create a kind of space of life-sustaining regularities within the chaotic space of the cosmos. Living organisms have interior milieus (cellular formation, organic functions) and exterior milieus (food to eat, water to drink, ground to walk on). 'Every milieu is vibratory, in other words, a block of space-time constituted by the periodic repetition of the component' (Deleuze and Guattari 1987: 313). All the milieus of the organism have their own patterns and these patterns interact with the patterns of the other milieus with which they communicate. The rhythm of the interactions between these different milieus 'does not operate in a homogeneous space-time, but by heterogeneous blocks' (Deleuze and Guattari 1987: 311). The periodic repetitions of the different milieus cannot be correlated according to the metre of regular time. Rhythm 'is the Unequal or the Incommensurable' of the differences among the periodic repetitions of distinct milieus. Thus, an organism emerges from chaos ('the milieu of all milieus') as vibratory milieus or blocks of space-time that create rhythms within the organism as well as with the milieus exterior to the organism. The refrain allows the territorialisation of milieus and rhythms that creates a home; the various rhythms of the body's components and their relations to interior and exterior blocks of space-time become homogenised into the lived experience of the organism. The organism as a self-regulating whole with its own spatial orientation can then be opened up to forces beyond it.

Deleuze and Guattari describe the initial emergence of a child's territories in *A Thousand Plateaus*:

A child in the dark, gripped with fear, comforts himself by singing under his breath. He walks and halts to his song. Lost, he takes shelter, or orients himself with his little song as best he can. The song is like a rough sketch of a calming and stabilizing, calm and stable, center in the heart of chaos. (Deleuze and Guattari 1987: 311)

It takes a while for a child to develop the sense of space through which she is able definitively to pinpoint different locations. Various kinds of refrains – of song, habitual activities, favourite words or phrases – help her to create a space that allows her to feel more at home. The spaces of sand and sun and water, grass and sky and trees, quilt and crib and room, are distinguishable not through the different locations they occupy (the Jersey shore located a two-hour drive from the backyard of a house that has her bedroom on the second floor), but through the different feelings and sensations associated with the routines that emerge in playing at the beach, walking in the backyard, and lying in bed. It takes the daily repetition of habitual activities (down the stairs to breakfast, up the stairs to bed) and repeated trips ('are we there yet?') before the different spaces of various activities can begin to be connected into one continuous and stable space. A rupture in the child's routine, a 'mistake in speed, rhythm, or harmony would be catastrophic because it would bring back the forces of chaos, destroying both creator and creation' (Deleuze and Guattari 1987: 311). The spaces of childhood not yet connected to the homogenised, regulated space of conventional reality is a fragile one. The patterns of bodily needs and satisfactions created in early infancy unfold into the rhythms of routines and habits that help the child to organise her surrounding environment into the enduring contours of home.

Individuals of all sorts need to sustain their power to affect and be affected. This requires maintaining patterns of self-regulation. But in addition to creating a space that allows one to sustain the comforting rhythms of familiar places, one must also be able to confront the new: 'one opens the circle a crack . . . One launches forth, hazards an improvisation. But to improvise is to join with the World, or meld with it. One ventures from home on the thread of a tune' (Deleuze and Guattari 1987: 311). Maintaining one's home-space requires repeating refrains that have become familiar, but to withstand the novel rhythms of life that always encroach, one must be able to improvise new refrains that bear some relationship to old rhythms. The normative subject of contemporary society tends to sustain itself through a form of self that staves off forms of repetition that entail continual becoming-other. In addition to the binary machines of personal and social identity (woman/man, daughter/son, black/white, Protestant/Jew), this means orienting one's experience of space and time in keeping with a socially sanctioned totalised whole of measurable units. Beneath the threshold of a reality represented through such coordinates are the heterogeneous space-times of the interior milieus of organic processes as well as the interactions of the milieus of the individual (symbolic as well as organic) with the myriad milieus with which it comes into contact. Deleuze and Guattari advocate the construction of nomadic 'lines of flight' in order to experiment with implicit connections currently imperceptible to the subject that could be actualised into new realities.

The nomadic subject able to supercede personal identity in keeping with virtual relations that defy conventional conceptions of space will perceive as well as think differently. Deleuze's notion of the virtual entails an unrepresentable reality conditioning what happens. A particular state of affairs occurs when bodies affect other bodies in specific ways. But bodies comprise more than what they actually do; they also comprise the potential to act differently given different circumstances. The virtual real is a transcendental field of virtual relations that exceed the constraints presented by actualised subjects and their objects.[1] If specific virtual relations actualise they result in states of affairs that exclude other states of affairs, but the excluded virtual relations still insist in what actualises with an implicit force that could yet unfold with a shift in circumstances. Both art and philosophy can foster nomadic subjectivity. Art creates 'percepts' to shake us out of our habitual responses to the world and open up other possibilities in perceiving and thinking by actualising virtual relations, thus rendering imperceptible forces perceptible. Philosophy or 'genuine thinking' (much of what passes for philosophical thought is, according to Deleuze, State thinking), actualises virtual relations of sense through the creation of concepts.[2] Deleuze and Guattari have created various concepts (for example, schizoanalysis, deterritorialisation, and constructing a body without organs) entailing the opening of individual self-sustaining patterns to dynamic flows of process that mutate those patterns into a becoming-other. But if such lines of flight are to lead to the proliferation of enlivening connections with the world rather than the demise of the individual (never mind the destruction of those around her), such construction must be done with care. It is never a matter of simply opening oneself to all the forces of the universe, but always of creatively evolving one's powers to affect and be affected by life in concert with surrounding forces.

The Smooth Space of Whale Hunting

Deleuze considers the implicit or virtual force of a process to be as important as its actual functioning. The singularities of a process have virtual relations with the singularities of other processes; when a process reaches a critical threshold that pushes it into another pattern of activity, thus actualising singularities that were previously only implicit, its power to affect and be affected changes as well. Herman Melville describes such a moment in his novel, *Moby-Dick*. When Ahab lies sick after losing his leg to the great white whale, he is forced into a period of inactivity. A critical threshold is reached, an 'interfusing' of body and soul that actualises a capacity in Ahab for becoming-whale.[3] From that point onward, he no longer merely hunts whales; he becomes obsessed with second-guessing the movements of one whale in order to enact his revenge. The virtual force of the other patterns processes could form is a dynamic aspect of present reality. Virtual powers of affecting and being affected are aspects of the past that constitute implicit forces of the present. These forces unfold in blocks of space-time that are only correlated to the space-times of others through territorialisation of mutant patterns into a regulated whole. If Ahab had territorialised the loss of his leg to that of a sea captain carrying out a job with certain risks, he would have pursued patterns of living – patterns of feeling, meaning, and action – that repeated refrains others could recognise. Instead, something – some configuration of forces at the physical and symbolic levels – pushes him to unfold the imperceptible force of implicit singularities into a course of action with a logic of its own.

In *A Thousand Plateaus*, Deleuze and Guattari say that, '[s]mooth space is filled by events or haecceities far more than by formed and perceived things. It is a space of affects, more than one of properties (Deleuze and Guattari 1987: 478–9). Smooth space is a space of multiplicities constructed through local operations involving changes of direction that may shift in keeping with the journey itself or the shifting nature of the journey's goal. Events of sense, haecceities, and affects are singularities of sense, movements, and sensation-emotion that retain their relations to the virtual real.[4] Human individuals as sentient language speakers with bodies that interact with other bodies are nodes of all three. An individual human being actualises specific configurations of meaning (Ahab is a sea captain, not an accountant), movement (Ahab on board a ship leaving Nantucket), and sensation-emotion (Ahab stands on deck determined to wreak revenge upon Moby-Dick). Events of sense, haecceities, and affects comprise virtual as well as actual relations of sense, movements, and sensations-emotions; they thus resonate with the virtual real where no power to affect or be affected has been excluded due to the specific forms an individual's life has taken.

What Deleuze in *Cinema 1* (1986) calls 'any-space-whatever' is a spatial haecceity freed from conventional location within a totality to which all spaces can be related. In the chaotic realm of the virtual, all movements are related to other movements. In a discussion of the concept of the movement-image inspired by Henri Bergson, Deleuze distinguishes movement from space: 'space covered is past, movement is present, the act of covering' (Deleuze 1986: 1). Spaces covered by movement are divisible and belong to a single, homogeneous space while movement 'cannot be divided without changing qualitatively each time it is divided' (Deleuze 1986: 1). Movements of what Deleuze and Guattari in *A Thousand Plateaus* call 'deterritorialisation', unfold with respect to one another rather than occurring within space as a void. They are acts of uncovering that are not referred to space conceived as a uniform area of measurable units within which changes occur.[5]

Organic life – including human life – requires sustained patterns where spatial relations are repeated. A haecceity is a specific configuration of relations that is individuated not through an absolute location in a space-time experienced or thought as a totalised whole, but rather through the relations themselves. When a film presents rain in a way that directs our attention to, 'not what rain really is, but the way in which it appears when, silent and continuous, it drips from leaf to leaf', it presents neither the concept of rain or the state of a rainy time and place.[6] Instead the rain 'is a set of singularities which presents the rain as it is in itself, pure power or quality which combines without abstraction all possible rains and makes up the corresponding any-space-whatever' (Deleuze 1986: 111). Cinema can 'think' things as they are in themselves by presenting them in relation to a virtual real rather than familiar activities (the camera zooms in, allowing our attention to linger upon the raindrops glistening on a leaf). We can then experience rain beyond the conventional refrains we attach to our personal selves. The haecceity of a rain event is not tied to a conventionally demarcated space located in a homogenised whole. Instead, it forms a link to other spaces that evoke a similar set of relations – a repetition of the configuration of molecules of water and air with their potential as well as actual capacities to affect and be affected (the raindrops glistening on the leaf evoke not how many miles I will have to walk to get home, but an infinitely variable configuration of leaf and rain that comprise the events of 'being rain', 'glistening', and 'being a leaf' in shifting context with other bodies that can affect or be affected by them).

A human individual can orient herself on a trip up a coastline in terms of the longitude and latitudes mapped out through social convention or through following the contours of rock and beach she discovers as she goes. In the former case, her local movements are charted with respect to already specified points (thus imposing a plane of organisation upon the movements that unfold). In the latter case, her space shifts at each moment as the multiplicities of which she is a part shift (rocks-sea-ship to sandy-beach-curved-in-sea-ship). Deleuze and Guattari advocate thinking of life in terms of multiplicities: 'Multiplicities are defined by the outside: by the abstract line, the line of flight or deterritorialisation according to which they change in nature and connect with other multiplicities. The plane of consistency (grid) is the outside of all multiplicities' (Deleuze and Guattari 1987: 9). A shift in multiplicities does not occur *in* space; rather it establishes a different configuration of the relations of processes in movement: slowly-evolving-rocks-choppy-sea-gliding-ship to relatively-faster-moving-sand-calmer-waters-ship-almost-at-a-standstill:

> Pure relations of speed and slowness between particles imply movements of deterritorialisation, just as pure affects imply an enterprise of desubjectification . . . The plane of organisation is constantly working away at the plane of consistency, always trying to plug the lines of flight, stop or interrupt the movements of deterritorialisation, weigh them down, restratify them, reconstitute forms and subjects in a dimension of depth. Conversely, the plane of consistency is constantly extricating itself from the plane of organisation, causing particles to spin off the strata, scrambling forms by dint of speed or slowness, breaking down functions by means of assemblages or microassemblages. But once again, so much caution is needed to prevent the plane of consistency from becoming a pure plane of abolition or death, to prevent the involution from turning into a regression to the undifferentiated. (Deleuze and Guattari 1987: 269–70)

A subject who orients herself with respect to movements rather than a retrospectively created construct of space actualises configurations of singularities that never settle into any one pattern. She experiences space not in terms of a totality to which it is connected (I walk across the lawn near the park and the highway), but rather pure relations of speed and slowness (grass under moving feet as wind lifts hair) that evoke powers to affect and be affected, both actual and potential (feet pushing against ground, could push off the ground or run). Pure affects are intensities – capacities to affect and be affected – not yet subjected to the homogenising dictates of conscious awareness.[7] Once an affect is experienced as a feeling or thought, it has already undergone a process of selection where some of its capacities have been emphasised at the expense of others. The nomadic subject is able to experience space in terms of haecceities and thus lengthen the gap between perception and action in order to resonate with imperceptible forces of affect. This can, in turn, lead to a creative response uniquely suited to the actual and virtual relations of the present situation rather than a repetition of habitual patterns of action developed in the past.

The whale hunting of the nineteenth century Herman Melville describes in *Moby-Dick* constitutes a multiplicity of men, ships and sea, that for the most part operates in smooth space. Unlike ships or planes with specific destinations and set schedules, the whaling ships of Nantucket deliberately cruise some of the most isolated waters of the globe in pursuit of the whale oil through which the ships' owners can make a profit. Although the captains of whaling ships make use of a quadrant by which they can ascertain their position according to fixed points of latitude and longitude, for the most part, life on a ship plays out in the unmarked space of the open sea. Although the set goal of a whale hunting venture is obtaining whale oil, the hunting of whales must unfold in keeping with the movement of the whales themselves. The ships go to the waters most likely to be frequented by whales, set their itineraries in keeping with whale sightings, and pursue the whales with which they actually cross paths. Waves play across the sea's surface or die down in rhythm with changing winds and currents. Whales travel great distances in their ceaseless search for food. Work on the ship is reoriented from day to day in keeping with shifting configurations of the ship, crew, sea, weather and whales.

Melville stresses the risky nature of the work; the tasks required to hunt a whale and extract its oil are so perilous that one false move at any point along the way means death to the men involved. Members of the crew must be prepared to improvise in keeping with shifting conditions. Ships are out at sea for years at a time, only receiving news and the occasional letter from home through chance meetings with other whaling ships. The sighting of a whale or another ship is relative to the movements of both the whale or ship and one's own ship. Days are marked in terms of whales caught, barrels filled with oil, number of whales sighted, or the occasional encounter with another ship. The seamen create a tenuous home on a ship open to the cosmic forces of the sea. As individual organisms with specific spatial orientations, the disparate space-time blocks of their bodies have been homogenised into distinct wholes. Melville presents the members of the crew as colourful personalities, each with a unique perspective of his own. The social space they share is created through tactile relations with one another and their environment in rhythms that unfold among them. They locate themselves not with respect to the town hall or church to which all the members of their town – whether they know them or not – have an ascertainable spatial relationship, but rather to the men with whom they work, the tasks they have to perform, and the whales (always in motion on an ever-changing sea) they pursue. They orient themselves less in terms of homogeneous space or chronological time than in terms of the shifting multiplicities of which they are a part.

Ahab is distinguished from his motley crew less by his eccentricities than the dangerous direction they have taken. Although at first his obsession with avenging himself against Moby-Dick is compatible with rhythms established by years of whale hunting, when Ahab relinquishes the 'scientific' use of the quadrant in navigating his space, he is well on his way to forsaking his men as well as himself for the sake of his obsession. By entering into a becoming-whale, Ahab risks the territorial refrains of whale hunting and becomes an anomalous member of the pack of whale hunters (Deleuze and Guattari 1987: 244–5); he still unfolds his actions in keeping with established rhythms of work, but those rhythms begin to deviate into ever more aberrant patterns. When Ahab abandons the quadrant, he abandons an already tenuous tie with the striated space of conventional life to pursue the smooth space of the nomadic subject to the limit point of the whale hunting multiplicity of which he is a part.

Ahab's reaction to the loss of his leg takes the form of a desubjectified affect – an intensity that has consequences for how one experiences a situation and thus for one's actions, but which is itself beyond the reach of conscious awareness. This 'irrational' rupture in his experience of conventional reality intimates the virtual real; his obsessive quest for vengeance has tapped into a virtual conjunction that resonates with what could be as well as what is. This deepening of the feeling of personal revenge into something larger constitutes a lengthening of the gap between perception and action that allows Ahab to resonate with the virtual real. Ahab experiences the space-time between the loss of his leg and the act that will avenge it as a virtual whole into which all possibilities – both rational and irrational – are telescoped. He attempts not simply to avenge himself, but to manifest the creative forces with which he resonates. He remembers his fateful encounter with Moby-Dick not in terms of the particular longitude and latitude where he lost his leg, but in terms of a space-time beyond representation. The wind on his face and the movement of the ship each time he stands on deck, sights a whale, or orders the lowering of the boats in pursuit of a whale resonate with the virtual relations of the fateful encounter as well as the actual effects of losing a leg.

Ahab's response to his engagement with Moby-Dick is one that defies description – he is inspired not by feelings that he can share, but by intensities that resonate with virtual relations not yet actualised. These imperceptible forces push him to do the unthinkable in defiance of the engrained patterns of years in his profession. He risks everything in order to find the act that can do justice to the intensities of his experience. As Ahab dies (thrown into the sea by the harpoon rope caught around his neck), his ship (having been attacked by Moby-Dick) goes down, killing everyone on board except Ishmael, the narrator of the book. Thus Ahab's line of flight, despite the intensity of its creative force, succeeds only in destroying his ship, his crew and himself.

When we locate things in terms of a conventional notion of space and time their identities can be fixed. A subject thinking according to the classic image of thought posits, 'the Whole as the final ground of being or all-encompassing horizon, and the Subject as the principle that converts being into being-for-us' (Deleuze and Guattari 1987: 379). This entails a 'striated mental space' in which 'all the varieties of the real and true find their place' (Deleuze and Guattari 1987: 379). This subject navigates a regulated space with coordinates that can identify objects. The nomadic subject who navigates smooth space 'does things differently'; she orients herself vis-à-vis a singular race rather than a universal thinking subject, and a horizonless milieu rather than an all-encompassing totality: 'A tribe in the desert instead of a universal subject within the horizon of all-encompassing Being' (Deleuze and Guattari 1987: 379).

Ahab is no longer the universal subject – the sea captain who surveys his ship and the ocean in terms of a totality within which he has a specific location. In his becoming-other he becomes many selves all of whom are connected only by the continuity of a line of becoming. His perceptions, affective responses and actions are no longer consolidated in terms of a self that remains the same over time with a specific location in a totalised space. The singularities selected to actualise – haecceities of movements, affects or intensities that constitute virtual relations in capacities to affect or be affected, and events of sense – follow aberrant lines and ametrical rhythms in defiance of conventional space, emotional reactions, or meanings. Ahab does not intend to destroy his ship, his men and himself. Despite his obsession, he attends to his duties for as long as he is able. Once Ahab passes a critical threshold, however, he no longer relates to his situation in terms of a personal self. He is a becoming-whale. He is a configuration of physical and symbolic forces tapped into a virtual real unfolding forces that were previously only implicit at the expense of the conventional meanings his life could be given. He thus orients himself not with respect to patterns of living already enacted in the past (for example, those of being the captain of a whale hunting ship) or the homogenised space-times of conventional life, but rather in keeping with haecceities and events freed from the regulations of normative expectations.

Becoming-Other and the Virtual Past

Deleuze's conception of individuality suggests that the self as a kind of thing with certain attributes is no more than a state of relative equilibrium comprising a convergence of multiple lines of force of myriad and heterogeneous elements that is always about to move into another state. These lines of force, for language speakers like ourselves, are composed of symbolic as well as physical elements. Just as a physical body can be at rest and a person feel a moment of stability as a self, so can a belief or obsession propel a body into motion. To conceive of the individual in terms of one of its states of equilibrium is to deny its immersion in a world of becoming where it both affects and is affected by other forms of becoming. Normative subjectivity tends to emphasise states of equilibrium and assimilate its space and time to socially recognisable coordinates. A grid-like conception of space suggests fixed coordinates with respect to which any and all movement can be mapped. This allows us to conceive of space as a uniform void inhabited by a shared reality. A chronological conception of time suggests a temporal grid of instants that allows the coordination of different temporal perspectives according to a set of logically compatible happenings. This allows us to conceive of the world in terms of static entities that can be located within a homogeneous container of time in the way that static objects can be located in space conceived as an empty container. Ahab, as a nomadic subject following a line of flight that changes the nature of the whale hunting multiplicity, experiences a deterritorialised space and time. It is the anomolous nature of the space-time block he shares with Moby-Dick that allows him to free himself from the refrains of life marked out with others. His example demonstrates just how enticing – and how risky – entering deterritorialised space-times can be.

Deleuze's (and Guattari's) notion of the virtual challenges conventional understandings of time. The past as a transcendental field of virtual relations includes relations that defy chronology; Ahab's trauma may have happened in the past, but in his obsessive pursuit of Moby-

Dick it is as if that past moment and the present are directly linked. For Deleuze, the past is always present – it insists in the present configuration of forces that inform our situation with virtual forces that may unfold in more than one way. Like the processes of a body or the speech patterns of a poem being read aloud, the past is brought into the present through the force of implicit patterns and relations that are never actualised as well as those that are. This past is not the representable past of a collective history, but a non-personal past that exceeds any narrative of a recognisable set of identities. And yet a novel, a painting, a theory can release some of these virtual possibilities by acting as a vector of force entering into a field of forces with unprecedented effects.

Deleuze's (and Guattari's) notion of the virtual likewise challenges conventional understandings of space. The transcendental field of the virtual relations of movements include relations that defy the notion of space as a universal grid within which objects can be located. Just as the events of sense have virtual relations that may never be actualised in an embodied thinker, so do spatial haecceities have virtual relations that insist in the experience of embodied perceivers even if they are imperceptible. While the normative subject experiences the perceptible reality of conventional space and time, the nomadic subject resonates with the imperceptible relations implicit in her experience. After Ahab's shift into obsession, he experienced each movement of his ship and cresting of a wave as a haecceity resonant with the force of space as a virtual whole; instead of a void within which he hunted a whale, his space was experienced in terms of haecceities resonant with the unrepresentable force of the virtual reality that condition any given whale hunt. Symbolic vectors converge with the forces of bodies, cities, states and the environment in ways that can consolidate habitual repetitions or set new patterns into motion. Deleuze's (and Guattari's) nomadic subject can orient herself through the establishment of 'refrains' that may creatively differ from established norms (Deleuze and Guattari 1987: 310–50). A nomadic style of subjectivity consists in the unfolding of patterns that are not referred to an external plan of organisation or conventional notions of space and time, but rather evolve from the force of patterns immanent to the individual in its specific milieu.

Ahab's encounter with Moby-Dick in conjunction with his years in the smooth space of life on sea led to the actualisation of a line of flight that unfolded according to a logic increasingly foreign to those around him – with disastrous results. One lesson one might take from this example is that it is by living in the shared block of homogenised space-time that we are able to coordinate a life we can live together. And yet, despite the horror of a path of action that destroyed not just Ahab, but his ship and crew, there is something about Ahab that fascinates us. The virtual real is always with us, no matter how regulated our lives become. Unmeasured and unmeasurable spaces beckon us beyond the reassuringly familiar spaces of our shared reality. For Deleuze, mutant spaces are always right here with us, beckoning us to take risks in our thinking as well as our living. It is such experiments in living, despite the risks they entail, that can, if we are careful, help us to evolve creatively with the becoming-other of life.

The nomadic subject orients herself not through the already established norms of socially sanctioned thresholds, but rather through the events of sense and haecceities of enfleshed memory. As Rosi Braidotti puts it:

> This intensive, zig-zagging, cyclical, and messy type of re-membering does not even aim at retrieving information in a linear manner. It simply intuitively endures . . . It destabilizes identity by opening up spaces where virtual possibilities can be actualised. It's a sort of empowerment of all that was not programmed within the dominant memory. (Braidotti 2002: 399)

Deleuze's approach entails attending to the imperceptible forces of meaning, of our bodies, and of the world around us in order to respond creatively to our situation in a way that is fully resonant with the present as well as the virtual past insisting in that present. In *Difference and Repetition*, Deleuze suggests that chronological time is rooted in the habitual contractions of organic response and he characterises a kind of time, the third synthesis of time, that entails superseding automatic responses in order to draw upon the generative field of the virtual. The subject able to live this third synthesis of time would change with time itself rather than mark out her movements with respect to a measurable chronology. Just as living the temporality of the third synthesis of time fosters a nomadic subject more interested in creative evolution than preserving a normative self, so does living the spatiality of smooth space foster creative attunement to aspects of our spatiality that defy regulation.

Where Ahab failed was not in his willingness to open himself to imperceptible forces in defiance of a homogenised space-time lived with others, but rather in his inability to allow his experiments to resonate with the experiments of others in a shared flight that took the enfleshed and symbolic memories of a community into account. He experiences his pursuit of Moby-Dick as something unique, an event stripped of its habitual connections to other whale hunts and instead resonating with unprecedented possibilities. Ahab's revenge is not just any revenge, but a revenge so singular that his own life, as well as the lives of his men, becomes trivial in comparison. The haecceity of harpoon hitting whale includes everything of importance to Ahab; it resonates with all the places and all the moments when he confronted – or did not confront – his deepest longings and deepest fears. In his obsessive quest for revenge, Ahab entered a smooth space constituted in relation to Moby-Dick. Ahab's spatial orientations were thus, in a sense, reduced from the smooth space created in relation to his ship and crew as well as the surrounding environment to those relations of movements concerning his own becoming-whale. Despite Ahab's openness to forces beyond the territorial confines of the established refrains of whale hunting, he is strangely isolated. His obsessive focus on Moby-Dick – a whale with which he is in actual contact for only short periods of time – excludes the force of his daily interactions with the men and environment of his daily life.

For a more constructive example of a nomadic subject on a line of flight with an alternative spatial and temporal orientation, we may need to turn to Virginia Woolf for guidance, who, according to Deleuze and Guattari:

> says that it is necessary to 'saturate every atom', and to do that it is necessary to eliminate, to eliminate all that is resemblance and analogy, but also 'to put everything into it': eliminate everything that exceeds the moment, but put in everything that it includes – and the moment is not the instantaneous, it is the haecceity into which one slips and that slips into other haecceities by transparency . . . One is then like grass: one has made the world, everybody/everything, into a becoming, because one has made a necessarily communicating world, because one has suppressed in oneself everything that prevents us from slipping between things and growing in the midst of things . . . Saturate, eliminate, put everything in. (Deleuze and Guattari 1987: 280)

Ahab's experience of space deepened to include not just the path of a voyage he had done before, but haecceities of whale and sea and ship resonant with spaces he had never experienced as well as those he had. Ahab may have been successful at eliminating resemblance and analogy (the refrains that might have normalised his behaviour) from his situation, but he failed to saturate his world with everything it included. Ahab experienced space in terms of pure relations of movements rather than a retrospective construct of a socially shared space, but the space-time block of Ahab and Moby-Dick excluded the improvised rhythms of Ahab's men. Thus the refrains connecting Ahab to humanity mutated and his becoming-other became a path of destruction rather than a creative evolution that could disseminate throughout the social field.

Any spatial orientation entails the territorialisation of distinct milieus into one whole, and thus the actualisation of specific singularities at the expense of others. As creatures of becoming we must improvise the rhythms that keep us connected with life without completely deterritorialising from the refrains that sustain our homes. The striations of a totalised space provide a collective refrain that may either drown out or help harmonise our improvisations. But the striated space of conventional spatial orientations is not the only alternative. The refrains we evolve in the improvisations of daily interactions could unfold a smooth space through 'an infinite succession of linkages and changes in direction' that create shifting mosaics of space-times out of the heterogeneous blocks of different milieus (Deleuze and Guattari 1987: 494). To saturate the moment, we must be willing to relinquish our attempts to embody the power of life as individuals and mutate our lines of flight in keeping with the improvisations of those around us. Attuning ourselves to life-as-becoming requires disorienting ourselves from established spatial norms in order to attend to spaces unfolded in the play of movement. But if we are not to destroy ourselves in the process, it also requires that our smooth spaces be created from the ametrical space-times of an open-ended humanity that we can unfold together.

References

Braidotti, R. (2002), *Metamorphoses: Towards a Materialist Theory of Becoming*, Cambridge: Polity Press.

Colebrook, C. (2002), *Gilles Deleuze*, New York: Routledge.

Deleuze, G. (1986), *Cinema 1: The Movement-Image*, trans. H. Tomlinson and B. Habberjam, Minneapolis: University of Minnesota Press.

Deleuze, G. (1989), *Cinema 2: The Time-Image*, trans. H. Tomlinson and R. Galeta, Minneapolis: University of Minnesota Press.

Deleuze, G. (1990), *The Logic of Sense*, trans. M. Lester, New York: Columbia University Press.

Deleuze, G. (1991), *Bergsonism*, trans. H. Tomlinson and B. Habberjam, New York: Zone Books.

Deleuze, G. (1994), *Difference and Repetition*, trans. P. Patton, New York: Columbia University Press.

Deleuze, G. (2001), *Pure Immanence: Essays on a Life*, trans. A. Boyman, New York: Zone Books.

Deleuze, G. (2003), *Francis Bacon: The Logic of Sensation*, trans. D. W. Smith, Minneapolis: University of Minnesota Press.

Deleuze, G. and Guattari, F. (1983), *Anti-Oedipus: Capitalism and Schizophrenia*, trans. R. Hurley, M. Seem, H. R. Lane, Minneapolis: University of Minnesota Press.

Deleuze, G. and Guattari, F. (1987), *A Thousand Plateaus: Capitalism and Schizophrenia*, trans. B. Massumi, Minneapolis: University of Minnesota Press.

Deleuze, G. and Guattari, F. (1994), *What Is Philosophy?*, trans. H. Tomlinson and G. Burchell, New York: Columbia University Press.

Massumi, B. (2002), *Parables for the Virtual: Movement, Affect, Sensation*, Durham: Duke University Press.

Melville, H. (1967), *Moby-Dick*, New York: Bantam Books.

Notes

1. Deleuze develops the notion of the virtual throughout his work. For example, see Deleuze 1991: 42–3, 82–3; Deleuze 1994: 207–14; Deleuze and Guattari 1994: 156–7; and Deleuze 2001: 25–33. For some recent helpful commentary, see Colebrook 2002: 97 and Massumi 2002 generally.
2. Among the forces affecting human existence is the force of sense. Deleuze (and Guattari) think of the sense of language as a virtual field that is actualised in the concrete words of embodied individuals. Concepts are events of philosophical thinking that 'hover' over concrete states of affairs; their sense can never be exhausted in a specific use of a term, but unfolds in concrete meanings actualised in shifting contexts. Specific meanings come into play when I think, speak, or write, but there are always other meanings virtually implicit in language that could be actualised.
3. To put it in Melville's words:

   > [E]ver since that almost fatal encounter, Ahab had cherished a wild vindictiveness against the whale, all the more fell for that in his frantic morbidness he at last came to identify with him, not only all his bodily woes, but all his intellectual and spiritual exasperations. The White Whale swam before him as the monomaniac incarnation of all those malicious agencies which some deep men feel eating in them, till they are left living on with half a heart and half a lung . . . [W]hen by this collision forced to turn towards home, and for long months of days and weeks, Ahab and anguish lay stretched together in one hammock, rounding in mid winter that dreary, howling Patagonian Cape; then it was, that his torn body and gashed soul bled into one another; and so interfusing, made him mad. (Melville 1967: 175)

4. In *The Logic of Sense*, Deleuze distinguishes events of sense from specific propositions and states of affairs. An event of sense – 'to hunt whales' – can be applied to any number of whale-hunting situations. Events are pure becomings that Deleuze aligns with an alternative conception of time – the time of Aion, 'the time of the pure event or of becoming, which articulates relative speeds and slownesses independently of the chronometric or chronological values that time assumes in the other modes' (Deleuze and Guattari 1987: 263). In the time of Aion events are connected in the incompossible whole of duration or the virtual real.
5. For a helpful description of the Bergsonian notion of space as a retrospective construct, see Massumi 2002: 6.
6. Deleuze 1986: 110, quoting Béla Balàzs.
7. See Brian Massumi's excellent and intriguing account of affects in 'The Autonomy of Affect' (2002: 23–45).

Chapter 10

Transcendental Aesthetics: Deleuze's Philosophy of Space

Gregory Flaxman

> Representation has only a single center, a unique and receding perspective, and in consequence a false depth. It mediates everything but mobilizes and moves nothing.
>
> Deleuze, *Difference and Repetition*

The Problem with Space

If space constitutes one of the most perplexing and elusive concepts in all of Gilles Deleuze's philosophy, this is undoubtedly because its conceptualisation never amounts to any kind of traditional definition. Even as Deleuze develops a whole variety of spatial modalities, from the 'smooth and striated' to the 'molar and molecular' to the 'derived and descriptive',[1] these discussions only serve to confuse any more general sense of space. What can we say with certainty about what Deleuze means by space *in itself*? We might respond here by suggesting that this question, auguring as it does the imposition of an overarching theory, promising the definition of space as a grand determination or metaphysical category, presupposes the very regime of representation to which Deleuze is opposed. From his earliest monographs on minor philosophers to his final elaborations of a philosophy of immanence, Deleuze never ceases to insist that representation begins by grafting order onto 'the delicate milieus of overlapping perspectives, of communicating distances, divergences and disparities, of heterogeneous potentials and intensities' (Deleuze 1997: 50).[2] In other words, representation swindles us of the very experience of difference, especially the difference of space, and for this reason the more apt question with which we might begin is this: how can we understand space in the context of Deleuze's desire to deterritorialise the ground (*Abgrund*) of representation and, thence, the regulated and regular determination of all perception?

Deleuze's work offers countless different lines of approach to this problem, but the project to open space to the intensity of differences, or rather to restore difference to space, can be most clearly understood by considering the way that Deleuze addresses Kant's critical philosophy. In part, the reason for this lies in Deleuze's own diagnosis of the malady of representation, the multifarious symptoms of which always include a return to the subject-form and, concomitantly, the elaboration of experience itself around certain inviolable conditions of possibility. Indeed, Kant appears to determine space according to these very principles of representation, such that the analysis of *a priori* principles (the subject) ensures space as the form of all appearance (the object) – and yet, Deleuze seems to suggest that were it not for certain stubborn predispositions, Kant might have hit upon the constituents for liberating space from its servitude to representation. In this respect, Deleuze not only returns to Kant's sense of space but seeks to transform its transcendental project by submitting the designation of internal forms and external objects to a radical revision: in effect, we might say that Deleuze dissolves the mutually reinforced separation of inside and outside, *Innenvelt* and *Umvelt*, so that we have neither a determinate space to inhabit nor determinate principles of space to inhabit us. In these circumstances, when the very concept of space is no longer sustainable, Deleuze presents the challenge of future philosophy, namely, to find new determinations with which to characterise the immanence of perception and thought.

Space without Sensation

Following in the tradition established by Nietzsche, Deleuze's attack on representation musters both its forcefulness and nuance by returning to the status of aesthetics in the metaphysical tradition. Most appreciably in *Difference and Repetition* but also elsewhere, Deleuze laments that the regime of representation tends to relegate aesthetics to the domain of possible experience. 'It is strange that aesthetics (as the science of the sensible) could be founded on what can be represented,' Deleuze muses (Deleuze 1997: 56). In other words, what Deleuze finds so strange is that philosophers would eschew sensation itself, or what he calls 'the reality of the real insofar as it is thought', and choose instead to consider, 'the categories defined as conditions of possible experience' (Deleuze 1997: 68). Signs of this aesthetic turn can be detected across a vast philosophical landscape, but like an earthquake whose tremors can be traced back to a great epicentre, so too can we trace this tradition to the project of Kantian metaphysics. In the *Critique of Pure Reason*, Kant announces that speculative reason must begin by cleansing judgement of the taint of all empiricism. For this reason, he adds, we must disavow the tradition of aesthetics that sought to reflect upon actual sensation under the auspices of taste:

> The Germans are the only people who currently make use of the word 'aesthetic' in order to signify what others call the critique of taste. This usage originated in the abortive attempt made by Baumgarten, that admirable analytical thinker, to bring the critical treatment of the beautiful under rational principles, and so to raise its rules to the rank of a science. But such endeavours are fruitless. The said rules of criteria are, as regards their chief sources, merely empirical, and consequently cannot serve as determinate a priori laws by which our judgments of taste must be directed. (Kant 1965: 66).

While critics invariably read this passage, arguably Kant's most famous footnote, in light of the remarkable change of heart that marks the subsequent *Critique of Judgment*, we need not look past the *Critique of Pure Reason* to feel a disquieting sense of contradiction. Kant's censure of all 'merely empirical' judgements adorns the text's opening section, the 'Transcendental Aesthetic', which purports to describe the means of our immediate (intuitive) relation to the world. Insofar as knowledge begins with sensation, Kant explains, the mind must be 'affected in a certain way' in order to provide the substance of thinking: 'Objects are *given* to us by means of sensibility, and it alone yields us *intuitions*; they are *thought* through the understanding, and from the understanding arise *concepts*' (Kant 1965: 65). Having said as much, however, the key to understanding the transcendental aesthetic emerges when we grasp that sensation is immediately differentiated from the means of its subjective sensibility. In his primer on *Kant's Critical Philosophy* (1963), Deleuze marks this distinction within the very notion of representation, cautioning that we must always discriminate between what is presented to us *qua* the sensible diversity of phenomena and the conditions of those presentations *qua* 'the pure forms of our intuition and our sensibility' (Deleuze 1990: 8).

Thus, while the *Critique of Pure Reason* begins by acknowledging sensation, this acknowledgement in turn provokes a consideration of our formal capacity to be affected: Kant displaces the consideration of actual sensations, which suffer from the vicissitudes of empirical circumstances and judgements, with an elaboration of the transcendental conditions of possibility defining what can be represented. The transcendental aesthetic extinguishes both the marks of empirical experience and of logical (or 'discursive') understanding in order to isolate the 'subjective constitution of our mind' (Kant 1965: 68), the very ground according to which we experience the world. This is the point to which our discussion has been driving, since we have finally arrived at the juncture when Kant's aesthetic can be understood as a particular means of elaborating the concept of space. In other words, we could say that the delimitation of aesthetics as a 'science of the sensible' determines space not as a singular arrangement or aggregate of sensations but, rather, as the form in which sensations can take place. 'In the transcendental aesthetic we shall, there-fore, first isolate sensibility,' Kant explains, the result of which is that we find, 'that there are two pure forms of sensible intuition, serving as prin-ciples of a priori knowledge, namely, space and time' (Kant 1965: 67). Far from being a simple existent characterising the world at large, space is defined (along with time) as the subjective form that precedes all such experience, and without this form the actual experience of space would be utterly meaningless; as Kant reasons, the absence of space is unimag-inable because space is the ground of all appearances.

Inner and Outer Sense

In order truly to understand the complexity of Deleuze's attempt to deter-ritorialise the ground of representation, which is by no means a simple repudiation of Kant's critical philosophy, we might begin here by consid-ering how the latter defines the form of space in light of the form of time. The reason for this lies in the critical divergence these forms undergo in the first *Critique* despite their ostensible symmetry. Indeed, the transcen-dental aesthetic initially appears to have divvied up the field of represen-tation between space and time, and this sense of proportion would seem to be confirmed by Kant's correlation of these determinations, respec-tively, with 'outer sense' and 'inner sense'. While these terms are more nebulous than they appear, we might follow Henry Allison here when he explains that 'by "outer sense" is meant a sense through which one can become perceptually aware of objects as distinct from the self and its states. Similarly, by "inner sense" is meant a sense through which one can become perceptually aware of the self and its states' (Allison 1983: 83). Thus, space is defined as the sense by which, 'we represent to our-selves objects outside us', and likewise time is defined as the sense by which, 'the mind intuits itself or its inner state' (Kant 1965: 67). The problem with this formulation, no less with the whole sense of symme-try pervading the transcendental aesthetic, is that objects outside of us ('*ausser mir*'), while in space, are no less in time. Whether representa-tions, 'have for their objects outer things or not', they all qualify as, 'determinations of the mind' that belong to our inner sense, that is, time. Thus, whereas space, 'serves as the *a priori* condition only of outer appearances', time 'is the formal *a priori* condition of all appearances' (Kant 1965: 77).

Readers of Deleuze will likely recall the various occasions on which he celebrates the 'great Kantian reversal' of time, and in large part the justification for anointing such a revolution can be traced back to the peculiar status of time as both inner and outer sense.[3] On the one hand, Deleuze credits Kant with reversing the ancient subordination of time to space, such that time is no longer defined according to, 'the cardinal points through which the periodical movements that it measures pass' (Deleuze 1990: vii). Freed from its identification with movement, time becomes, 'the form of everything that changes and moves'. On the other hand, though, we have already seen that this reversal is predicated upon an understanding of the subject according to which time also serves as the form of inner sense, of our inner perceptions and changing states. Unlike the exposition of space, which implicates subject and object in a mutually separated distinction, the exposition of time elaborates the imbrication of outer sense and inner sense. Yes, time lays the groundwork for outer appearances, such that time is no longer simply tantamount to a mode of succession or movement, but this only occurs because time migrates into the subject, running like a crack or fault line through the transcendental structure. When Kant says that time, 'is nothing but the form of inner sense, that is, of the intuition of ourselves and our inner state', we must understand him to mean that the empirical ego itself is bathed in time, affected by the waves and fluctuations of time and, thereby, divided from the ideality of apperception (the 'I') which demands the syntheses of time (Kant 1965: 77).[4]

Is it possible to imagine a correlative revolution of space? In the preface to *Kant's Critical Philosophy*, Deleuze observes that the definition of sensibility henceforth entails that, '[b]oth space and time have to find completely new determinations', as if to suggest that the transcendental aesthetic had liberated space as well.[5] But by the time that Deleuze returns to the problem of Kant's metaphysics in *Difference and Repetition* (first published in 1968), he seems to have accepted that such 'new determinations' have been left to future philosophers to create. Whereas the Kantian form of time determines the conditions of representations but also forms the becoming of consciousness, space is never granted any such reciprocity: the *a priori* principles of space continue to determine the conditions of possibility of space as outer sense, but at no point do we grasp that outer space can give rise to new forms of perception. Is it really possible to provide a transcendental account of space that refuses the conditions determined by idealism, which is to say, the 'original representation' of space? In a sense we must admit that for all Deleuze's discussion of the historical repression of time in favour of space, space itself is no less subjugated, no less limited, and that any philosophy of space must begin by transforming the very presuppositions according to which space itself has been traditionally determined.

Extension

In order to inaugurate this project, to realise the potential redistribution of what is called space, let us return to the most reductive and pessimistic circumstances of Kant's transcendental aesthetic, the point at which no alternative seems possible and space has been surrendered to an inalterable *a priori* form. We can best grasp this state of affairs by returning to the question of representation and, in particular, the divestment of sensation from the sensible. As we have noted, Kant's foray into sensation only serves to clear the ground for an even more radical retreat from the sensible, for if the transcendental aesthetic establishes our receptivity to sensation it ultimately does so in order to distinguish what part of representation cannot be attributed to the affections we encounter. In the specific context of representation, Kant seeks to clarify the distinction between sensation and the sensible in terms of, respectively, matter and form. The first is always *a posteriori*, depending as it does on an empirically given sensation, while the second, identified with space, 'must lie ready for the sensations *a priori* in the mind' (Kant 1965: 66). Only when the latter has been evacuated of the attributes of sensation as well as the discursive temptation of the understanding, of all that is empirical and all that is ideal, can we speak of a pure intuition:

> Thus if I take away from the representation of a body that which the understanding thinks in regard to it, substance, force, divisibility, etc., and likewise what belong to sensation, impenetrability, hardness, colour, etc., something still remains over from the empirical intuition, namely, extension and figure. These belong to pure intuition, which, even without any actual object of the senses or of sensation, exists in the mind *a priori* as a mere form of sensibility. (Kant 1965: 66)

In a sense, Kant's procedure strikes us as counter-intuitive, since the form of pure intuition empties space of the very properties that we tend to consider important or even necessary. It is hard to imagine much of anything depending 'upon/ a red wheel/ barrow/ glazed with rain/ water', or any other object in space for that matter, when it is divested of colour, texture, and all other marks of sensation. And yet, it is at the point when we reach this pure sensible form that we may begin to grasp what Kant truly signifies by space. The transcendental aesthetic not only elaborates space as an *a priori* condition of possibility but also renders it, as we now see, an essentially Euclidean or geometrical substrate, for the divestment of sensations entailed by the science of sensibility deprives space of the dimension of depth. In this respect, of course, Kant is no different from the predominant tradition of representation, which considers space primarily in terms of extension (*res extensa*) and, thereby, renders it a kind of tableau upon which appearances are projected like the images of a magic lantern. In the theatre of this perception, we can speak of high and low, left and right, but the question of depth is always and inevitably botched because it is rendered extensive (that is, depth is extension from another perspective). As Deleuze writes, 'what is missing is the original, intensive depth which is the matrix of the entire space and the first affirmation of difference: here, that which only afterwards appears as a linear limitation and flat opposition lives and simmers in the form of free differences' (Deleuze 1997: 51).

It is wise to recall here Deleuze's frequent reference to Malraux's insistence that the human is a slow being composed of a remarkable accumulation of velocities – that the speed of our bodies must be measured against the sluggishness of our perception. In essence, difference cannot be explicated without ceasing to be difference because explication *qua* representation constitutes the very process of extension whereby difference suffers annihilation. 'Difference is the sufficient reason of change only to the extent that the change tends to negate difference,' Deleuze says, adding that difference would never be so suspect if it didn't seem to rush headlong into suicide (Deleuze 1997: 228). Representation orders space by distributing a fog of extensity over the swarm of differences that, as Deleuze says, constitute the genetic element of space, the singular objects and organisations of which cannot impress themselves on perception, *as* perception, because they are so quickly covered up. What would it mean to define space differently, to define space as depth, rather than to determine it solely according to the diversity of extension and figure?

Intensity

The impoverishment of space by representation returns us to the fate of sensation, for if we are ever to go beyond or beneath extensity we are bound to slough off the transcendental conditions of possibility in favour of the singularity of sensation – as Deleuze would say, of *this* percept or *that* affect. Deleuze's solution lies, first of all, in returning to a different sense of aesthetics from the one we have heretofore explored, namely, the sense of aesthetics that is properly concerned with the theory of art. 'The elementary concepts of representation are the categories defined as the condition of possible experience. These, however, are too general or too large for the real. The net is so loose that the largest fish pass through,' Deleuze writes in *Difference and Repetition*.

> No wonder, then, that aesthetics should be divided into two irreducible domains: that of the theory of the sensible which captures only the real's conformity with possible experience; and that of the theory of the beautiful, which deals with the reality of the real insofar as it is thought. (Deleuze 1997: 68)

As we have mentioned, this project is already broached by Kant himself in the *Critique of Judgment*, where the ready-made legislation of the faculties over experience gives way to the exploration of sensation and the emergence of an original accord between the faculties themselves. As Deleuze writes, the third critique, 'does not restrict itself to the perspective of conditions as it appeared in the other two Critiques: with the *Critique of Judgment*, we step into Genesis' (Deleuze 2004: 69). Nevertheless, the project to retrieve differential and genetic sensation from its condemnation at the hands of representation could be said to have been raised to a new level of philosophical invention and intensity in Deleuze's own work. The experience of depth, as opposed to mere extensity, demands the retrieval of the 'other' sense of aesthetic experience which is not mediated by condition of possibility but, instead, turns upon the 'reality of the real insofar as it is thought'.

Hence, we find that across the swath of his work that Deleuze consistently returns to the arts, and especially what could be called 'the arts of depth', in order to provide the basis for a philosophy of sense. In other words, he begins from the point of view of the work of art as experimentation with sensibility in order to define, in each particular case, the operative transcendental conditions. The artwork thus consists in an experiment in experience, a form of 'experientiation'. In *Difference and Repetition*, Deleuze outlines, 'a crucial experience of difference and a corresponding experiment' which articulates the beginnings of a way out of the dominance of extension:

> every time we find ourselves confronted or bound by a limitation or an opposition, we should ask ourselves what such a situation presupposes. It

presupposes a swarm of differences, a pluralism of free, wild or untamed differences, a properly differential and original space and time . . . (Deleuze 1997: 50)

For a moment, then, let us imagine that beneath the ground of representation and the surface of extension another experience of space lurks. In other words, we must not presuppose extension but, rather, presuppose that extension is the second-order process, the sorry representation of difference from an impoverished perspective.[6] Thus, while extensity always covers the ground of space, extensity *qua* space is always implicated in depths – not simply as its other dimension but as the dimension that implicates space, that forms what Deleuze has called its 'implex'. 'No doubt depth is also a possible length and size,' Deleuze says:

> but this possibility is only realized in so far as an observer changes place and gathers into an abstract concept that which is length for itself and that which is length for others: in fact, it is always on the basis of a new depth that the old one becomes length or is explicated in length. (Deleuze 1997: 229)

In other words, even as depth is transformed into extensity, into length from another perspective, Deleuze suggests that perspective itself is born out of depth, from the depths of perception. After all, the extensity of objects and our capacity to grasp them would be impossible if those objects did not issue forth from the recession of shading and shadows, if they did not differentiate themselves from the tableau of extensity. 'The law of figure and ground would never hold for objects distinguished from a neutral background or a background of other objects unless the object itself entertained a relations to its own depth', which is to say, a sense in which the essence of any object were its own self-differentiating depth, or rather the self-differentiation in depth of the object. The ground (*fond*) of all homogenous extensity would hardly be possible if it were not the 'project of something deeper (*profond*)' (Deleuze 1997: 229).[7]

Unlike the homogeneous field of extensity, then, the intensity of depth is tantamount to difference, and Deleuze goes so far as to consider the very notion of 'difference of intensity' to be tautological. 'Every intensity is itself differential, by itself a difference', such that the disparity of difference, of intensity, or the difference of intensity, constitutes the, 'reason of all phenomena, the condition of that which appears' (Deleuze 1997: 222).[8] Whence the great formula of *Difference and Repetition* that, 'difference is not diversity, but difference is that by which the given is given, that by which the given is given as diverse'. We tend to take for granted that difference presupposes a ground of resemblance, and the tradition of representation essentially codifies this belief, but Deleuze's argument consists in suggesting that representation derives from the genetic force of difference – that extension emerges from difference. Deleuze's reversal, then, consists in taking the intensive nature of difference, and the differential nature of intensity, to constitute the conditions for the sensible. The sense or sensibility of depth, which explicates extensity and which is all too often covered up by extensity (no less by the whole consideration, philosophical and otherwise, of 'appearances'), is inseparable from the 'power of diminution of intensity' that we experience. As Deleuze often repeats, 'Intensity is simultaneously the imperceptible and that which can only be sensed', just as 'depth is simultaneously the imperceptible and that which can only be perceived' (Deleuze 1997: 230–1).

From Space to Spatium

But why, we might ask, is the genetic power of difference so evasive? Why have Kant and a whole tradition of philosophy failed to intuit difference and created, instead, the conditions for an impoverished diversity (manifold)? The answer to this riddle, we now see, can be understood when we realise that intensity remains inextricable from extensity, which in turn cancels the appearance of difference by virtue of producing general qualities (that is, physical qualities, or *qualitas*, and perceptible qualities, or *quale*). 'In short, we know intensity only as already developed within an extensity, and as covered over by qualities' (Deleuze 1997: 223). This remarkable thesis cannot be read without understanding its promotion of depth as perhaps Deleuze's most profound reversal of Kant, whose 'mistake' was to define, 'all intuitions as extensive quantities' and, thereby, to, 'reserve intensive quantity for the matter which fills a given extensity to some degree or another' (Deleuze 1997: 230). Hence, space itself is relegated to an *a priori* condition, the form of intuition, and so the sensible substance of appearances is all too easily subsumed according to the laws of a transcendental idealism. Difference, 'is cancelled in so far as it is drawn outside itself, in extensity and in the quality that fills extensity', though extensity would not exist without the genetic force of difference itself, which 'creates extensity and this quality' (Deleuze 1997: 228).

In this context, it is worth wondering whether we can even speak of space any more. Perhaps only as a kind of conceptual reminiscence. In the contortions and distortions of modern art and modern cinema, the metaphysical ground of space is foreclosed, and this is why Deleuze's calls for 'new determinations of space and time'. We cannot reconcile aesthetics without also revising our sense of space, and – even more to the point – we might say that the very reconciliation of aesthetics must begin from the very point of revising space. The collections of lines, angles, and objects – the distribution of singularities ('shining points') – would not result from *a priori* conditions but, instead, would form the constituents of an intensive 'spatium' in which perception and thought are immanent, in which depth (say, depth of field in the cinema) is no less an intensive quantity. Admittedly, as Deleuze cautions, it is possible to go too far in the direction of the sensible, to lapse into the ocean of pure sensation and pure difference. This procedure, the 'inverse' of traditional attempts to ascertain the conditions of possibility for sensation, 'is not much better, consisting of the attempt to withdraw the pure sensible from representation and to determine it as that which remains once representation is removed (a contradictory flux, for example, or a rhapsody of sensations)' (Deleuze 1997: 56).

Rather, the project to revise the determination of space and, more generally, to restore aesthetics to its place in a philosophy of sensation must develop a delicate methodology that neither determines sensation in advance nor pretends to be able to filter sensation from an already constituted difference. In a sense, the problem, as Deleuze lays it out, should be read in light of Kant's own problematic in the transcendental aesthetic or, rather, as a transformation of the constraints of a science of sensibility. On the one hand, as we have repeatedly seen, Kant is concerned to formulate the transcendental aesthetic without drawing upon empirical sensations, such that the forms of sensibility will be *a priori*. But on the other hand, as Kant maintains, the transcendental aesthetic cannot be deduced because even the *a priori* forms of sensibility cannot aspire to a 'discursive' or 'general status' without completely removing them from the realm of sensibility. This is why the transcendental aesthetic is neither induced from empirical judgements nor deduced from logical premises but, rather, is subject to an exposition (*expositio*), which Kant defines as, 'the clear, though not necessarily exhaustive, representation of that which belongs to a concept: the exposition is metaphysical when it contains that which exhibits the concept as given *a priori*' (Kant 1965: 68).

We might say that Deleuze's conceptualisation of space leads him to undertake his own transcendental aesthetic, but whereas Kant resolves to exclude the purely empirical and the purely logical, Deleuze resolves to bring together the two senses of the aesthetic – the transcendental and the empirical. As Deleuze says elsewhere, 'the conditions of experience in general must become conditions of real experience', such that the work of art forms in each case its own transcendental conditions – conditions that do not precede experience but arise from it. Everything changes once we determine the conditions of real experience, which are not larger than the conditioned and which differ in kind from the categories: the two senses of the aesthetic become one, to the point where the being of the sensible reveals itself in the work of art, while at the same time the work of art appears as experimentation' (Deleuze 1997: 68).[9]

References

Allison, H. E. (1983), *Kant's Transcendental Idealism: An Interpretation and Defense*, New Haven: Yale University Press.

Deleuze, G. (1990), *Kant's Critical Philosophy*, trans. H. Tomlinson and B. Habberjam, Minneapolis: University of Minnesota Press.

Deleuze, G. (1997), *Difference and Repetition*, trans. P. Patton, New York: Columbia University Press.

Deleuze, G. (2004), 'The Idea of Genesis in Kant's Esthetics', trans. M. Taormina, in D. Lapoujade (ed.), *Desert Island and Other Texts*, 1973–1974, Los Angeles and New York: Semiotext(e).

Kant, I. (1965), *The Critique of Pure Reason*, trans. N. K. Smith, New York: St Martin's Press.

Notes

1. As this brief list indicates, what we call space appears in Deleuze under the auspices of different modalities and determinations, the result of which is that we can never settle on any certain sense of what space entails – and this, as I argue, is precisely Deleuze's point. In other words, space as a concept is inseparable from its singular instantiation. 'Space and time display oppositions (and limitations) only on the surface, but they presuppose in their real depth far more voluminous, affirmed, and distributed differences' that cannot be subsumed under a concept. Of this 'difference in depth', Deluxe proffers a list of different kinds of space – 'geometrical, physical, biophysical, social and linguistic' – each of which, presumably, must be counted as a different dimension of what is called space (see Deleuze 1997: 51).

2. Even on those occasions when representation seems to entertain the multiplication of perspectives within space, Deleuze says, those points of view are reducible to so many permutations because, 'representation already includes precisely an infinity of representations – either by ensuring all points of view on the same object or the same word, or by making all moments properties of the same Self' (Deleuze 1997: 56).

3. See Deleuze 1990: vii.

4. As Deleuze writes of this Kantian organisation in *Kant's Critical Philosophy*, on the one hand:

> the Ego itself is in time, and thus constantly changing: it is a passive, or rather receptive, Ego, which experiences changes in time. But, on the other hand, the I is an act which constantly carries out syntheses of time, and of that which happens in time, by dividing up the present, the past, and the future at every instant. The I and the ego are thus separated by the line of time which relates them to each other, but under conditions of a fundamental difference. (Deleuze 1990: viii).

5. In Deleuze's own philosophy, we might say, space does find new determinations, not only in the particular aesthetic media that he considers (painting, theatre, cinema) but also in the general consideration of movement that characterises his work. Whereas representation always demands the return to a unique perspective, Deleuze argues in *Difference and Repetition* that movement, 'implies a plurality of centers, a superimposition of perspectives, a tangle of points of view, a coexistence of moments which essentially distort representation' (Deleuze 1997: 56).

6. As Deleuze writes, in a related context, 'The negative is the image of difference, but a flattened and inverted image, like the candle in the eye of an ox – the eye of the dialectician dreaming of a futile combat' (Deleuze 1997: 51).

7. Far from being another dimension of extensity, then, depth indicates the intensive field (*plan*) from which extensity issues: 'Depth as the (ultimate and original) heterogeneous dimension is the matrix of all extensity, including its third dimension considered to be homogeneous with the other two' (Deleuze 1997: 229).

8. The diverse or manifold is produced by difference, by the irreducible inequality and disparity that haunts God's perfection like a remainder. Thus, as Deleuze says, it is not God's perfect calculations which form the 'principle of sufficient reason' for the world but, rather, the imperfection of those equations – the always present, always unrecoverable difference – that makes the world behind God's back, as it were.

9. What is Deleuze arguing with respect to space? In a sense, Kant anticipates Deleuze's own transcendental empiricism in his elucidation of space and time when he considers possible objections to his own exposition. Those who:

> regard space and time as relations of appearances, alongside or in succession to one another – relations abstracted from experience, and in this isolation confusedly represented . . . are obliged to deny that a priori mathematical doctrines have any validity in respect of real things (for instance, in space) or at least to deny their apodeictic certainty.

Insofar as Kant means geometry by 'mathematical doctrines', and insofar as the Euclidean notion of space and the Newtonian notion of space-time on which Kant bases so much of his exposition have been largely dismantled, we have no real trouble with this objection. What should interest us, however, is the conclusion that Kant draws about this transcendental empiricism:

> on this view, indeed, the a priori concepts of space and time are merely creatures of the imagination, whose source must really be sought in experience, the imagination framing out of the relations abstracted from experience something that does indeed contain what is general in these relations, but which cannot exist without the restrictions that nature has attached to them. (Kant 1965: 81)

Chapter 11

The Space of Man: On the Specificity of Affect in Deleuze and Guattari

Claire Colebrook

> The relation between mathematics and man may thus be conceived in a new way: the question is not that of quantifying or measuring human properties, but rather, on the one hand, that of problematising human events, and, on the other, that of developing as various human events the conditions of a problem.
> (Deleuze, *The Logic of Sense*)

The Sense of Space

How do the spatial metaphors adopted by Deleuze and Foucault in their early work relate to a theory of actual space? When Foucault, in *The Order of Things* (1970), detailed a series of historical *a priori*, he set himself the task of uncovering the 'table' across which the terms of thought were distributed. He also referred to spaces of knowledge, and concluded with reflections on the history of thought as defined by various 'foldings' producing an interiority and exteriority. One of the many texts to which Foucault's work was responding was Edmund Husserl's *Crisis of the European Sciences* (1970) which, as Derrida noted, unwittingly exposed the ways in which a humanised and architectonic conception of space underpinned the transcendental project (Derrida 1989). A common, objective, presentable and scientifically meaningful world was the implicit *telos*, not only of all acts of meaning but also of the very idea of meaning as such. In order for phenomenology to establish consciousness as the temporal synthesis that constitutes a world, and that posits that world as objectively present for others both now and in the future, one must presuppose a space of man: a world whose sense, truth, order and geometry must always be presentable (even if not present) for any subject whatever. Any cultural, historical or ethnographical relativism relies upon a general horizon, common world or pre-cultural 'we' within which relativity takes place.

Whereas Derrida argues that this architectonic assumption of a human space in general underpins philosophy as such, which necessarily presupposes that all sense can ultimately be brought to presence, Foucault (1970) argues that this transcendental concern is historically specific. Prior to modernity space was heterogeneous: selves were constituted morally, defined according to their territory and its norms (Foucault 1970: 328); but it is with the transcendental project that any local appearance of man is seen as an empirical realisation of a general humanity. An entirely new spatial metaphorics explains the existence of actual spaces: there can only be this localised world here because humanity is just that transcendental movement that will unfold itself through time in all these concrete dimensions. Now, in his later work on Foucault, Deleuze suggests that we can move beyond Foucault's charting of those human or actual spaces that unfold from a transcendental principle of space in general – the phenomenological idea of consciousness as the genesis of space – towards a 'superfold'. The argument goes something like this (Deleuze 1988: 131). First, there is the era of the unfold: any actual appearance of life is seen to be a finite expression of an infinity. Human beings are fragments of the cosmos. Second, in the nineteenth century, with the emphasis on 'man', we encounter the fold: 'man' is finite, but his subjection to the world is precisely what produces his historical, linguistic and political development. A sense of time, space, language and life in general is brought into being only because finite man can turn back and come to recognise the ways in which he is enfolded by life; he is that border where local determination understands itself as localised. In these first two eras of knowledge the very style of our thought is oriented by spatial relations, the way in which we imagine what it is to think. The very idea that thought alters historically, that it has an orientation or spatial imaginary is what opens up the 'superfold'. By confronting all those events from which thought emerges, by thinking how there can be perceptions of spaces, we no longer presuppose an infinity to be represented; nor a finite being who constitutes 'his' human world (as in phenomenology) but an 'unlimited finity'. Each located observer is the opening of a fold, a world folded around its contemplations and rhythms. There are as many spaces or folds as there are styles of perception. If a fold is the way perceptions 'curve around' or are oriented according to an acting body, then the *thought* of these curves produces a life that can think not just its own human world – the space of man – but the sense of space as such.

What united Husserl in the 'Origin of Geometry', and Derrida with Foucault in their criticism of phenomenology was the problem of the emergence of sense. Phenomenology had argued that all perception and communicable meaning presupposed a horizon, a world of possibilities which would then be given repeatable form and ideality in the structures of sense. The laws of geometry may, therefore, have been inscribed by Euclid but their *sense* transcends any specific subject and concerns any subject whatever. Sense emerges from a local time and space but then allows for the thought and being of what is true for space and time in general. For Derrida this horizon of 'any subject whatever' presupposes a normative image of humanity, a subject oriented towards the disclosure of an objective and scientifically manipulable world. For Foucault, this horizon fails to confront the 'Outside', the *unthought* events that orient the horizons of sense or milieus within which we move and think. The problem of sense, then, is the problem of the way in which *actual spaces* – the milieu in which we orient ourselves and live – are doubled by a space of sense, a 'distance' or distribution from which we can think or live localised times and spaces. It would be far too simple, then, to say that phenomenology uses the concept of 'horizon' metaphorically, or that the 'territory' is figural in *A Thousand Plateaus* (1987). Rather, the very difference between literal and figural – the very possibility of thought – emerges from *both* the movements of bodies *and* the images those bodies produce of each other.

As early as 1969, in *The Logic of Sense*, Deleuze contrasted two geneses of sense: the first is Husserlian and is static. Sense is released by an event that passes from a 'noematic attribute' – seeing something as something – but then releases the perceived for all time; one sees in the here and now (the actual) a potential that could be perceived for all time (the eternal and pure singularity, singular because not entwined with a world of relations). The noematic attribute of sense is the event, for we see not just what actually *is*, but also the seen as it might be remembered, imagined, recalled, repeated, hallucinated. Any perceived redness becomes a 'to red'. It is in this sense that the surface of sense is only 'quasi-causal', sterile and incorporeal; it is the image of bodies produced from an encounter, but is also no longer bound up with bodies and mixtures. Sense is the event that emerges from an encounter, a sense of red, a potential or power 'to red . . .'. Deleuze's static genesis is therefore close to phenomenology in arguing that the condition for any perceived or actual world is a virtual distance. But whereas Husserl saw sense as a predicate – judging the world to be thus – Deleuze sees sense as the verb, releasing from this world of effected relations – this territory, assemblage or mixture – the potential for other relations, other worlds. In addition to the surface of production, or the space that is produced from the encounters of singular powers, there is also the *metaphysical surface*, which is the image of those powers *not* as they are actualised but as they might be. We could say, for example, that even the minimal laws of geography form a metaphysical surface, extracting from relations certain powers *to relate*. But once we *thought* this genesis of a metaphysical surface, this doubling of the actual world with its sense, then we would be obliged to consider the potential of other worlds or a counter-actualisation.

The second genesis is dynamic: how is it that this expressing or sense-constituting perception emerges? How is the eye capable of surveying a world, not just as its own but as it would be, or could be, for any subject whatever, for all time? Here, Deleuze draws upon a psychoanalysis of partial objects; bodies begin as flows of forces and desire, mouth and breast, mouth and finger, excrement and anus. This is a schizoid position of forces, and is made up of parts and fragments. But in the subsequent depressive position the surface is overtaken by a height, the height of the good object that presents the forces with an image of wholeness and integration, a proper point from which the surface is surveyed. If there is a surface of sense that we can describe statically (as the difference between actual images and the image as it would be for others beyond this here and now), this is only possible because of the dynamic relations of bodies. The mouth becomes an organ of speaking, producing a subject whose world is now no longer that which it sees for itself, but is that world as it is surveyed. If we have a horizon, lived world, context or actual space, this is because an event has occurred in the peculiar mixtures of human bodies. The Body without Organs is *first* just that depth produced by the forces that take in and spit out partial objects; but with the elevation of the 'good object' the body without organs becomes a 'full depth'.

If we move forward to the politicisation of this genesis in *Anti-Oedipus* we are given a further distinction: *legitimately*, the Body without Organs is effected from the production of forces. (So, to draw upon a 'field metaphysic' that goes back at least as far as Spinoza: life is force, the play of forces, and the interplay of these forces produce zones or sites of qualities, intensities. It is not that there is a space that is then qualified; rather, forces produce qualities and qualities produce fields or spaces, 'blocs of becoming'). The Body without Organs is produced 'alongside' the connections of desiring flows. The zones add up to a series of spaces; but this whole is never given, for there is always the potential for further connection and production. Legitimately, the Body without Organs is this effected depth. Illegitimately, however, one can come to believe that the

Body without Organs was the original subject or ground, from which finite territories or zones were formed. In psychoanalytic terms, the desires of bodies create partial objects or attachments, which are then structured by Oedipus: the breast is the breast of the mother, the penis is the phallus of the father, and all this is necessary because if we are not submitted to structure we will fall back into the abyss of pre-Oedipal indifference. The Body without Organs is assumed to be that ground or life *against which* human structure defines itself. Politically, this error is that of presupposing that from all the territories and regimes of signs which do effect a possibility for *thinking* territoriality as such, or an absolute deterritorialisation, we imagine that there is in existence an ultimate territory, a unity within which and from which local spaces are lived.

Absolute territorialisation is, then, the *potential* of sense, the potential of the brain to think the genesis of spatiality from within a local space; not just this image as it is here for me, folded around my body, but imaging as such. Humanity is not, as in phenomenology, the finite point in the world from which the world is unfolded. But human life, in the form of the thinking brain *is* the site where the potential for space – the intuition of inhuman foldings of space – can be actualised and counter-actualised. For Deleuze, then, the human or the potential of the brain is always more than a constituted image within sense; it is also that image that allows us to think the potential of imaging as such (Deleuze 1995: 42). Just as Foucault's genealogy of man was accompanied by an affirmation of the self as that which can turn back upon itself, problematise itself and thereby open new ways of thought, so Deleuze will affirm Foucault's 'superman' who no longer turns back upon himself but opens out to forces that will 'free life' from *within himself* (Deleuze 1988: 132). Indeed, as Deleuze notes in his work on Foucault, to *think* requires moving beyond formations of knowledge and dispersed visibilities to the 'non-place' from which 'what we see' and 'what we say' emerge (Deleuze 1988: 38). This 'outside' is not *spatially separated* from the world we live; rather, the 'outside' is nothing more than the relations of forces through which we live, see, and say (Deleuze 1988: 84). There is space, the experience of space, only because of a non-spatial 'outside' that is nothing more than a play of forces (Deleuze 1988: 86).

The Ethics of Space

There is a perception we could have in reading Deleuze and Guattari that the molecular is good, while the molar is bad, that affect is liberating and

mobilising while meaning or conceptuality is rigidifying. Such a moral-
ising reading would be enabled by placing Deleuze and Guattari in the
tradition of post-1968 difference thinkers who resist the lure of identity
and who, supposedly, grant an essential radicalism to the non-semantic
per se. On such an understanding, conceptuality, ideality and form are
ways of retarding and normalising the flow and force of life, while the
random, singular or unthought release life into its open and infinite
potentiality. The relation between time and space would, accordingly,
also be historicised and politicised. Philosophy has privileged a uniform
space of points, a space that may be measured or striated precisely
because any point in space is equivalent to and interchangeable with any
other. These points are achieved either by the division of uniform matter,
or by the location of bodies across the plane of matter. Time is then
regarded as the measure of movement or points within this uniform field.
Western metaphysics has always privileged a fixed world of forms, a
spatial unity and a pre-given order over the processes and events that
produce that order. When we read Deleuze and Guattari's seeming celebration of smooth over striated space (Deleuze and Guattari 1987: 353),
of multiple plateaus rather than a line of history (Deleuze and Guattari
1987: 393), of artisans rather than architects (Deleuze and Guattari
1987: 402), and of nomadology rather than sedentary phenomenology
(Deleuze and Guattari 1987: 380), this would seem to suggest that we
move from a dualism that privileges a founding term – spatial coordinates, measuring time, order – to an affirmation of the singularities from
which all dualisms and orders emerge. As in Derridean deconstruction,
we would recognise any moral or binary opposition as effected from a
differential field not governed by any dominant term. In terms of space
this would seem to suggest that space, far from being a field within which
points are mapped, is better conceived as a plane of singular affects and
events that is, in Western thought, reactively coded as one general territory.

However, the emphasis in post-Deleuzian theory on affect, singularities and nomadology misses the affirmative understanding of sense,
mind and philosophy that sits alongside Deleuze's critical project.
Throughout his work Deleuze is at pains to point out that he is not advocating a 'return' to primitivism, and this has been accepted well enough.
However, the celebration of the minor term in Deleuze and Guattari's
non-dualist binaries does seem to suggest a preference for the affective,
singular, haptic and embodied over sense, conceptuality and ideality.
Alongside the critique of the normalisation of space in the figure of a
unified humanity, there is another *problem* in the post-1968 affirmation

of difference: the problem or positive possibility of the whole, the power of a singular thought to imagine space in general. Certainly, *post*-structuralism concerned itself with the disruptive question of genesis: how is any field, system of differences or plane of knowable terms generated, and how does one term explain, and thereby occlude, the genesis of any structure? But there is also an affirmation of the structural possibility of this genesis: how does any field or set of relations produce a point or image of that which exceeds the set? For Deleuze and Guattari, it is time to approach the problem of genesis and structure differently (Deleuze and Guattari 1987: 242): a structure is a set of external relations, the way in which life is viewed or generated from some point. A structure is one side of a stratification; the other side is *that which is structured*, but this determinable content is *not undifferentiated or formless*. And so for Deleuze and Guattari we need to move beyond structures on one side and structured on the other to the abstract machine from which both are unfolded. This would mean taking account of the process of differentiation – the dynamic unfolding of difference – that subtends differenciation, or the actual and realised distinctions between terms (Deleuze 1994: 206–7). It should be possible to think immanent tendencies, the way in which different expressions of life unfold different spaces, relations, fields or trajectories, 'the immanent power of corporeality in all matter' (Deleuze and Guattari 1987: 411).

Genesis and Structure

Structuralism presented itself as a break with the Western epoch of metaphysics that had grounded beings and identities upon some prior plane from which they emerge; differences were no longer differences within space. Rather than accepting that differences were grounded on a prior order and distributed across a field, structuralism described the emergence of any field from the differentiation of points or terms. The idea of difference without positive terms allows us to imagine a differentiating field that produces points only in relation to each other and that have no intrinsic orientation. Space would, then, be the effect of a synthesis of points, not a container or ground. Space is the effect of relations. This would apply both to space in a metaphorical sense, such as the space or field of a grammar or social structure, and literal space. Geometry is not a pre-given and ideal order of a space that bears its own laws; rather, our space is constituted through the sense we make of it, the mapping of our field of orientation. Structure therefore privileges *external* relations or movements over points. There is nothing in any point or being itself (no intrinsic relation) that would determine how it behaves or constitutes itself in relation to other points. However, as long as structure is seen in terms of a differentiating system of pure relations it fails to account for the *genesis or internal difference of those relations*.

While Deleuze also insists on the externality of relations – that nothing fully determines how any potential will be actualised – he refuses to reduce relations to a single structure. Rather, life is a plane of potentialities or tendencies that may be actualised in certain relations but that could also produce other relations, other worlds. We can make this concrete by way of a very crude example. The power to be perceived as located in geometrical space – to be actualised in a system of relations between points – is certainly one way in which a body or matter might be actualised. So, a line that makes up a grid on a plan or diagram *is* a line by virtue of this realised set of relations. But such a line might also be drawn on a canvas, overlaid with other lines or set beside blocks of colour, no longer being a line but becoming other than itself – a shading or border. This means that there is a potential for sense (within, say, linearity) that cannot be exhausted by any single relation. In contrast with the idea that space or the world is constructed from sense – socially or culturally constituted – spatiality opens sense, for any location bears the potential to open up new planes, new orientations. Rather than seeing space as effected from sense, as realised from a system of orientation or intending, Deleuze sees spatiality as an opening of sense, as the potential to create new problems. Deleuze is critical of the subject of philosophy for whom space is a form imposed on the world, but he is also resistant to reducing space to actually constituted spatial planes. What needs to be thought is not this or that plane, nor this or that realised system of relations, but the potential to produce planes, the 'planomenon', *and* our capacity to think or encounter that potential.

A singularity is the potential to produce relations, but these relations cannot be determined from the singularity alone, for it is always possible that new encounters will open up new relations. Consequently, there can be no point from which spaces are drawn, because a point only takes on its determination with the unfolding of a certain space (an unfolding that could always be redrawn). A singularity is, however, a tendency or potential and for this reason a space or field is always more than its relations; there are always singularities or potential that could open further spaces *or* allow for the thought of any space whatever, space as such, or the sense of space. In *What is Philosophy?* Deleuze and Guattari argue for the primacy of architecture in relation to the arts and this is because art works with the plane of composition, all those affects and percepts that fill out any space. The plane of composition in art is more than a spatial metaphor, for any work of art is a struggle with those perceptions, affects and sensed encounters that are 'lived'. Art does not express the 'lived' but releases from the lived the impersonal power from which any oriented and located life emerges. The plane of composition comprises the potentials of sensibility that an artist must somehow locate in a material (in this time and in this space), while producing a monument, such that this sensation as it would be felt comes to stand alone, for all time.

We might contrast this productive, composing and architectonic model of art – art as the creation of relations that allow for the preservation of sensation without reference to a 'lived' body – with a received understanding of deconstruction. For Derrida deconstruction is not itself a method so much as an inhabitation and solicitation of all those texts that present their structures, differences, borders or relations, while repressing that which generates structure. There will always be, within any field or space, a closed set of terms *and* an unthinkable supplementary term that borders or closes the set. If we imagine how this might provoke the practice of spatial arts, such as architecture, then we can follow Mark Wigley by suggesting that any experienced or actual space must repress, forget or disavow that spatialising tracing which marks out the border between inside and outside, which generates the field but cannot be located within the field (Wigley 1993: 191). More concretely one could strive, as Bernard Tschumi has done, to bring this thought of quasi-transcendental difference into practice. *Le Parc de la Villette* (1987) aims to decentre space by producing a distribution of points without hierarchy. According to Tschumi, the various points that create the grid system of the park preclude the thought of a centre or realised intention. Without hierarchy or centre the various points will then enter into a series of multiple relations, such that the character of the space produced is not determined or organised beforehand. Further, by overlaying other distributions such as a series of surfaces and then a series of lines, no system of distributions is elevated above any other; unity is avoided. The points therefore work against a dominating ratio that would present space as an expression of design – certainly not an expression of a subject. If the points were in some ways pure form or pure difference, this would be a set of relations without positive terms, without overarching form, allowing other systems of relations – including actions and the participation of other designers – to produce new relations. Most significantly, Tschumi insists that the, 'project aims to unsettle both memory and context,' and is therefore exemplary of a resistance to the idealisation of space, the use or experience of space in terms of an ideal sense that would precede its punctual event:

Not a plenitude, but instead 'empty' form; *les cases sont vide* La Villette, then aims at an architecture that *means nothing,* an architecture of the signifier rather than the signified – one that is pure trace or the play of language . . . a dispersed and differentiated reality that marks an end to the utopia of unity. (Tschumi 1987: viii)

In contrast to this pure distribution and relation of points – 'differentiated reality' – Deleuze puts forward the idea of external relations that cannot be confused with the singular powers from which those relations are effected. Relations are not the effect of a process of differentiation or distribution. Rather, the power to differ expresses itself differently in each of its produced relations, with each effected point or term bearing a power to exceed itself, and to establish a new relation that would then create a new space. Put more concretely, we might imagine a certain power to differ – light – producing a spectrum of colours, such that these differences are effects of this intensity of difference; but we then might imagine colours entering into relation with the eye, thereby producing a visibility that can create new terms and new relations. Any space or plane, then, is the unfolding of matter, with relations being effected by specific expressions, which are events of specific powers *to relate*:

[T]here is an extraordinarily fine topology that relies not on points or objects but rather on haecceities, on sets of relations (winds, undulations of snow or sand, the song of the sand or the creaking of the ice, the tactile qualities of both). It is a tactile space, or rather 'haptic', a sonorous much more than a visual space. The variability, the polyvocality of directions, is an essential feature of smooth spaces of the rhizome type, and its alters their cartography. (Deleuze and Guattari 1987: 382)

This is what Deleuze draws from Spinoza: if life is desire or striving, and has no static being outside this striving, then encounters or relations need to be referred back to desires or intrinsic powers to differ.[1] There are not points or positive terms that are differentiated or distributed in a uniform space; nor is there spatiality or punctualisation *as such* which can only be thought after the event. Rather, each relation is expressive of a power that bears a potential to enter into further relations, such that a field is not a distribution of points so much as the striving of powers to become and that become *as this or that quality* depending upon, but never exhausted by, their encounters.

Even so, while this yields an affirmation of the affective or material over the formal, the *production* of space rather than its orienting sense, there is also an affirmation in Deleuze's work of the thought, philosophy and sense of affect. Indeed, Deleuze's historical work with Guattari offers a genealogy of globalism: how certain affects such as the white face, viewing, subjective eyes, and labouring and subjected body constitute the 'man' of modernity and single territory of capitalism. There is nothing radical *per se* about affect, but the *thought* of affect – the power of philosophy or true thinking to pass beyond affects and images to the thought of differential imaging, the thought of life in its power to differ – *is desire, and is always and necessarily radical*.[2] The power of art is ethical: the power not just to present this or that affect, but to bring us to an experience of 'affectuality' – or *of the fact that there is* affect. Art is not a judgement on life but an affirmation of life.

Space in General

Deleuze's concepts of the molecular, affect, haecceity and multiplicity, far from striving to think a spatiality that lies outside the field it determines, allow the thought of a self-distributing plane, a space that unfolds itself, and that does not require and expel a supplementary absent and spatialising force. Deleuze's difference is not radically anterior and unthinkable; it is the immanent pulsation of life that expresses itself infinitely and that can be affirmed in the *thought of life*.

The idea of space as the effect of a radically absent force of spatialisation that lies outside the field it spaces – even while this outside can only be thought *as* outside once terms are spatialised – is itself a peculiar event, affect and multiplicity. Why is it that today we see ourselves as subjected to the signifier, as inhabiting a law or system of relations imposed by an Other who does not exist? There is, if you like, a space of white Oedipal man, a space that has expressed itself in a pure geometry, a geometry oriented by the sense of a space that would be the law for any body whatever, a space that is nothing more than a capacity for axiomatic repetition. In response to this space of man and pure geometry Deleuze suggests that far from returning to a primitive geometry, and far from adding one more dimension to the plane that might allow us to think space in general, we ought to multiply the dimensions of space in order to maximise its power. From that critical endeavour we can then go on to ask, as Deleuze and Guattari do, what a plane is, such that it can think its own folds and dimensions. Philosophy creates the plane of thought which, in its Deleuzian form, strives to think the emergence of all planes, and this is why *A Thousand Plateaus* can describe life through planes of science, geometry, geology, literature, politics, metallurgy, history and linguistics: all the ways in which life folds upon itself in order to imagine and give form to itself, all the different matters of form, all the ways in which matter manners or articulates itself.

Univocity and Equivocity

Both Foucault's *The Order of Things* and Deleuze and Guattari's *Anti-Oedipus* historicise the emergence of man, pointing out that man is not just one being in the world among others, even if the human knower has always been somehow privileged. Man is defined through what Deleuze refers to as an equivocal ontology, or what Foucault describes as an 'ontology without metaphysics' (Foucault 1970: 340). That is, there is no longer a world of inherent or intrinsic differences which human knowledge may either come to know and map (as in the classical era), or which can be recognised and reflected in the self's relation to a cosmos. For Foucault, prior to modernity, space is the surface upon which knowledge and difference are placed, and time allows those dispersed spaces, not to be constituted and synthesised, but to be recognised. In modernity, however, this world of dispersed differences is now torn apart by a point of opacity and radical difference. Being does not bear its own truth or metaphysics; there is a point outside being – life – that is other than the world but which gives the world its truth, order or differentiation (Foucault 1970: 265). Difference and unfolding are located within man. To go back to Husserl's argument for transcendental consciousness: we can no longer naïvely use the truths of geometry as though they simply represented the truth of space. We have to recognise the temporal constitution of these truths by consciousness. Consciousness just is a capacity for spatialisation through time that can be recognised as having no proper space, and that must at once be located in a specific culture and epoch, but also differentiated in its potential from any concrete locale. Here, the difference, space and surface of the world are unfolded from one point within the world – life – a point that can never have its space within the horizon it unfolds:

> It is always against a background of the already-begun that man is able to reflect in what may serve for him as origin. For man, then, origin is by no means the beginning – a sort of dawn of history from which his ulterior acquisitions would have accumulated. Origin, for man, is much more the way in which man in general, any man, articulates himself upon the already-begun of labour, life and language; it must be sought for in that fold where man in all simplicity applies his labour to a world that has been worked for thousands of years, lives in the freshness of his unique, recent and precarious existence a life that has its roots in the first organic formations, and

composes into sentences which have never before been spoken (even though generation after generation has repeated them) words that are older than all memory . . . Far from leading back, or even merely pointing, towards a peak – whether real or virtual – of identity, far from indicating the moment of the Same at which the dispersion of the Other has not yet come into play, the original in man is that which articulates him from the outset upon something other than himself . . . (Foucault 1970: 331)

It is in equivocal ontologies, according to Deleuze, that man as a signifying animal is the point from which system, difference and structure are given. Man everywhere is subjected to the same formal structure of differences, law, exchange and signification – with the world and real being nothing more than the plane upon which system takes hold. In modernity, one moves from *expression* to *signification*: from a world where differences are real and distinct and give birth to signs, to a world where each event has its ground and origin in one organising system. From real and distinct differences one moves to formal difference, and to an idea of humanity that is nothing more than a formal function. Man is not a being within the world so much as a capacity to signify, exchange and communicate.

It is not surprising that Deleuze, like Foucault, makes much of the pre-Kantian experience of multiple folds and spaces. In his book on Leibniz and the fold Deleuze draws attention to the ways in which the Baroque plays upon the intrinsic differences of possible perceptions. Each point in the world is a monad, a perception that unfolds the world from itself without the requirement of a shared and anticipated space that is synthesised into the future. To say that 'monads have no windows' is to say that a world is perceived and unfolded without the assumption or presupposition of perception in general. One has not yet troubled oneself or given man the responsibility for the genesis of space from his own time; one has not yet seen each perceiver as the effect or sign of a perception in general. Perception is not the condition, genesis or origin of the spatial and temporal world; there are spatialities and temporalities of each monad. At one end, God is the full and clear perception of all space; at the other, are the singular perceptions of infinity, each monad's perceptual grasp of the infinite that transcends it. By contrast, modern 'man' stands, not for one perceiver among others, but for a purely formal power to perceive that also bears the imperative to perceive as any subject whatever. The deterritorialisation that frees the perception of space from its own locale is reterritorialised onto consciousness in general, the subject for whom space is everywhere subject to the same formal and geometric logic. Man speaks as one who is already subjected to a system that gives him being, and who must in essence already be tied to any other possible speaker:

> The classical image of thought, and the striating of mental space it effects, aspires to universality. It in effect operates with two 'universals,' the Whole as the final ground of being or all-encompassing horizon, and the Subject as the principle that converts being into being-for-us. (Deleuze and Guattari 1987: 379)

From univocity, where space and perception are spread across a time and surface that transcends the human knower, equivocity establishes a single and formalisable condition of spatiality – the logic of the subject – which is both inescapable and unmasterable. Both Foucault and Deleuze note that this historical shift does not just have political implications but needs to be seen as the very negation of the political. Although they both have a common target – the equivocal ontology whereby consciousness is the substance from which the world's spaces are constituted – Foucault and Deleuze differ as to the possibility of the repoliticisation of space.

Husserl had already argued that the formalising or idealising power of geometry allows one to repeat the truths of space to infinity. One establishes a science through an orientation or problem which goes beyond the given to its future and repeatable potential. Sense, for both Husserl and Deleuze, is this radical incorporeal power to release what is essential in an event from its material locale. The constitution of formal geometrical space therefore emerges from a certain *sense*, striving or project. For Husserl this is the sense of one humanity, occupying a single territory and history of truth and knowledge. Whereas Foucault and Derrida are critical of this one conscious life, this presupposed 'we' or ground of consciousness, Deleuze affirms the power of thought and philosophy to intuit life as the source of difference, folds, relations and spaces. Sense, philosophy, intuition, thinking and concepts all name the power to unleash other territories by imagining the given as an expression of a life that exceeds any of its fixed terms, and imagining the potential that can be unfolded from that expressive power.

'Man', or the modern subject of psychoanalysis or linguistics, closes down thinking if he is seen as the point from which differences and relations unfold. Accordingly, space, seen as the field occupied, measured and constituted by this man of consciousness, is a field of interiority – a space within which we think, a space reducible to perceptions of this specific organism. Such a space operates from a combination of sense and affect. There are the affects of Western man, the images that organise a plateau or constitute the social unit: the white face of the viewing subject, the black holes of eyes expressing an interior, a body dominated by speech and identified through its familial position as *either* mother or father (Deleuze and Guattari 1983: 96–7). That is, the investing perception of a certain body part – the apprehension of the power of the face as organising centre – unfolds a sense of space, a way of orienting a field crucial to the territory of man: 'The faciality function showed us the form under which man constitutes the majority, or rather the standard upon which the majority is based: white, male, adult, "rational", etc., in short, the average European, the subject of enunciation' (Deleuze and Guattari 1987: 292).

From the specific affect of speaking man as subject and centre, Deleuze and Guattari then describe the expansion or extrapolation of this affect to form a sense of space and time in general. The central point enables equivocity, where one privileged term is the organising ground of the other; man becomes the substance upon which other terms depend *and* he also enables a single temporal plane:

> Following the law of arborescence, it is this central Point that moves across all of space or the entire screen, and at every turn nourishes a certain distinctive opposition, depending on which faciality trait is retained: male-(female), adult-(child), white-(black, yellow, or red); rational-(animal). The central point, or third eye, thus has the property of organizing binary distributions within the dualism machines, and of reproducing itself in the principal term of the opposition; the entire opposition at the same time resonates in the central point. The constitution of a 'majority' as redundancy. Man constitutes himself as a gigantic memory, through the position of the central point . . . (Deleuze and Guattari 1987: 292–3)

And all this is achieved at the expense of the line: movement, desires and trajectories are subordinated to the terms or points they produce. The effects of relations and desires – points – are taken as original, and in the constitution of *an* origin Memory supplants memories:

> What constitutes arborescence is the submission of the line to the point. Of course, the child, the woman, the black have memories; but the Memory that collects those memories is still a virile majoritarian agency treating them as 'childhood memories', as conjugal, or colonial memories. (Deleuze and Guattari 1987: 293)

Deleuze's project is the expansion of sense beyond its localisation in man, the expansion of the potential of geometry beyond its purposive or architectonic sense. The transcendental project, the striving to think the sense of space, has yet to be carried out beyond its dependence on man.

The space of humanity has been constituted from the perception of an upright man of reason who regards all others as potentially or ideally just like himself. A radical striving towards sense must be transcendental and empirical: transcendental in its refusal of any image of thought or consciousness, and empirical in its observation of the different perceptions opened from different affective encounters. Sense is the potential to imagine other perceptions of the infinite, and the striving to think space positively; not the link between two points, but the power of life in its striving to create trajectories that open series or plateaus.

One might think here, positively, of sacred land. Claims for the sacredness of land by indigenous peoples are not just examples or instances of the various ways in which 'we' (humanity) grant space significance. For the key difference is that space here is not 'significant' – not seen as a marker, symbol or image of cultural memory. Whereas Western understandings of monument use space to mark an event, and do so in order to call future humanity to recognise and retain its past, sacred land is *both* infinite – demanding recognition from others – and inherently affective. The infinite it opens is deemed to be real, and not simply a relative cultural construction; but at the same time this infinite cannot be known or appropriated by just any other. Indigenous Australian claims to the sacredness of land locate memory or spirit in the land itself, which is not a signifier of the past, so much as the affirmation of the ways in which bodies and land are created through their affective connections. A people is a people because of *this* land, and this land bears its affect, resonance and spirit because of the dreaming of *this* people. At the same time, in accord with the positive reality of sense, the dreaming, spirit or genius of space transcends present individuals and opens up into the future, requiring further creation and demonstration. There is not *a* time or *a* space, which is perceived here in one sense, there in another. There are distinct modes of sense, different ways in which perceptions imagine, intuit and constitute an infinite.

Conclusion

Deleuze's project is both critical and affirmative. Like Foucault and Derrida he is critical of the assumed centre of a constituting consciousness or single body from which relations emerge. But Deleuze also wants to argue that the transcendental project – the striving to think space or life in general – needs to be carried beyond its human territory.

The subject as universal humanity who operates on the single spatial and temporal plane of capitalism represents a distinct passage from affect to formal function. The white man of reason has no race, no body, no beliefs; he is nothing more than a power to relate to and recognise others. Capitalism is cynical and axiomatic; no body, image or desire governs its domain. Man is the communicating, rationalising and labouring potential in us all. There is an abstraction from all tribalism and affective relations: territories are no longer constituted through investment in certain bodies or images. But this is possible only because one affective body – the image of Oedipal man who is nothing more than a power to abstract from his body and speak – now allows the axiom of one global humanity. The production of one who is other than his bodily desire – the gender-neutral, disembodied subject of modernity – is the white, Western man of reason.

The body of signifying, capitalist man is the body of reason, speech, communication and submission to a law that one recognises as one's own, and therefore as the law of all others. One's true being is that of 'any subject whatever', an affective investment in a body whose desires are now pure functions, who can recognise in all others the same human life, the same potential to liberate oneself from mere life and become fully human. Man is that body or point of life liberated from life, a desire not for this or that image or affect, but a desire to be other than affect. On the one hand, then, this subject of formal geometry and the space of humanity is reactive: a desire that wills itself not to will and in so doing submits itself to the negation of desire. One constitutes oneself as a point in humanity across one universal space and time. In so doing, however, desire is deprived of its own power, reterritorialised or subordinated to one of its affects. The power to intuit or sense perceptions beyond one's own purview is halted by the inclusion of all other perceivers as already within one's own space and time. Deleuze's own project is *neither* the inhabitation of a specific text or event of space – determining the points from which a space is drawn or delimited – *nor* the assertion of an absolute deterritorialisation. Rather, from the thought of the constitution of this or that space from this or that desire, or from the thought of the potential of sense, one can think space as such in its infinite divergence: a thousand plateaus.

References

Deleuze, G. (1988), *Foucault*, trans. S. Hand, London: Athlone.

Deleuze, G. (1990), *The Logic of Sense*, trans. M. Lester with C. Stivale, ed. C. V. Boundas, New York: Columbia University Press.

Deleuze, G. (1992), *Expressionism in Philosophy: Spinoza*, trans. M. Joughin, New York: Zone Books.

Deleuze, G. (1993), *The Fold: Leibniz and the Baroque*, trans. T. Conley, London: Athlone Press.

Deleuze, G. (1994), *Difference and Repetition*, trans. P. Patton, New York: Columbia University Press.

Deleuze, G. (1995), *Negotiations: 1972–1990*, trans. M. Joughin, New York: Columbia University Press.

Deleuze, G. and Guattari, F. (1983), *Anti-Oedipus: Capitalism and Schizophrenia*, trans. R. Hurley, M. Seem and H. R. Lane, Minneapolis: University of Minnesota Press.

Deleuze, G. and Guattari, F. (1987), *A Thousand Plateaus: Capitalism and Schizophrenia*, trans. B. Massumi, Minneapolis: University of Minnesota Press.

Deleuze, G. and Guattari, F. (1994), *What is Philosophy?*, trans. H. Tomlinson and G. Burchill, London: Verso.

Derrida, J. (1974), *Of Grammatology*, trans. G. C. Spivak, Baltimore: Johns Hopkins University Press.

Derrida, J. (1981), *Dissemination*, trans. B. Johnson, Chicago: University of Chicago Press.

Derrida, J. (1982), *Margins of Philosophy*, trans. A. Bass, Sussex: Harvester Press.

Derrida, J. (1989), *Edmund Husserl's Origin of Geometry: An Introduction*, trans. J. P. Leavey Jr, Lincoln: University of Nebraska Press.

Foucault, M. (1970), *The Order of Things*, London: Tavistock Press.

Foucault, M. (2001), 'Space, Knowledge and Power,' in J. D. Faubion (ed.), *Power: Essential Works of Foucault 1954–1984*, trans. R. Hurley et. al., Harmondsworth: Penguin, pp. 449–64.

Husserl, E. (1970), *The Crisis of the European Sciences and Transcendental Phenomenology*, trans. D. Carr, Evanston: Northwestern University Press.

Heidegger, M. (1967), *What is a Thing?*, trans. W. B. Barton Jr and V. Deutsch, Lanham: University Press of America.

Tschumi, B. (1987), *Cinégramme Folie: Le Parc de la Villette*, Princeton: Princeton Architectural Press.

Wigley, M. (1993), *The Architecture of Deconstruction*, Cambridge: MIT Press.

Notes

1. Accordingly, there is a quantitative distinction among beings that allows for intrinsic difference. All these numerically different instances of white are still *of whiteness*, a power to differ that is essential and can be seen as really distinct only because it expresses itself over and over again. Space as extension allows for 'extrinsic individuation' or the difference of this *from* that; but intensive space as intensive is just the power of essential differences to express themselves, to repeat themselves in all their difference and thereby establish one expressive plane:

   > Only a quantitative distinction of beings is consistent with the qualitative identity of the absolute. And this quantitative distinction is no mere appearance, but an internal difference, a difference of intensity. So that each finite being must be said to *express the absolute*, according, that is, to the degree of its power. Individuation is, in Spinoza, neither qualitative nor extrinsic, but quantitative and intrinsic, intensive. (Deleuze 1992: 197)

2. In *Anti-Oedipus* (1983), Deleuze and Guattari argue that desire is always revolutionary. Desire is not the desire for this or that lost object, or this or that supposedly natural need. Desire is the power for life to act, where action, movement and striving are not determined in advance by any proper end or intrinsic relation (Deleuze and Guattari 1983: 377).

Chapter 12

The Desert Island

Tom Conley

One of Gilles Deleuze's earliest pieces of writing could be imagined as a manuscript that its author, a shipwrecked sailor having washed up on a deserted island, wrote and illustrated with a map on a piece of paper, scrolled tightly into a coil, and then pushed down the neck of a bottle he corked and tossed into the ocean. But unlike the marooned soul on the beach living in the hope that a crew aboard a passing ship might find the bottle bobbing in the waves, read the words and look at the map in order to change the course of their voyage, retrieve the forlorn author and bring him back to the haven of a mainland, the isolated man encrypts his words in a glass container and sends them seaward. He throws the bottle into the sea to let it follow a course and reach a destination of its own.

'The Desert Island' (in French as 'Causes et raisons des îles désertes' [literally, 'Causes and Reasons of Desert Islands'] now in English translation as "The Desert Island") was penned in the 1950s. Purportedly written for a special issue of *Nouveau Fémina* on the theme of desert islands, the manuscript copy of 'The Desert Island' never reached the address which, it was supposed, was written on its containing envelope. When David Lapoujade and his team of editors retrieved the pages and used them to inaugurate an assemblage of the philosopher's essays written in France and elsewhere between 1953 and 1974, Deleuze had been dead for seven years. The ms. in a bottle was recovered, and a text that until the turn of the twenty-first century had been private finally became public. The piece has since become an event and, as an event, a marvellous reflection on the vitality and force of the spaces Deleuze invents in all of his philosophical and critical writings.

The unpublished essay on desert islands has appeared almost literally out of the blue. The decision to title the collection of thirty-nine essays *L'Ile déserte et autres textes: Textes et entretiens 1953–1974* [The Desert Island and Other Writings: Texts and Discussions 1953–1974] attests to a sense of its import in the work at large. Is the article a piece of juvenilia in which many of the themes of the later work find imperfect but jewelled expression? Is it a miniature 'Combray' in a copious and moving architecture of writing, ending with *Critique et clinique* in 1993, that bears resemblance in volume and force to Proust's *A la recherché du temps perdu*? Has it remained, before it appeared in print, a 'empty square' in a checkerboard that allowed an infinite permutation and variation in the creative drive in the philosopher's work in general? Affirmative responses to these questions would be likely and reassuringly welcome, but only if the early writings were not taken to determine and predict what would be thought, in the philosopher's career, to follow or to evolve from the first writings. Reflective space would need to be retained for a position from which it could be argued that the early work is as genuine and as complex as the later material, and that in sum it would be useless to apply a model of 'phases of development' or 'evolution' in Deleuze's writing as might the specialist in embryology.

A positive answer to the questions would in greater likelihood serve to inform the reader of Deleuze's lasting identification with issues of space and geography. It is in this sense that the paragraphs that follow will take up a reading of Deleuze's 'Desert Island'.

The philosopher whom Alain Badiou has rightly called an ontologist is an adept of the science of being insofar as he is a geographer and a philosopher of space (see Badiou 1997). The beginnings of the imaginative spatial ontology that will assume other – and often protean – forms are coordinated and plotted with commensurate complexity in this early article. To see how they are and in which directions they move will be the concern of the paragraphs that follow.

As always with Deleuze, the island is something that is thought, something created by virtue of being selected, classified and thus provisionally isolated or pigeonholed. Reflection on the causes of the island is what prompts the philosopher to discover that the act of selection and isolation constitutes not an instance of creation but of re-creation. The discovery of the originary and founding world that would be the piece of land surrounded by water is an effect of a variation and a repetition. The island is found within the process that makes it liable to be contemplated in the first place. It is from its inauguration as both identity and difference that one critic calls his own Caribbean world that of a 'repeating island'. In any given locale the island would be a reiteration making possible what we imagine to be the topographies of our world and our lives (see Benitez-Rojo 1996). Deleuze's essay does not broach subjectivity in terms of the experience of local or sentient space, but it does chart a multi-faceted or multi-layered ground plan of the relation of sensation and imagination to location.[1] It shows that our imagination tends to make space tantamount to being insofar as being can only be thought of in terms of becoming, in other words, within the flow, force and vitality of repetition and recreation.

It suffices to review the essay to discern its inherent cartography and implications for what concerns Deleuze and space. It begins with a quadrant defined by two species of island and two ways – one based on science and the other on the imagination – of comprehending them. What scientific geographers call *continental islands* are 'accidental' (and possibly *accidentées*, with anfractuosities seen as jagged edges) or 'derived' (having been separated from a *rive* or shore). They are born of 'a disarticulation, of an erosion, of a fracture', and they are survivors of the swallowing up or the 'engulfing of what used to retain them'.[2] By contrast, *oceanic islands* are 'originary, essential islands: sometimes they are formed by corals, they offer us a veritable organism – sometimes they surge up from under the sea, they bring to the open air a movement from the lower depths; some emerge slowly, others disappear and come back, they can't be annexed' (Deleuze 2002: 11). The sentences with which the geographical definitions are crafted betray an insular and unsettling style. They are open-ended, in a loose syntax, in which the verbal components are effectively isolated from each other. They appear almost incontinent or of such an oral texture that they make the ear imagine the words in their spoken delivery where, as such, sentences do not exist; where, in other words, a flow of expression prevails, and where, inasmuch as one descriptive is added to another, clauses, like waves, follow and fold upon and over each other.

The tenor of the description of the two kinds of island complicates the opposition of the continental to the oceanic species. It is at once scientific and mythic. The 'derived' islands are brought forward *before* their 'originary' counterparts are defined. If they withstand – or, in the highly organic idiolect that makes their seemingly inorganic matter resemble living flesh – they 'survive' being eaten or swallowed by the continents that had formerly 'retained' or kept them under their jurisdiction. The drift of Deleuze's sentence suggests holds that the derived islands had been *de facto* engulfed, under the dominion of land, before they escaped the clutches of the continent. By a short stretch of the imagination the derived islands can be figured as sailors who survive, both *on* and *as* the islands where they are. They are the fruits of the shipwreck of a continental vessel or a mutiny that separated them from the tyranny of continental land. The gist of Deleuze's French suggests the narrative of an upheaval or a founding separation that, paradoxically, defines their originarity: '[E]lles sont séparées d'un continent, nées d'une désarticulation, d'une érosion, d'une fracture, elles survivent à l'engloutissement de ce qui les retenait' (They are separated from a continent, born of a disarticulation, of an erosion, of a fracture, they survive being swallowed up by what retained them).

That is why it seems strange that oceanic islands would be called 'originary, essential', in view of the creative rupture that formed their derivative coequals. In the style of the description these islands would be errant, mercurial beings, tricksters perhaps, even Chaplinesque forms that pop out of and disappear into the ocean that would engulf them. They surge out of what elsewhere Deleuze calls an 'originary' world of lower depths or 'bas-fonds'.[3] They cannot be colonised or 'annexed' to the continent. They could be figured possibly as craters of volcanoes that draw elemental force from the earth into the atmosphere. They might also be countenanced as great accretions of calcium that coral vegetation has so accumulated in submarine places that they have become reefs and indeed patches of *terra firma*.

In all events the opposition between the two kinds enables Deleuze to mobilise inherited Aristotelian world-pictures for the purpose of creating a geography of force and intensity: 'These two kinds of islands, originary or continental, attest to a profound opposition between the ocean and the earth.' In this context the historian of geography recalls that in many diagrams of the celestial spheres the world is at the crux of ten concentric circles that describe, after earth and water at the core, air and fire, and then the lunar and planetary spheres.[4] In these configurations globe is seen in dark and light patches that depict aqueous and telluric regions roughly comprising a sum of oceans and continents. To this inherited image Deleuze adds, however, that 'the elements generally detest each other, the one is horrible to the other. In all this, nothing very reassuring'.

What had been flux and flow, bearing witness to symmetry and complementarities of all things in God's creation, is turned into war and conflict in a way that renews a sense of geographical adventure known to the Renaissance, a moment when earthly beginnings are recreated and rehearsed. The two elements of the elementary region, held within the circles of air and fire, are earth and water. They are folded upon each other and are offered to the eye as 'the diverse layers of the egg or the onion' (Broc 1980: 68ff.). Albertus Magnus' providential hypothesis argued that in the beginning the earth was covered with water, but that God left a part of the earth uncovered to allow man and animals to live.

The scientific counterpart to the theological explanation was based on the perception that certain of the circles were of different axes, such that earthen circumference, although inscribed in the aqueous surround, exceeded its container at the North Pole. Copernicus ratified the point by, 'showing that there do not exist two distinct spheres, one of earth and the other of water that "penetrated each other"', but that in their place is a single terrestrial sphere whose depressed surfaces are the basins of the seas.[5] Theories of the balance and flow of water moving about masses of land, thanks to the speculation that there existed an austral continent inhabited by the Antipodes, were defined in new terms of a general geography that included: island, peninsula, cap, isthmus, and continent.[6] The seas and rivers of the earth were thought to be in a dynamic process, due to a marvel of nature by which oceanic currents descend from certain places to others, and that as a result and a verification of the hypothesis rivers both flow into the sea and the sea (eventually and by often strange itineraries) into rivers. Yet speculation among cosmographers was so varied that there reigned as much conflict in the attributed causes of the places and movements of masses of water and land as the places and movements themselves.

Deleuze vitalises inherited cosmography when he personifies the land and the sea. In his polemology these contrary bodies are mutual enemies who use strategies to win over each other. The sea that covers much of the earth, 'takes advantage of the slightest sinking of the highest structures' of the land itself, while the earth that lies under the sea can terrorise its adversary by cutting through and renting its aqueous surface. As a consequence no inherited explanation of the character of the planet goes without conflict and struggle. It follows, too, that the 'causes' and 'reasons' for islands are themselves at war with each other, and that the condition of possibility of a deserted island would be based on a truce in the ongoing conflict of land and water.

The two other elements in the quadrant, the points of view of science and of the imagination are clearly interwoven in the discourse of the distinction being made between the earth and water. But the imagination, he argues, had already pre-empted the scientific explanation in its greater psychogenesis of islands.

The élan of humans that lead them toward islands takes up the double movement that produces the islands in themselves. To dream of islands (with all the attendant anguish and joy) is to dream of separating oneself, that one is already separated, far from continents, that that is alone and lost – or else to dream that one begins again at zero, that one recreates, that one recommences. There were derived islands, but the island is also what one derived toward, and there were originary islands, but *the island is also the origin*, the radical and absolute origin. (Deleuze 2002: x)

Recreation and separation are warring forces, like the nature of the composite elements of islands, in which are reproduced the movements at the basis of the causes for islands. The man on the island he calls deserted is no more separated from the world than the island is at a distance from a supposed continent from which it was detached. No longer does the island create itself by piercing the surface of the sea from the bottom of the earth than the man, standing aloof and alone on a shoreline, would recreates the world on the basis of what he perceives to be the island and its surrounding waters.

The radical implication of the crisscrossing of terms is that in his isolation a 'man' ascribes to his being two different origins, one of the creation and the other of the being of the island. Man reenacts the originary and derived creation of islands through the imagination of beginnings that geology and cosmography had ascribed to the birth and evolution of the core elements of the terrestrial sphere. Little distinction is made between the subject as supremely thinking creature (of science and imagination that can furnish an adequate ontology for itself) and the forces of the earth itself, whether organic or inorganic (that create a sense of conscience and of being apart or separate from any necessary presence of man). The island, like whoever desires it, is of a conscience unto itself, 'la pure conscience de l'île' (the pure conscience of the island) (Deleuze 2002: 13), being at the same time of the perceiver and the perceived alike.

At this moment in the text there occurs an event that anticipates much of Deleuze's work concerning the invention of space. When he causes barriers to erode between the subject and object in the form of man and the island Deleuze implicitly engages new reflections on *habitus*. What, why, and where the desert island? Its causes and reasons move with the syntax that makes both the place and the hypothetical man's desire to be there it a product of the imagination. Deleuze argues that to say an island is inhabited does not mean it is no longer deserted. It can be deserted where it is inhabited. The trope that leads men to the island reproduces that of its own creation prior to or after human intervention. By being separate and separated from the sea, the continent, and 'man', it remains in a creative condition. The space that it creates of itself is reflected in the syntactic shifts in the sentence that opine to imagine the sensation of the shipwrecked sailor's attraction to the island:

[I]l n'y a qu'à pousser dans l'imagination le mouvement qu'amène l'homme sur l'île. Un tel mouvement ne vient qu'en apparence rompre le désert de l'île, en vérité il reprend et prolonge l'élan qui produisait celle-ci comme île déserte; loin de le compromettre il le porte à sa perfection, à son comble. (It suffices to push into the imagination the movement that man brings upon the island. A movement of this sort only seems to break the desert from the island, in all likelihood it takes up and prolongs the élan that produced the latter as a desert island; far from compromising it he brings it to its perfection, to its zenith.) (Deleuze 2002: 13)

When the desert is broken from the island, all of a sudden we realise that the relation of the adjective, *déserte*, to its substantive, *île*, undergoes a tectonic shift. The island was a continent inasmuch as it contained a *desert*, say, what we imagine to be an quasi-infinite expanse of sand in the torrid zone of Africa. In the eyes of the person driven by an *élan vital* the island – in all its implied immensity as a desert – would be as such only when the perceived is separated from what he or she perceives – the desert island – from within the imagination. If men were:

> sufficiently separated, sufficiently creative, they would only give to the island a dynamic image of itself, a conscience of the movement that produced it, to the point that through man the island [*à travers l'homme l'île*] would finally takes conscience of itself as deserted, with or without humans. The island would only be the man's dream, and the man, the pure conscience of the island. (Deleuze 2002: 13)

Deleuze's words move the centre of subjectivity in the perceiver to the island itself as a creative force. Inhabitation, or a sense of being and becoming-in-the-world, begins when the illusion of mastery of the island is renounced in favour of letting the space realise a consciousness of its own.

At this juncture, in the revealing formula that makes the island the dream of man and 'l'homme, la pure conscience de l'île', in the apposition that makes conscience something shared by man and the island alike, there is created – or recreated – a space that becomes as such when perceiver and perceived exchange roles. The parataxis anticipates what Deleuze later calls the 'space' that becomes the momentary product of an 'event' in the context of another desert and an island – in this instance a pyramid that pierces the surface of the barren landscape – when Napoleon's troops march across northern Egypt. In question is *prehension*, the 'act of taking hold, seizing, or grasping' an object of one kind or another. 'Living beings prehend water, earth, carbon, and salts. The pyramid at a given moment prehends Bonaparte's soldiers (forty centuries are contemplating you), and reciprocally' (Deleuze 1988: 106). Space is created when the soldiers realise, whether in paranoid fantasy or in reality of military encounters, that the pyramids are observing them. When the 'datum' that would be a pyramid erupts from the floor of the desert the object of the soldiers' sensory predication turns into a subject and the soldiers into the predicate or object of the pyramid's gaze.

Deleuze's pregnant remarks in *Le pli* (1988) are close to those that concern the invention of space in 'Causes et raisons de l'île déserte'. Like the pyramid, the desert island exists before and after the advent of humans or their incursions in the world. The island is a '[c]onscience of the earth and the ocean (. . .), ready to recommence the world' (Deleuze 2002: 13). Such is what applies in *Le pli* to the event and the space it produces. In the context of Leibniz and Baroque philosophy he refines what is imagined in the scenario of the shipwrecked sailor on the sand and shore of the desert island. The datum or prehended object becomes, 'itself a preexisting or coexisting prehension, and the event, a "nexus of prehensions"' (Deleuze 1988: 106). Each new prehension (a subjectifying force, the marooned sailor taking stock of his situation on the island) becomes an object (a datum or a sailor that the sailor sees being seen by the island) that turns into a public fact for other prehending forces that would objectify it. Thus the event is 'inseparably the objectification of one prehension and the subjectification of another' (*pli* Deleuze 1988: 106), such that both the pyramid and the island are at once a public and a private affair, something simultaneously, 'actual and potential, entering into the becoming of another event and the subject of its own becoming' (*pli* Deleuze 1988: 106).

Space is experienced as the intensity of the event and perhaps, too, as its inseparability from its duration. For this reason (or cause) in his work on the desert island Deleuze is led, it seems, to remark that 'man' as such is preceded by himself and that, 'such a creature on the desert island would be the desert island inasmuch as the island is imagined and reflected' (Deleuze 2002: x) – or imagines and reflects itself – in its initial movement, that is, in its action of prehending its inhabitant. It might be said, too, that the space of the island is born at the singular point where the man and the place are at once in contact and apart from each other. The philosopher has shown that the rebirth of the island owes to the independence of the consciousness of the two prehending bodies, on the one hand the shipwrecked sailor and, on the other, the beach on which he stands.

The argument is further complicated when Deleuze notes that a desert is not a necessary attribute of a deserted island. The surrounding waters of the sea become the 'desert' surrounding the *egg-like form* of the island. The adjective becomes a substantive when it is assimilated into the smooth space of the sea, and by implication the island-egg becomes an adjective when it is put into the service of a description of the ambient milieu. With the deserted island is born an isolated or insular, but also infinitely extensive desert. The sea turns into a aridly expanse of sand and the island an embryo or a contained world of wonders – 'with the most vivid springs, the most agile fauna, the most dappled flora, the most astonishing foodstuffs, the most living savages, and the shipwrecked man as its most precious fruit' (Deleuze 2002: 14) – that would be a figment of imagination, and not a product entirely of either mythology or geology.

Could it be inferred as a result that Deleuze's island belongs to a Mediterreanan or, more specifically, an Aegean archipelago? For up to this point in the essay attention is focussed on the island as matter and space in the field of the imagination. What is it to 'meditate' the causes and reasons of an island? Does it have to do with the origins of philosophy, as he later showed with Félix Guattari, in the Mediterranean?[7] If the sea can become a desert and the island an embryo of concepts, it can be said that the philosopher is speculating on a place 'in the middle of the earthen lands', *mésogeios*, a mass of land far from the sea, in contrast to *mediterraneus*, a term that the Romans used to designate the sea they called their own for the reason that it is in the 'middle of the lands' (François de Dainville 1964: 101).

The desert and its island become an object of mediation and meditation. Montaigne, the sceptical philosopher known to champion epistemology over ontology, argued that 'le mediter est un puissant estude et plein, à qui sçait se taster et employer vigoureusement' (meditation [but also the act of meditating implied by the infinitive noun] is a powerful and full study for those who know how to sense and employ themselves vigorously) before he immediately adds, 'j'aime mieux forger mon ame que la meubler' (I prefer to forge my soul than to furnish it) (Montaigne 1962: 797).[8] In the context of the essay in which the remark is made Montaigne describes his tower, the space in which he writes and thinks, at the same time that he speculates on the art of dividing and separating entities for the purpose of getting to know them by virtue of relating and comparing them to one another. To classify is to separate and, in the same thrust, to recreate and to recommence. His *estude* or study could be at once his object and action of reflection – his art and science – as well as the room in which he thinks and writes. It could be at once the space he forges, a sea of infinite extension, and the desert island of his tower, the place he inhabits to the degree that its conscience is congruent with his own. By comparative means the island becomes the space where philosophy works and acts, a study that is the conscience of its surroundings.

In his essay Deleuze reaches the Aegean archipelago by way of a literary itinerary that bears resemblance to what Montaigne equates to be the identities of mediation and meditation. The desert island is populated with myths, argues Deleuze, and belongs more to mythology than the science of geography. Inasmuch as most people prefer not to understand their myths they need literature to intervene and to, 'interpret ingeniously the myths that can no longer be understood', especially at those moments when myths cannot be either dreamt or reproduced. Two novels built from the theme of the desert island, Jean Giraudoux's *Suzanne et le Pacifique* and Defoe's *Robinson Crusoe*, attest to the end of mythology. In the latter, a book so insufferably boring that 'it is sad to see children still reading it', (Deleuze 2002: 15), the protagonist, an exemplar of the Protestant ideal, treats the island as if it were a piece of private property: 'The mythic recreation of the world from the very being of the desert island gives way to a reconstruction of everyday bourgeois life based on capital investment' (Deleuze 2002: 15). Every healthy reader, he avows, would wish that Friday the slave would finally cannibalise Robinson in order to have the narrative averte the assimilation of the mythology of the desert island into the puritan ethic. By contrast, Suzanne's desert island in Giraudoux's creation is a place where mythology dies because the objects in the heroine's midst reproduce the commodities that circulate in modern cities. Tepid and tasteless, she is not in the company of originary figures of the likes of Adam, 'but of young cadavers, and when she discovers living men, she loves them with a uniform affection, in the manner of priests, as if love were the minimum threshold of her perception' (Deleuze 2002: 16).

These two novels vividly adduce the failure of the inhabitant of a desert island to reach the power of myth in a space in which myth abounds. They attest to the death of myth that in Deleuze's essay broader reflection on desertic space is brought forward to revive and re-energise. Giraudoux's and Defoe's two works, genial symptoms of a parabola that leads from myth to the novel, incite an implementation of what might be called the theory and practice of the desert island.[9] In the concluding paragraph of the essay Deleuze begins, as if in a manifesto, '[t]he stakes involve recovering the mythological life of the desert island'. As a corollary, 'returning to the movement of the imagination . . . turns the desert island into a model, a prototype of the collective soul' (Deleuze 2002: 16). The latter is implied not to be a social movement but an immanent presence of energy and vital force. Vital force is made manifest less through the creation of the island than its *recreation*, its rebirth or renaissance after a catastrophe following its birth. One principle of a creative repetition and variation is brought forward through the imagination of the island, a mountain (or both at once) pushing above the sea, where survivors of an originary deluge recommence life as such. Another comes through a 'cosmic egg' that leads to the creation of Mediterranean islands – Circé and Calypso – where a separation of genders promotes recommencement through parthenogenesis, and where, in 'an ideal of the recommencement there is something the precedes commencement itself' (Deleuze 2002: 17), which takes up the latter in order to deepen it and to have it recede in time.

The desert island, no matter if it is in the Pacific or in the Mediterranean, becomes the emblematic place where there can be perceived originary myths and the concurrent forces that generate them. Once it is thought of in this way the desert island becomes the vital space of creative difference and repetition. Surely, in the historical parabola of Deleuze's writing 'Causes and Reasons of the Desert Island' figures as a parable for the longer work on difference and repetition or a threshold, following his comparisons of eggs to Bodies without Organs, for the distinction of 'smooth' and 'striated' spaces (Deleuze 1968; Deleuze and Guattari 1980). More importantly, in the unconscious register of concepts and the words that are conveyed in a language that is continually being born of itself, Deleuze's *île déserte* can be imagined as something insular, insular to the degree that it remains, in respect both to itself and other entities, entirely singular. Desert islands in the early essay comprise a figurative geography of *singularities* in other writings. They can be said to belong to a cartographic genre, the 'island-book' or *isolario*, with which a good deal of Deleuze's work is directly or indirectly affiliated.[10] In these works, written and illustrated at the time of discovery and global expansion, the world is conceived not as continents and their ambient oceans and seas, but as a quasi-infinite number of islands, each of an unknown (or expanding) sum bearing unique traits in comparison with other islands.

It may be, in the fashion of a projective conclusion, that the island could be imagined as a space of singularity. If indeed Deleuze calls 'singularity' the 'power of the Idea', then the deserted island is one of a thousand sites of both difference and repetition (Deleuze 1968: 41). For Deleuze the island is not a geographical representation but, rather, a plot-point and a plateau for any of the philosopher's lines of flight and of migration. The island becomes an enchanted space where concept continually moves in all directions and reinvents itself.

References

Apian, P. (1529), *Cosmographia*, Antwerp: R. Bollaert.
Badiou, A. (1997), *Gilles Deleuze: La Clameur de l'être*, Paris: Hachette.

Benitez-Rojo, A. (1996), *The Repeating Island: The Caribbean and the Postmodern Perspective*, trans. J. Maraniss, Durham: Duke University Press.

Broc, N. (1989), *La géographie de la Renaissance (1420–1620)*, Paris: Bibliothèque Nationale.

Deleuze, G. (1968), *Différence et répétition*, Paris: PUF.

Deleuze, G. (1983), *Cinéma 1: L'image mouvement*, Paris: Minuit.

Deleuze, G. (1988), *Le pli: Leibniz et le baroque*, Paris: Minuit.

Deleuze, G. (2002), *Causes et raisons des îles désertes et autres textes: Textes et entretiens 1953–1974*, ed. D. Lapoujade, Paris: Minuit.

Deleuze, G. and Guattari, F. (1980), *Mille plateaux*, Paris: Minuit.

Deleuze, G. and Guattari, F. (1992), *Où est-ce que la philosophie?*, Paris: Minuit.

De Montaigne, M. (1962), *Oeuvres complètes*, ed. M. Rat and A. Thibaudet, Paris: Gallimard/Pleiade.

Finé, O. (1532), *Protomathesis*, Paris: G. Morrhij and I. Petri.

Finé, O. (1553), *Le sphère du monde*, Paris: Vasconsan.

Finé, O. (1558), *La théorique des cieulx et sept planètes*, Paris: G. Cavellat.

François de Dainville, S. J. (1964), *Le langage des géographes*, Paris: Picard.

Gallois, L. (1963), *Les géographes allemands de la Renaissance*, Amsterdam: Meridian Reprint.

LeviStrauss, C. (1992), *Histoire de lynx*, Paris: Plon.

Lukacs, G. (1971), *Theory of the Novel: A Historico-Philosophical Essay on the Forms of Great Epic Literature*, trans. A. Bostock, Cambridge: MIT Press.

Tuan, Yi-fu (1990), *Topophilia: A Study of Environmental Perception, Attitudes and Values*, New York: Columbia University Press.

Notes

1. By contrast it is informative to appose the work of Yi-fu Tuan, including *Topophilia* (1990), to that of Deleuze. From the experience of space Tuan obtains concepts or mental maps that, in turn mediate its discovery and perception.

2. Deleuze 2002: 11. Further reference to this article will be made in the text. For the purpose of the rhetoric of this article all allusion is made to the French texts. Their translations into English are my responsibility. This essay was begun before the 2004 publication of an English edition, *Desert Islands and Other Texts (1953–1974)*, translated by Mike Taormina (Cambridge and London: Semiotext(e).

3. In a comparative treatment of the films of Erich von Stroheim and Luis Buñuel, Deleuze notes that the originary world:

   > does not exist independently of determined milieus, but inversely causes that world to exist with characters and traits that come from higher up, or rather from an even more terrifying depth [*fond*]. The originary world is a beginning of the world, but also an end of the world, and the irresistible downward slope of the one to the other: it is what carries the median area, and also what causes it to be a closed, absolutely hermetic milieu, or else what opens it ever so slightly onto an uncertain hope. (Deleuze 1983: 176–7)

   The movement can be called Chaplinesque because, in a memorable sequence of *The Idle Class* (1924), a film that figures prominently in Deleuze's pantheon, the tramp escapes apprehension by the police by jumping into and out of thick masses of shrubbery. He baits the law as he evades it.

4. Illustrated in Pieter Apian 1529; and Oronce Finé's works, including the

Protomathesis (1532), *Le sphère du monde* (1553) and *La théorique des cieulx et sept planètes* (1558).

5. Broc 1980: 68, following Lucien Gallois 1963: 145.
6. Broc 1980: 69. A comparative history of each of these terms is included in Chapter 2 (hydrography) of François de Dainville 1964: 97–115.
7. In their chapter, 'Geo-philosophie' in Deleuze and Guattari 1992.
8. For the relation of ontology to epistemology, based on the remark, similar to what Deleuze makes of a man and an island, that, 'we have no communication with being', see Lévi-Strauss 1992: 218–20.
9. In this respect Deleuze follows closely György Lukács (1971), in which immanence (of epic and myth) are compared to a lapsarian condition (of the modern novel).
10. A comprehensive study of the genre is contained in Frank Lestringant (2003), *Le Livre des îles* (Geneva: Droz, 2003).

Chapter 13

What the Earth Thinks

Gregg Lambert

What is 'Geo-Philosophy'?

Before examining the concept of space in Deleuze and Guattari's philosophy, one would first have to ask what the Earth thinks. In other words, if the Earth had a philosophy, what would it be? If the Earth had a political philosophy, moreover, would it be a political theology or perhaps something more resembling a political geology? In responding to these questions, I will argue that we must understand that what Deleuze and Guattari call 'geo-philosophy' is a partial solution to the language and the concepts of historical materialism, the creation of an alternative language and conceptual plane that is equal to the question of the Earth (the only true Universal!), that is, the creation of a geo-materialism, or of a political geology. In light of this thesis, we might be led to wonder how to evaluate a recent work like *Empire* (Hardt and Negri 2000), which seems much more of a 'compromise formation' in this regard, a marriage of the old language of historical materialism with the geological metaphors borrowed from Deleuze and Guattari's second volume of the 'Capitalism and Schizophrenia project', and in particular, the concept of 'deterritorialisation' which is put to extensive use in this later work. Of course, Hardt and Negri recognise the need to renovate the conceptual language of Marxism in order to confront the latest stage of capitalism and the new reality of globalisation, which is why they borrow heavily from Deleuze and Guattari's language of geo-philosophy, even while they choose to keep the old narrative framework of 'Universal History' in order to tell the story of 'passing through Empire, to get to the other side' (Hardt and Negri 2000: 206). Although I would not be the first to observe that *Empire* is the most recent attempt to rewrite Marx's *Grundrisse* for a contemporary leftist audience, I would point out that in many respects this revision takes its model from Deleuze and

Guattari's own *Anti-Oedipus* (1983), and not as much from the subsequent plane of concepts that is proposed in *A Thousand Plateaus* (1987). In fact, the second volume of the 'Capitalism and Schizophrenia project' eschews many of its earlier strategies with regard to the concepts of Marx and Engels, and the concepts of 'Universal History', in particular, and instead seems to opt for a more pure conceptual plane of geo-philosophy (perhaps alluding to Marx's own shift from the Hegelian-influenced early writings to the new abstract machine of political economy that is invented in *Das Kapitale*).

If Deleuze and Guattari come to speak more of a political geology than in terms of a political theology, this is what makes their talk of emancipation somewhat distinct from both traditional Marxism, and also 'new-age' versions like that found in *Empire*. Nevertheless, it is important to notice that the question that each of these approaches continues to share is the fundamental social problem of how to create a revolutionary movement of desire and, at the same time, to ward off the intoxicating fantasies associated with what Deleuze and Guattari refer to as the 'full body of the Despot', or with the return of a new 'State-Apparatus'. Thus, their viewpoint runs counter to the appeal to 'theological forms of sovereignty', even those by an oppressed people, who often dream of a new despot, or identify with the return of what Foucault defined as 'a pastorale form of governmentality', such as the Hebrew state, or the Christian Monarchy (Foucault 1997: 68). This hope, according to Deleuze and Guattari, often turns out to be the same one that always leads us back to the theology of the State-Form (the benevolent nation or 'Father land', the 'Good Despot', the household order of *pater familias*). Their frequent critiques of the theology of the State-Form, and of the desires and superstitions that are often attached to its avatars (including various national and racial ideologies), can be understood to belong to the Spinozist tradition of political philosophy, a tradition that has preoccupied Negri as well, and can be formulated in terms of a certain question from *Anti-Oedipus* that also appears in the following passage from *Empire*:

> A long tradition of political scientists has said the problem is not why do people rebel but why they do not. Or rather, as Deleuze and Guattari say: 'the fundamental problem of political philosophy is still precisely the one that Spinoza saw so clearly (and that Wilhelm Reich rediscovered): "Why do men fight *for* their servitude as stubbornly as though it were their salvation?"' (Hardt and Negri 2000: 210)

Of course, their response to this problem always surrounds the question, 'how to create a Body without Organs?' and, at the same time, 'to avoid another judgement of God'; or, in plainer terms, how to encourage new social formations of power that do not fall back into repressive states of individual desire?

In an earlier interview conducted for the journal *Actuel*, Guattari clarifies the following with regard to this problem:

> The whole question turns on a State apparatus. Why would you look to a party or a State apparatus to liberate desires? It's bizarre. Wanting improved justice is like wanting good judges, good cops, good bosses, a cleaner France, etc. And then we are told: how do you propose to unify isolated struggles without a State apparatus? The Revolution clearly needs a war-machine, but that is not a State apparatus. It also needs an analytic force, an analyzer of the desires of the masses – but not an external mechanism of synthesis. What is liberated desire? A desire that escapes the impasse of individual private fantasy; it's not about adapting desire, socializing and disciplining it, but hooking it up in such a way that its process is uninterrupted in the social body, so its expression can be collective. (Deleuze 2004: 227)

In another interview that occurs during the same period after the publication of *Anti-Oedipus*, French anthropologist Pierre Clastres (who is cited often by Deleuze and Guattari) summarises the brilliant thesis that he discovered operating throughout Deleuze and Guattari's arguments, one that responds directly to the problem of the return of the repressive apparatus of the State-Form to hinder any revolutionary movement of desire – the thesis of the primitive horde.

> Yes, the State exists in the most primitive societies, even in the smallest band of nomadic hunters. It exists, but it is ceaselessly warded off. It is ceaselessly prevented from becoming a reality. A primitive society directs all its efforts toward preventing its chief from becoming a chief (and that can go as far as murder). If history is the history of class struggle (I mean in societies that have classes), then the history of a classless society is the history of their struggle against a latent State. Their history is the effort to encode the flows of power. (Deleuze 2004: 227)

One can see how this fundamental intuition from the chapter 'Savages, Barbarians, Civilized Men' is fashioned into a major operational thesis of *Empire*, a 'strategy' which is revealed from the viewpoint of the Universal History of a classless society that ends with 'the Multitude' successfully encoding power without resorting once again to the State-Form. After all, what is a Multitude but a primitive *socius* that already dwells in the interstices of late-capitalism, over-coded by globalised flows of capital, at the virtual fringes and the multiple points where 'deterritorialisation' occurs in a non-unifying and essentially nomadic form of collective phenomena? At the same time, it would not be difficult to prove that Hardt and Negri's fundamental thesis is secretly nostalgic, basically an attempt to ward off the consolidation and return of state sovereignty through forging new alliances with the 'diabolical powers' that have always been just outside the gates of *Empire*, even in the somewhat desperate hope that this will bring about a new Rubicon. At one level, this hope can be understood as a expression of 'new-age' millennialism, one that combines postmodern desires for hybridity and 'anthropological exodus' with the epic dimension of a new *race* – and I use this word intentionally to describe the concept of the 'Multitude' – that will emerge from the 'outside' to bring about the 'Fall of Empire'. In other words, as they write, 'a new nomad horde, a new race of barbarians, will arise to invade or evacuate Empire' (Hardt and Negri 2000: 217).[1]

If the problem of the State-Form of Sovereignty has been one of the most difficult questions to resolve historically, then there is good reason that it appears in Deleuze and Guattari's final work *What is Philosophy?* (1997) as the first and final question of what they define as geo-philosophy, since the fundamental problematic of 'how to make a philosophy with the Earth' already appears across a ground that is occupied by concrete social formations and by the historical societies that appear today more and more like throws of the die over the same ground. And each time, we might say, the solutions can only be deemed as partial and unresolved, since each solution that is actualised can only be as good as what Spinoza first defined as the 'common notions' that comprise the ideal image of freedom belonging to each historical society. In other words, each time we can only say that the solution to the problem of society itself could only have been as good as the plane of concepts it occupied, and which constituted its historical ground. As Deleuze remarked many times, concepts do not fall from the sky ready-made; rather, they are pieced together from earlier concepts, for 'every concept relates back to other concepts, not only in its history but in its becoming and present connections' (Deleuze and Guattari 1997: 19). Therefore, in order to understand better the composition of the plane of concepts proposed by Deleuze and Guattari's 'geo-philosophy', and how both its possible becoming as well as its present connections must be distinguished from previous traditions of political philosophy (and from Marxism, in particular), in the following passages I will attempt to situate and to contextualise Deleuze and Guattari's concepts by exploring the following questions: what is the Earth? (moreover, what are 'strata' or what Deleuze and Guattari describe as the processes of 'stratification')? What is a *socius* (in particular, the stratification engendered by a primitive territorial-machine, and of a State-Form)? And finally: what, actually, is meant by the concept of 'deterritorialisation'?

A Conspiracy of the Earth? A fragment from Hesiod

Taking up our first question, I wish to return to a very early source: Hesiod's *Theogony*. Although some might immediately believe this to be a Western source, there are many early Egyptian, Babylonian and Northern African hints and traces so that things get confused and contradictory. In any case, in one of the original creation myths assembled by Hesiod, there is the story of the Earth (Gaia), and Heaven (Ouranos), and a certain progeny called Kronos (who is figured as the archaic forerunner of Time). In this story it is said that Gaia is covered up by Ouranos, so much so that he never lifts his body from her day and night but constantly fornicates and pushes Gaia's progeny into the inner recesses of her body until, as the Greek has it, Gaia is all 'crowded out', stuffed up with her own generations, to the point of bursting. It is at this point in the story that something strange occurs. A third party comes onto the scene, Kronos, who mysteriously is reported to be the first progeny of Gaia and Kronos – and of course, don't ask these stories to make sense, since we must imagine that one of Gaia's children managed to escape the eternal rape of Heaven, and the marriage bed of his two parents![2] It is said that Gaia devised a 'crafty, evil device' (*techain*), or conspiratorial plot, with Kronos to rid her of her unwelcome suitor, and sent him to hide in a place of ambush (*loxos*, the ancient twin of *logos*). The next time Ouranos came, figuratively I imagine, Kronos leapt from his place of ambush and castrated his father, Heaven, which is why the world was divided in two from that point onward, so that no part of Heaven actually touched the Earth.[3]

If this act of separation was not terrible enough, he then spread the seed from Ouranos' bloody genitals over the entire surface of Gaia: 'The drops of blood fertilize Gaia and generate Furies, Giants and Melian nymphs; the severed parts fall into the sea' (Kirk and Raven 1957: 35). Thus, from these seeds sprang the race of Titans (the bastard sons of Heaven), who would later assume the roles of poetic figures the earthly powers, the monarchs and despots, the Caesars and, finally, modern nation-states. Although, of course, the last can only be pre-figured allegorically in Hesiod's original fable, today, we might perceive the countenance of a new Heaven in the obese figure of globalisation, the giant colossus with two backs who lies a little too heavily on the Earth and which internalises all desiring production within its ever-expanding body. It is because this new figure of Heaven appears more powerful and all-encompassing than Gaia's previous suitors, moreover, that recently there has been a noticeable loss of faith, among the intermediate surface dwellers, in the existence of a new *place* of ambush, in the return of old Kronos or in the idea of forging a new conspiracy with the Earth.

I do not recount this early myth of Greek theodicy here simply to be dramatic. I would argue that one can find in the writings of Deleuze and Guattari a version, if not a revision, of Hesiod's fable in the description of the Earth whose body is said to be bloated (*trop gros*), pock-marked by territories, over-burdened and weighted down by the despotic forms of sovereignty and theological forms of the state. So many Heavens have been invented to lie heavy on the Earth, like obese lovers that cover her body day and night. In fact, we might think of each Heaven as the representation of a distinct stratum, and the multiple strata that pile on top of one another as the multiplication of layers or plateaus in the geological diagram that Deleuze and Guattari employ in their conception of 'stratification' as *the* problem of political geology, and of the Earth as suffering from too much stratification. Here, I will refer to the definition offered by Professor Challenger, a character drawn from the novels of Arthur Conan Doyle and Edgar Rice Burroughs, who first appears in *A Thousand Plateaus* to expound upon the concept of stratification.[4] According to Challenger:

> Strata are layers, Belts. They consist of giving form to matter, of imprisoning intensities or locking singularities into systems of resonance and redundancy, of producing on the body of the earth molecules large and small and of organizing them into molar aggregates. Strata are acts of capture, they are like 'black holes' or occlusions striving to seize whatever comes into their reach. They operate by coding and reterritorialisation upon the earth: they proceed by code and by territoriality. The strata are judgments of God; stratification in general is the entire system of the judgment of God (but the earth, or the body without organs, constantly eludes that judgment, flees and becomes destratified, decoded, de-territorialized). (Deleuze and Guattari 1987: 40)

A surface of stratification is defined as, 'a more compact plane of consistency lying between two layers' (Deleuze and Guattari 1987: 40). But, as they also observe, 'strata always come in pairs', one serving as a substratum for the other. This can be readily illustrated in Hesiod's fable, with Gaia (the Earth) forming the substratum of Ouranos (Heaven); however, something comes between them, the surface occupied by Kronos, the surface that exfoliates from the bloody genitals of Ouranos, which represents an original point of deterritorialisation that produces surface through which peoples and territories are first distributed.

Prior to this event there was no surface, and no 'space', strictly speaking; or rather, between the two layers or strata represented by the body of Ouranos lying on Gaia 'day and night', there was no exterior place for Gaia to produce new strata as these were constantly crammed back into the inner recesses of her ever more crowded and populous body. It was only through the intervention of Kronos who came between this ancient pair of strata that the idea of an *externalised plane*, separated from the immediate joining of the two primitive strata, was first possible. The contradiction we have noted, the externalisation of the surface Kronos occupied as a place of ambush prior to the division of earth and sky into two separate strata, can thus be interpreted as the retroactive image of the 'act' created afterwards as the necessary condition of its possibility. Moreover, the original Greek meanings of *techain* (as plot, or secret pact between Gaia and Kronos) and *loxos* (a place of ambush, hidden away from Ouranos) also point to the political and strategic determination of a surface or place, even (non) place, from which the revolt against Heaven unfolded – two external relations to power or domination whose utopian meanings are obvious: (1) Conspiratorial plot or 'crafty device' invented by a revolutionary assemblage (or what Deleuze and Guattari later call 'a war machine'); (2) a utopian (non) place that constitutes the virtual point of emergence (or 'point of deterritorialisation') of new strata, and particularly those strata that concern us, which are composed of humans (but not exclusively, since they also include vegetable, mineral and even machinic phyla as well) and are defined less by species than by a distribution of strata that takes the distinctive form of a *socius*.

Social Bodies, or the Principles of Territoriality

In turning to our second question, specifically, we are interested in two types or organisations of a *socius* frequently discussed in *A Thousand Plateaus*: the primitive territorial-machine and the State-Form. From the perspective of the Earth (the immobile continuum, the ground of production, the Body without Organs), so-called 'human societies' only appear as coded blocks (either mobile or static), or as inscriptions organised into distinctive patterns of cities and territories, more recently into populations. The Earth is tattooed by the societies which emerge to represent the points of its surface that are over-coded, and human beings do not appear 'on the surface', as they are attached to it by their organs (by their eyes, their hands, their mouths, their genitals, by their great and over-developed anuses) in order to make *another* meta-body. It is at this point, as with Aristotle, that human beings cease to be defined primarily as biological entities and become elements of an entirely different assemblage called a *socius* or 'social machine'. In turn, this creates the condition for the emergence of the great territorial machines that have distributed themselves across the surface of the Earth which have bodies of human beings as their parts; and their organs are now attached directly to the Earth through the intermediary of territorial signs, which are composed of matter drawn from the hybrid inscriptions of soil and blood. It is from these primitive territorial machines that the great races and the territorial bands emerge and strap themselves to the Earth's body like lines that criss-cross the Dogon egg, carving out internal neighbouring zones, remote exterior precincts, frontiers and wastelands, boundaries and borderlines, and what Kant earlier described as the 'vast spaces of communication' (the oceans, deserts, the air) that lie between the doorsteps or porticos of the *domus*, the homeland (*Heimat*), the native soil (*nation*). Far from being a static notion, the concept of space that this process of stratification express is wildly productive. The specific characteristic of space that the processes of stratification express can be defined as a *viz activa*, by the tendency to proliferate and to multiply and become a 'manifold', something that Deleuze later explores through the concept of 'the fold' (*le pli*). Throughout this process, however, the Earth must be defined as a Thing that remains consistent, immanently connected through all its points or surfaces (interior and exterior), or rather a plane of consistency that becomes more compact and hardened the more strata or layers are produced. In other words, with each new surface actually produced through stratification, the Earth withdraws even further into itself, becoming more impenetrable and *In-Itself*. (I will return to comment on this tendency below when we come back to the notion of 'deterritorialisation'.) Human societies can therefore be described as 'mega-machines' that cover the Earth – we recall the description of Ouranos, 'he stretched himself, and spread all over her' – and thus comprise its new surfaces of inscription and encoding. The question I have raised above concerns whether these surfaces can be arranged successively in a historical description, or whether their arrangement must be sought in the distinctive process of stratification itself.

The description of societies as 'mega-machines' requires us, once again, to clarify all this talk of machines in Deleuze and Guattari's writings. Simply put, a 'machine' is actually a much more accurate manner of speaking of societies as being, in fact, composed of the relations of production and surfaces of inscription (or what they call recording); that is, the relations of production and recording that are inscribed directly onto bodies which form the different surfaces of social machines. As they write: 'The social machine is literally a machine, irrespective of any meta-phor, inasmuch as it exhibits an immobile motor and undertakes a variety of interventions: flows are set apart, elements are detached from a chain, and portions of the tasks are then distributed' (Deleuze and Guattari 1983: 41). Of course, this description refers back to Marx's image of the relations of production that take on distinctive characteristics at each stage of the evolution of capital. Human societies are made up of lines, some of which are segmented and appear hard and easily noticeable on a surface of inscription-recording; however, others are more supple and appear further down (such as the flows of desire that are inscribed in the infrastructure of production itself), or take the shape of flows that circulate over the entire surface (flows of money, for example, that circulate in patterns that are difficult to perceive on first glance). Of course, there have been many different machines, as many as different organisations of the *socius* determined by the relations of pro-duction, from the primitive territorial machine, to the despotic feudal machines, to the machines of the nation-state, to the globalised machines of late-capitalism. In each case, 'flows are set apart, elements are detached, and tasks distributed'; however, in each case as well, new strata are produced that bear distinctive characteristics and new elements, which is why Deleuze and Guattari constantly emphasise the notion of 'territory' in distinguishing between different strata, or arrangements of the *socius*, in order to observe 'what has changed' in passing from one level, or stratum, to the next.

At the same time, according to Deleuze and Guattari, it is only from the current perspective of this last machine that we can speak of the wholesale dismantling of all the machines that preceded it – thus, of the decline of the nation-state machine and its gradual incorporation into the machinery of global capitalism which today covers the Earth and constitutes a new surface of inscription and recording (or memory), and which unites all events and bodies into one *mega-machine* at 'the end of History'. Thus:

> It will be necessary to await capitalism to find a semiautonomous organiza-tion of technical production that tends to appropriate memory and repro-duction, and thereby modifies the forms of the exploitation of man; but, as a matter of fact, this organization presupposes a dismantling of the great social machines that preceded it. (Deleuze and Guattari 1983: 141)

This is why they often claim that capital is perhaps the most 'miracu-lous' of all previous social machines, since it appears that everything that happens has been pre-ordained to happen for its benefit, to bring it into being and to make it the internal presupposition of every previous *socius*. As Deleuze once remarked: 'The first capitalists are waiting there like birds of prey, waiting to swoop down on the worker who has fallen through the cracks of the previous system. This is what is meant by primitive accumulation' (Deleuze 2004: 268). However, this is partly an illusion that belongs to the 'History of Capitalism' itself, that is, to the idea of Universal History which is completely consistent with the encoding of capital and its specific line of development onto the full body of the Earth, of the process of stratification in which it plays the role of an *'Urstaat'* that organises every other social form that preceded it, even those that are remote in time or place, and some that have yet to be invented ('the most ancient and the most recent forms of exploitation of man by man') (Deleuze and Guattari 1983: 140). On the contrary, following the observations by Maurice Godelier, Deleuze and Guattari argue against what could be understood as the underlying theoretical assumption that belongs to the current thesis of globalisation: rather than the West's line of development being universal because it recurs everywhere else, it must be understood as universal because it has recurred nowhere else: 'it is typical therefore [only] because, in its singular process, it has obtained a universal result' (Godelier, quoted in Deleuze and Guattari 1983: 40).

To describe the class of the 'universal' as 'typical', or general, is very different from saying it is determining 'in all cases'. (This recalls the problem of logic based on syllogism.) On the other hand, many current theories of globalisation (including, I might add, the theory of 'Empire') continue to mistake the two types, or species of universality, which can be defined in terms of the distinction between 'totality' and 'singularity' (or the contingency of the Western line of development). Why is it, one might ask, that most critiques of the capitalist system insist on the universality of the first kind, that it has and will continue to recur everywhere else according to the line of development first established in the West, rather than developing the critical insight that its form of universality corresponds to a line of development that belongs to the West and 'could recur nowhere else'? In other words, the more that the current critiques of capitalism continue to 'universalise', and the more they pretend to speak from the position of the full body of the Earth, the more they continue to perpetuate the myth of globalisation according to one line of development, that is, according to a singular process of stratification that encodes the entire surface of the Earth – *that stretches itself, and spreads all over her*! In fact, the *singular universality* that belongs to the Western line of development is expressed in the form of *absolute imperium* that characterises its political organisation of democratic states, but all along a line of a singular interest that must find its own limit 'at a certain point' in other organisations that are always located 'outside' the West.[5] As Deleuze and Guattari write:

> if we say that capitalism determines the conditions and the possibility of a universal history, this is true insofar as capitalism has to deal essentially with its own limit, its own destruction – as Marx says, insofar as it is capable of self-criticism (at least to a certain point: the point where a limit appears, in the very movement that counteracts this tendency). (Deleuze and Guattari 1983: 140)

In this regard, we see that the problem of 'the West' is, in a certain sense, equivalent to the problem of 'Oedipus' in Deleuze and Guattari's argument – when viewed as a form of universality that captures desiring-production, recoding all deterritorialisation according to its own singular axiomatic, which becomes 'typical' as a result. 'The West' produces the *universal* as its own 'plane of immanence,' and then *'rejoices over the evil deed'* (Hesiod). And yet, *'the whole of Oedipus is anal* and implies an individual overinvestment of the organ to compensate for its collective disinvestment' (Deleuze and Guattari 1983: 143). Would it not be conceivable to apply this same statement to the future of the Western line of development (or 'the history of capitalism' heretofore), somewhat analogically or speculatively from the current moment, but rather once other systems and future instruments of capital begin to disinvest from its overarching myth of stratification, that of *absolute imperium*?

As Deleuze and Guattari argue, therefore, it is only from the perspective of the full body of the Earth (or 'the absolute point of deterritorialisation') that the idea of Universal History can first appear not only as 'retrospective' (with respect to its own line of development), but also 'contingent, singular, ironic and critical'. This remark is important with regard to the possible manners in which capitalism may encounter its own limit 'outside' or 'beyond the line' of its own internal development, and specifically the development of Western capitalist societies. In some sense, the limit in question concerns the appearance of its universality when viewed from the perspective of other societies, which could only appear as 'contingent, singular, ironic, or critical' – in other words, as finite arrangements of interest that always flow back to 'the West'. Hence, the critical remark made by Godelier above is extremely important for perceiving how the form of juridical sovereignty that underlies Western democratic institutions and ideas – and the idea of universality especially – has functioned as the immobile motor of the expansion of the Western line of development in the form of *absolute imperium*. As Godelier observes, even the theoretical idea of socialism (developed, in part, in compensation for the forms of exploitation that belong 'retrospectively' to 'the History of Capitalist Socities') now confronts other societies and 'cause them to leave behind the most ancient as well as the most recent forms of exploitation of man by man' (Godelier, quoted by Deleuze and Guattari 1983: 140n.). But we might ask: to *leave them behind for what*, if not for the new forms of exploitation that belong to the technical process of the production of capital, and for the benefit of 'an arrogant breed who are our Masters' (Deleuze 1995: 181) and alongside the creation of new exploited classes that populate the different regions of the earth today? This is what Godelier refers to as, 'the authentic universality of the West's line of development' (Deleuze and Guattari: 1983: 140n.); and, of course, we should not only accept this remark as ironic and critical, but see that it is made to show how the 'authenticity' of Western notions of universality (but also social justice, equality, fraternity, and so on) are appearing more singularly, from the perspective of other societies, in light of their difference from actual practices.[6] Finally, this is also what Deleuze and Guattari suggest by the statement that capitalism must, 'deal with its own limit, its own destruction' (Deleuze and Guattari 1983: 140), and this would occur precisely at those points where its own 'authenticity' is constantly being placed in crisis, where its expression of Universal History appears against the background of its difference from other lines of development, in the realisation that this history could indeed recur nowhere else, and would no longer cause other societies to 'leave behind' the forms of exploitation of man by man. Such is already the case, I would argue, in different regions of the world and in certain 'other societies' where there is a preference for 'primitive territorial machines' (that is, from the perspective of 'the West' concerning the so-called return of 'archaic religious fundamentalisms') over the adoption of 'Western ideas', including the idea of socialism.

Political and economic theorists have already perceived that the history of capitalism in the West is contingent on a certain line of development, one that is completely dependent on *expansion*, that is, on an 'immobile motor of deterritorialisation' and a process of stratification that displaces the limit internal to the capitalist *socius* onto different segments of the Earth and, in particular, that always confronts this same line in the 'other societies' it encounters and in the new forms of exploited labour that it has created in its attempt, as Marx said, 'to go still further'. At the same time, I recall the critical diagnosis of this tendency that is offered by Deleuze from the 1973 interview 'Capitalism and Desire':

In every respect, capitalism has a very particular character: its lines of escape are not just difficulties that arise, they are the very conditions of its operation. Capitalism is founded on a generalised decoding of every flow . . . It did not create any code; it created a kind of accounting, an axiomatic of decoded flows, as the basis of its economy. It ligatures the points of escape and moves ahead. It is always expanding its own borders, and always finds itself in a situation where it must close off new escape routes at its borders, pushing them back once more. It has resolved none of the fundamental problems. It can't even foresee the monetary increase in a country over a year. It is endlessly re-crossing its own limits, which keep on appearing farther out. It puts itself in alarming situations with respect to its own production, its social life, its demographics, its periphery in the Third World, its interior regions, etc. *The system is leaking all over the place.* (Deleuze 2003: 270, my emphasis, G. L.)

Deleuze and Guattari constantly emphasise, it is the very same principle of deterritorialisation upon which this form of capitalism depends as its 'immobile motor' is the same one that has always haunted each society in which it historically appeared as the terrifying nightmare from which it cannot awaken. This is because in each instance of deterritorialisation that allows the capitalist *socius*, 'to displace its own limit further out, and to move on' (across the surfaces of the earth), there always appears a frightening tendency of this process to veer toward a point of 'absolute de-territitorialization'.[7] This produces, as they have frequently argued, the extremely peculiar, if not 'singular', expressions of *dread* that can be found at the basis of Western religious, sexual (or familial), political and philosophical institutions: specifically, the dread of 'decoded flows'. In fact, the more that the West has expanded by displacing its own interior limit onto the full body of the Earth, the more vulnerable Western societies have become 'to a dread they feel for a flow that would elude their code' (Deleuze and Guattari 1983: 142), a feeling (or 'I feel') that has returned in the heart of all its social institutions. This, in a nutshell, is the entire thesis of *Anti-Oedipus* concerning the strange union of desire with this singular feeling of dread which stems from the decoded flows that haunt the capitalist *socius* from an 'outside' it has first produced, a strange amalgamation of desire and dread that finds its universal apotheosis in the obese figure of Oedipus, who appears according to a fine phrase by Artaud, like 'a dead rat's ass suspended from the ceiling of the sky' (Artaud, quoted in Deleuze and Guattari 1983: 143).

Year 0: The End of Capitalism

As an experiment, let us imagine tomorrow the Earth is struck by a giant meteor that extinguishes all biological life and every *socius* distributed across its full body. The question would be whether the Earth itself would ever even notice this as an event, but would remain absolutely indifferent, the immoveable and glacial entity that has terrified every society trembling on its surface? Would the Earth be concerned whether the life forms that occupied its body were that of a human *socius*, or to employ a beautiful phrase first coined by Jonathan Schell in *The Fate of the Earth,* merely a 'Kingdom of insects and grass', or even if some-day it returned to a purely mineral environment without atmosphere or vegetable life? Would this not be one way of envisaging 'the End of Capitalism'? Certainly! But perhaps this raises the point that Deleuze and Guattari continued to make in their work – that the end of capitalism (or 'the end of history', as the dominant myth that belongs to capitalist societies) is not and has never been the most critical limit to achieve. 'Every civilisation and every epoch have had their ends to history. It's not necessarily insightful or liberating. The moments of excess, the celebrations, are hardly more reassuring' (Deleuze 2004: 266). And it is not by chance that contemporary popular culture is replete with fantasies concerning the end of the world, from *Independence Day* to *Armageddon* and the *Terminator* and *Matrix* series. Ironically, we are always having the same collective dream – 'the end of capitalism' – even Republicans and capitalists share the same dream! In other words, whence the popularity of this collective fantasy except that it issues from the dread that already determines the internal limit of the capitalist *socius* itself, but a dread that is recorded on bodies by culture as expressions of desire, jubilant intoxication, delirium and moribund fascination? For Deleuze and Guattari, it is the Earth ('the Body without Organs', or 'the Deterritorialized, the Glacial, the Giant Molecule') that provides us with the glimpse of the absolute limit. If anything, one sees from the perspective of this limit a supreme and terrifying indifference to the 'end of history', if not the fundamental image of terror itself, which is nothing less than the petrifying face of the Death Drive. Nothing! Absolutely nothing! This, in my view, is what the Earth thinks about the current *socius* that is tattooed across the surface of its full body, and which after all, is only a very temporary and minor skin irritation.

In conclusion, therefore, let us return to the idea of a political geology, or to our original question: if the Earth had a politics, what might it be? Certainly, following Deleuze and Guattari, of course the answer would be a politics of 'deterritorialisation'. A politics of Gaia-Kronos.[8] However, we must return to make one small correction. It would appear from the illustration offered above that the Earth can simply be defined as a primitive stratum, perhaps even the first or the 'original stratum'. On the contrary, Deleuze and Guattari do not define the Earth as a stratum, 'original' or otherwise, but rather as a more compact plane of consistency that lies between layers or strata: 'In effect, the body without organs [which has already been identified as the Earth in the earlier passage cited above] is itself the plane of consistency, which becomes compact or thickens at the level of the strata' (Deleuze and Guattari 1987: 40). This is how they avoid the charges of a 'return to Nature', as if they were saying that the plane of consistency (including the consistency of desire) is a 'natural state' that exists prior to the moment of stratification which causes it to deviate from its true unitary composition or to become 'outside itself within itself'. This would just be an inverted Hegelianism, and perhaps we were led astray here by the moral associations of rape in the story of Hesiod. There is always a danger in using fables (or 'fictions') in explicating concepts, which are made up of lines and not of images, and which is why we need to restore a proper degree of abstraction to the image of the Earth offered earlier on.

From our earlier description, we seem to have two mutually exclusive propositions in defining the Earth. On the one hand, it is defined as 'absolute deterritorialisation', and Professor Challenger has already described the Earth, or the Body without Organs, as what constantly 'flees and becomes destratified, decoded, deterritorialized'. On the other hand, the Earth has also been defined as, 'the plane of consistency that thickens and compacts between strata'. This would appear to be contradictory if the movement of deterritorialisation was always opposed to formations of congealment or stratification (or what Deleuze and Guattari call 'reterritorialisation'). But, as they write: 'Absolute deterritorialisation is not defined as a giant accelerator; its absoluteness does not hinge on how fast it goes. It is actually possible to reach the absolute by way of phenomena of slowness and delay' (Deleuze and Guattari 1987: 56). Consequently, thickness and density also resist stratification, as much as a surface that is characterised by dispersion and by externalised elements, and we might imagine that deterritorialisation must also be figured as those points that are impermeable and infinitely dense that can occur within any strata, forming 'black holes' or points where the Earth becomes too dense and undifferentiated. In each case, the process of stratification fails to 'capture' matter and transform it into a surface of encoding; the Earth no longer functions as a 'substratum', but comes undone and goes adrift, or reappears 'outside' the strata themselves; however, this is only an illusion caused by the failure of its particular matter to be articulated by the process of stratification.

The point of all this is, again, to be discovered in the thesis of Professor Challenger: that the Earth absolutely resists all stratification, always veering toward a point of 'absolute deterritorialisation', and it is this degree of resistance that appears in the residues that constitute the relative and varying degrees of deterritorialisation that belong to the strata themselves. Thus, absolute deterritorialisation (the Earth) appears twice, or is doubly articulated, and 'appears relative only after stratification occurs on that plane or body' (Deleuze and Guattari 1987: 56). This is why, according to Deleuze and Guattari, 'there is a perpetual immanence of absolute deterritorialisation within relative deterritorialisation', and why 'the plane of consistency [the Earth] is always immanent to the strata' (Deleuze and Guattari 1987: 56–7). Returning to apply this insight to the fable by Hesiod, the Earth must be figured as both a, 'prisoner to stratifications, and enveloped in a certain specific stratum that defines its unity of composition' (Gaia) and, at the same time, as that 'most unformed, destratified element that belongs to its plane of consistency' (Kronos). This removes any remaining hint of naturalism from Deleuze and Guattari's geo-philosophy, since the Earth can only be defined as the mobile continuum between two states of deterritorialisation, the plane of consistency that appears between relative and absolute deterritorialisation or as the tipping point that causes one state to pass into another. But again, the strata themselves are only residues of these passages from one state to another, which is why they are constantly haunted from within by the movements of relative deterritorialisation that always threaten to become absolute. Therefore, the Earth can only be defined by this degree of imbalance, or disequilibrium, in the same way that any surface of stratification (of territory, or the stratified surface of the Earth under capitalism) is always found to be animated by deterritorialised and decoded flows; this is Deleuze and Guattari's thesis concerning capital, for example, which is said to be 'leaking everywhere' and 'endlessly crossing its own limits', which it keeps pushing farther out. At the same time, it is precisely through this fact that the Earth is always expanding its own borders, as Deleuze argues, and 'always finds itself in a situation where it must close off new escape routes, and push them back' into its own body (Deleuze 2004: 270). Thus, if the couple formed by Gaia-Ouranos would form one image of the Earth (in which the Earth is shown to expand by internalising all strata into her bloated body), then the couple figured by Gaia-Kronos could provide another image (in which the Earth suddenly exfoliates all its strata on a surface that has no unity, but is characterised by an essential dispersion). And yet, these two images would not be opposed to one another, since one would form the internal presupposition of the other in the same way that every movement of deterritorialisation produces the conditions for reterritorisation, recoding, or for new stratifications, and every reterritorialialisation always foresees new possibilities of deterritorialised flows and even takes steps in anticipation of these flows and seeks to capture them, and to internalise them once more. But in each case, these possibilities appear as unprecedented and take on new character and new revolutionary potential. As Deleuze said: 'So, you see, there is hope' (Deleuze 2004: 270). This would be the hope of causing one state to pass into another, without going too far, of tipping the Earth over and causing it to spill out onto another plane of consistency, which would be the critical perspective of geo-philosophy. Is there a possibility of a new conspiracy with the Earth, one that would be different from the conspiracy of 'Totality'?

If, as Deleuze once observed, the philosophy of the future must become a species of science fiction, then this trait would be even more pertinent to characterise a geo-philosophy, or a philosophy of the Earth. It is for this reason that it cannot take the form of a political theology, since its concepts are unfolded on a ground that knows nothing of transcendence, but only of an 'outside' that is much older than history. Let us, for example, try and imagine the year 0. On this plateau, we might ask: what would be the characteristics of the *socius* that currently distributes itself across a surface of the Earth. After a long process of anthropological exodus, what of desire or power, the composition of the strata, the inevitable processes of stratification? The question of Empire? If such a question could be asked any longer, it would only occur further down, well beneath the surface, congealed and hardened at some distant level of the interior stratum. Perhaps it will have become the question of anthropologists and natural historians, but not of politics, for that is a question that is always reserved for the surface, and I imagine this will be just as true then, as it is now. The most critical point of view is only achieved in thinking of surfaces, in terms of which surface we occupy now or the one emerging just next to us, and not in terms of 'the culture of memory' that belongs either to the past or the future, since 'revolution has nothing to do with an attempt to inscribe oneself in a movement of development and in the capitalisation of memory, but in the preservation of a force of forgetting and a force of underdevelopment as properly revolutionary forces'(Deleuze 2004: 278–9). The future is not a surface that unfolds from deep within the strata. Rather, the future is an egg, or a Body without Organs. The Earth, in any case, as Deleuze and Guattari have remarked many times, does not have a future, but only a 'becoming' (or many becomings). And 'What is the Earth in the process of becoming now?' is perhaps the only critical question that, today, remains for us to answer.

References

Deleuze, G. (1990), *The Logic of Sense*, trans. M. Lester and C. Stivale, New York: Columbia University Press.
Deleuze, G. (1994), *Difference and Repetition*, trans. P. Patton, London: The Athlone Press.
Deleuze, G. (1995), *Negotiations*, trans. M. Joughin, New York: Columbia University Press.
Deleuze, G. (2004), *Desert Islands and Other Texts: 1953–1974*, trans. M. Taormina, New York: Semiotext(e)/MIT Press.
Deleuze, G. and Guattari, F. (1983), *Anti-Oedipus: Capitalism and Schizophrenia*, trans. R. Hurley, M. Seem and H. R. Lane, Minneapolis: University of Minnesota Press.
Deleuze, G. and Guattari, F. (1987), *A Thousand Plateaus: Capitalism and Schizophrenia*, trans. B. Massumi, Minneapolis: University of Minnesota Press.
Deleuze, G. and Guattari, F. (1997), *What is Philosophy?*, trans. H. Tomlinson and G. Burchell, New York: Columbia University Press.
Foucault, M. (1997), *Ethics: Subjectivity and Truth*, trans. R. Hurley, New York: The New Press.
Hardt, M. and Negri, A. (2000), *Empire*, Cambridge: Harvard University Press.
Kirk, G. S. and Raven, J. E. (1957), *The Pre-Socratic Philosophers*, Cambridge: Cambridge University Press.

Notes

1. One historical counter-argument can easily be made to the final vision of the Multitude in Hardt and Negri's argument, since Deleuze and Guattari also observe that the profound movement of 'deterritorialisation', and the collective expression of desire and delirium, need not always assume the form of a positive (or 'joyous') emancipation of political subjectivity. Deleuze and Guattari often refer to the Crusades as a historical example that could be offered as an alternate reading of 'the great flows of Humanity' that one finds forecasted in the final section of *Empire*. As Guattari remarked in the same interview cited above:

   > The crusades were indeed an extraordinary schizophrenic movement . . . It didn't always work: the Venetian Crusade wound up in Constantinople, and the Children's Crusade veered off to the South of France and quickly lost any sympathy the people had for it. Entire villages were captured and burned by these 'crusading' children, whom the regular armies finally had to round up, either killing them or selling them into slavery . . . (Deleuze 2004: 270)

   However, the really critical question that I would raise with regard to the concept of the Multitude is whether the anthropological thesis concerning primitive societies expounded by Clastres represents a critical intuition of the potential political phenomena of contemporary forms of nomadism in late-capitalism, or whether it merely functions poetically, as a theoretical fiction alluding back to Deleuze and Guattari's creative use of this thesis concerning the schizoid and deterritorialised flows of desire.

2. Kirk and Raven note that the details of Hesiod's version suggest that Ouranos did separate from Gaia, 'at least in the daytime', but it, 'is probable that in other versions of the story Ouranos covered Gaia day and night (as Rangi covers Papa in the Maori myth), so that in a manner of speaking "the sky and earth were one form"' (Kirk and Raven 1957: 35).

3. The original text reads:

> All that came from Gaia and Ouranos, the most dire of children, from the beginning were hated by their own begetter; and just as soon as any of them came into being he hid them away and did not let them into the light, in the inward places of Gaia; and Ouranos rejoiced over the evil deed. And she, prodigious Gaia, groaned within, for she was crowded out; and she devised a crafty, evil device . . . she sent him [Kronos] into a hidden place of ambush, placed in his hands a jagged-toothed sickle, and enjoined on him the whole deceipt. Great Ouranos came bringing night with him, and over Gaia, desiring love, he stretched himself, and spread all over her; and he, his son, from his place of ambush stretched out his left hand, and with his right he grasped the monstrous sickle, long and jagged-toothed, and swiftly sheared off the genitals of his dear father, and flung them behind him to be carried away . . . (Kirk and Raven 1957: 35)

4. Although less known than his Tarzan novels, Burroughs created a series of novels in which a scientist and an adventurer travel by mechanical machine through the Earth's crust to find another Earth ringed inside the Earth's core with its ball of fiery plasma as a secondary sun, which is called Pellucidur. Whether or not this allusion was conscious on Deleuze and Guattari's part, I am assuming that their invention of Professor Challenger is based on the hybrid fictional character of the nineteenth-century geologist-explorer of the Earth's strata.

5. One cannot say, for example, that the current line of development of capitalism in Chinese society is identical to what took place in Europe or America. This would reduce, by an appeal to the over-arching myth of 'totality', the myriad effects of globalisation (a term used to represent the entire ecumenon of globalised markets), and often reasserts the universality of the Western line of development according to the allegory of 'the centre' and 'the periphery'. For Deleuze and Guattari, it is not a matter of a totalising centre and a localised, remote and external region, but rather a 'non-place' (*non-lieu*) that de-territorialises this form of stratification.

6. It is not by accident that the most recent critiques of capitalist societies have been reoriented around locating a critical limit that is internal to capital itself, and to developing their analysis from a position of immanence, rather than transcendence, or from the perspective of external synthesis of a social agency. This even forms a certain *sensus communis* that many theories today all share, having benefited from Deleuze and Guattari's earlier intuitions concerning the productive limit of capital itself, and from the intuition that the most critical relation to capitalism is not external, but is rather immanent to capitalist processes of encoding desire directly at the level of bodies. As Deleuze argued:

> Ideology is not important here: what matters is not ideology, nor even the 'economic/ideological' distinction or opposition; *what matters is the organization of power*. Because the organization of power, i.e., the way in which desire is

already economic, the way libido invests the economic, haunts the economic and fosters the political forms of repression. (Deleuze 2004: 263)

7. It is important to observe that Marx in the *Grundrisse* first adopted this image of absolute deterritorialisation in order to portray the successive transformations of capital itself, which purportedly always encounters its own limit as the inherent condition of its evolution and historical transformation, all the way to the end when this limit will potentially become externalised in a new form. That is, if there is a necessary limit internal to capital itself, which functions both as the condition of its production and reproduction and as the moment when capital exhausts itself and 'turns about' into another form (that is, the moment of *crisis*), it is a limit it had first of all to *steal* from the Earth – as the absolute '*In Itself*', the immobile continuum, the ground of production.

8. Or the politics of 'Friday-Speranza'. In fact, Deleuze's early reading of Michel Tournier's novel *Vendredi, ou les limbes du Pacifique* echoes, in an uncanny manner, the original fable by Hesiod and ends with the Speranza (the Earth) being emancipated from the 'sad sexual economy' of Robinson Crusoe, the global personification of European colonisation, an event which is brought about by the figure of 'Friday'. See Deleuze 1990: 301–20.

9. Deleuze and Guattari have often referred to Marxism as a 'culture of memory', one whose theoretical practice always proceeds by the 'capitalization of the memory of social formations' (Deleuze 2004: 278). As I have argued throughout, this would have to be distinguished from the theoretical practice proposed by Deleuze and Guattari's notion of 'geo-philosophy', which proceeds through the cultivation of a force of forgetting that they already find in the processes of deterritorialisation and reterritorialisation, and in the example of the Earth. Perhaps this practice might more resemble the science of 'the Solarians' from Stanislav Lem's novel *Solaris*, which is why I referred to Deleuze's early statement from the preface to *Difference and Repetition* that a future philosophy would have to be partly a novel of detection and partly science fiction (Deleuze 1994: xxi). But, as I asked in the beginning of this chapter, would this not be the genre of philosophy that one already finds in *A Thousand Plateaus*?

Index